623.451954 STI

Stine, George Harry

ICBM : the making of the
weapon that changed the
world

# ICBM

*Rocket Power and Space Flight*
*Earth Satellites and the Race for Space Superiority*
*Man and the Space Frontier*
*The Handbook of Model Rocketry*
*The Third Industrial Revolution*
*The Space Enterprise*
*Space Power*
*Confrontation in Space*
*The Hopeful Future*
*The Silicon Gods*
*Bits, Bytes, Bauds, and Brains: The Untold Story of the Computer Revolution*
*Handbook for Space Colonists*
*On the Frontiers of Science: Strange Machines You Can Build*
*The Corporate Survivors*

# I
# C
# B
# M

## THE
## MAKING
## OF THE
## WEAPON
## THAT
## CHANGED
## THE
## WORLD

### G. HARRY STINE

 ORION BOOKS, NEW YORK

To Daniel O. Graham, Lieutenant General, AUS (Ret.)

Published by Orion Books, a division of Crown Publishers, Inc., 201 East 50th Street, New York, New York 10022. Member of the Crown Publishing Group.

ORION and colophon are trademarks of Crown Publishers, Inc.

Manufactured in the United States of America

Library of Congress Cataloging-in-Publication Data
Stine, G. Harry (George Harry)
   ICBM : the making of the weapon that changed the world / G. Harry
Stine. — 1st ed.
     p.   cm.
   1. Intercontinental ballistic missiles—Design and construction—
History.   2. Ballistic missiles—United States—Design and
construction—History.   I. Title.
UG1312.I2S75   1991
623.4′51954—dc20                                                    90–49136
                                                                        CIP

ISBN 0-517-56768-7
10 9 8 7 6 5 4 3 2 1

First Edition

# *Contents*

# *Preface*

This book is more than just the history of the intercontinental ballistic missile (ICBM). It contains several lessons about how to make and manage high technology, not just for a high-technology weapons system but for any application in any area of government, business, finance, and industry. It concentrates on the technology of the ICBM to provide a focus. I began my professional career as a scientist-engineer fascinated by technology. However, as my career unfolded, I became involved with the management of people in addition to the development and application of technology. The summer of the year before I graduated from college with a bachelor's degree in physics, I had an exciting job at White Sands Proving Ground, New Mexico, working with the first operational ballistic missile, the German *Aggregat Vier* (A.4), which was known to the world and to those of us at White Sands by the appellation given to it by Dr. Joseph Goebbels of Nazi Germany, *Der Vergeltungswaffe Zwei* or the V-2. As I kept track of the growing rocket and guided missile program over the years, I became aware that how the people and the technology were managed was just as important as what the technology would do.

The story of the development of the ICBM has never before been brought together in a single volume. ICBM development in the United States has been rather sketchily documented in various books dealing with individual ICBM systems that eventually were used as space launch systems. Furthermore, this historical documentation has concentrated on the technological issues. The development of Soviet ICBMs has never even been told. In fact, many of the details have never been revealed. It has been left to those of us in the western nations who are interested in Soviet rocketry to attempt to piece together these histories from snatches of news reports, interviews with some of the engineers and military men involved, collections of randomly scattered details that have appeared in other books and articles often unrelated to the subject of ICBMs, and what we know must have taken place because engineers everywhere must think and decide and behave in much the same way when it comes to a technical problem. Engineers work with the same immutable laws of the universe no matter where they live. A bridge in Moscow must be designed the same way as a bridge in Washington or Beijing.

Whether the reader is involved in modern research and development, leading a government high-tech project, or educating the next generation of people who will have to run and live in a world with even higher technology, the ICBM story will reveal patterns and methodologies—both the successful and unsuccessful ways—developed by people to get other people to do what is necessary in a high-risk, high-technology endeavor, facing strong and often unknown competition from many directions. The development of the ballistic missile was an activity in which all sorts of people from idealists to madmen have been involved for all sorts of reasons. We find all of both the best and the worst of human nature. Life and death decisions, often involving entire nations, have had to be made.

One of the striking issues of the history of the ICBM is the high cost one pays for neglecting long-range planning in favor of short-term goals. Another lesson is the amazing and seemingly impossible things that can be done if one utilizes long-range planning and then sets out in an opportunistic fashion to get from What Is to What Can Be. Another is that a good working product made with existing technology is better than a perfect product that may be made with future technology at some time in the future. Yet another is that an emerging technology usually progresses much faster than forecast or even planned, often to the detriment of those who bet heavily on a conservative technological forecast.

We shall see a side issue to the development of the ICBM as we progress through the story of the people who were behind this weapon. In both the United States and the Soviet Union, the people who were responsible for the development of the ICBM began working on rockets because rockets were perceived as the only way to achieve a higher goal: the conquest of space. The various ICBMs were therefore pressed into service as the initial space launch vehicles. It is becoming apparent now, nearly fifty years after the first flight of the German A.4, that this was probably the right way to go at the time for unmanned space missions but the wrong way to go in the long run for manned activities. The reason can be set forth very succinctly: No successful transportation system in history has been based on the principle of shooting people from one place to another. The space transportation we have in 1990 is firmly based on the doctrines, procedures, and technologies of the artillery officer and the gunner's mate. This is why it is so expensive, dangerous, and circuslike. And why it is also so controversial, because if it's too expensive or difficult to get people into space, you don't know what people can really do in space to make money or defend the nation. As the ICBM hopefully fades from the weaponry scene because of the deployment of ballistic missile defense systems by various nations, it will also fade from the space transportation scene except for those unmanned missions for which it makes economic sense to shoot things into orbit atop long-range artillery shells. But it is highly unlikely that we will be able to develop a safe, economical, and successful commercial system based on an extension of the circus-stunt technology of shooting daredevils out of cannons. However, this will not be the first time that human beings have made a false start and had to return to square one.

In a way, we can be thankful that the ICBM came along when it did and made early space exploration possible. However, tying our future in space to the coattails of ever-improved artillery shells means not much of a future in space at all.

The ICBM may have given us the breathing space necessary to sort out the confusion of World War II and a tantalizing glimpse of what the space frontier might offer.

Certainly, no one can argue the fact that the ICBM has changed the history of the world.

Fortunately, I was able to do all the research necessary for this book from my own personal reference library and by consulting my archival collection of reports, clippings, drawings, and photographs. All the photographs and drawings herein have come from my own collection which I started in 1951. It has been fascinating to have had even a small role in the making of history and to be able to draw some conclusions from what went on. As for the real long-term consequences, one is reminded of the reply given by the late historian Will Durant when he was asked what he thought the consequences of the French Revolution were: "It's too early yet to know."

# ICBM

# What Is a Ballistic Missile?

"ICBM" means many things to many people, and in some situations the meanings are slightly different. To talk intelligently about the history of the development of the ICBM and about the people who turned an idea into reality as a weapon, we need to start not only at the beginning of this history but also at the roots of the idea. This is especially true of the definitions we'll use because they are the basic concepts that make the ICBM the weapon that it is. If we understand the weapon, we can then have a better chance of attempting to control its future use or to develop defenses against it when it is used.

ICBM is an acronym. It stands for "InterContinental Ballistic Missile."

Initially, it was known as an "IBM." But, since that acronym was already the initials of a large computer corporation, it was modified to ICBM in about 1955.

An ICBM is a specific type of the general class of a self-propelled, extremely long range ballistic missile. Barring some unforeseen technical development, it is perhaps the ultimate form of the ballistic missile.

Basically, a ballistic missile is an artillery shell in common with all missile weapons developed and used since the dawn of the history of hunting and warfare. In Chapter 2, the development of the missile weapon from the rocket to the early ICBM will be covered in detail.

1

However, an artillery shell isn't a ballistic missile in the sense in which we'll use the term in this book.

A ballistic missile may have an effective range from less than a kilometer to as many kilometers as you wish to design and build it for. Artillery shells fired from large-bore rifled cannon may have ranges of up to thirty kilometers.

An ICBM differs from all other artillery shells and ballistic missiles because of its extremely long range. By "long range," we mean that it may be launched from any place on earth and hit a target at any other location on earth.

The ICBM started as a short-range (200 kilometers) ballistic missile and grew until it became a ballistic missile with intercontinental and then worldwide range. Thus, an ICBM is a special, ultimate category of ballistic missile.

A ballistic missile differs from an artillery shell or other missile weapon in several important ways.

Unlike an artillery shell, a ballistic missile isn't fired or launched from a gun barrel. An artillery shell requires a long tube open only at one end. This tube is built strong enough to contain the expanding gases from the chemical combustion of its propelling charge. The expanding propellant gases thus accelerate the shell to its final velocity, which occurs just as the shell leaves the open end or mouth of the tube.

Although some smaller ballistic missiles may use short launching tubes to help direct their flights, a ballistic missile doesn't use a gun barrel in the same manner as an artillery shell does. A ballistic missile is still accelerating or gaining speed when it leaves its launching tube. Furthermore, a ballistic missile is rocket-propelled. This is the major difference between a gun-launched artillery shell and a ballistic missile.

A rocket-propelled ballistic missile carries its own propellant along with it. This propellant burns more slowly than the propellant used in the closed tube or barrel of a gun. Since the ballistic missile can take longer to come up to its ultimate speed, this lessens the sudden shock of launching and allows less robust parts to be used in a ballistic missile's construction and internal operating parts. A lower acceleration also reduces the aerodynamic drag of a ballistic missile because it passes through the densest and lowest part of the earth's atmosphere at a lower speed. If enough propellant is carried in the ballistic missile to allow it to achieve a final velocity of about 7,600 meters per second, its range will be infinite and it can be aimed to hit any place on earth.

Imagine a planet with a very high mountain on which a cannon is emplaced to fire in a horizontal direction. ("Horizontal" in this case means at right angles to a line drawn through the cannon to the center of the planet.) Load the cannon with a small amount of gun propellant (powder) and an artillery shell. When it's fired, the shell will come out of the gun barrel and immediately begin to fall toward the center of the planet. On earth, it falls with an acceleration of 980 centimeters per second per second because this is the acceleration of gravity on our planet. Therefore, at some distance from the gun on the mountain, the shell will strike the surface of the planet. Repeat the experiment using more gun propellant or a lighter shell; this time the shell will come out of the gun barrel with higher velocity and travel farther before it strikes the ground. If you put enough propellant in the gun, the shell will be fired with enough velocity so that it goes halfway around the planet before it strikes the ground. The ultimate, of course, is to get the shell to emerge from the gun with enough velocity to permit it to fall all the way around the planet without hitting the ground. In this last case, it has become an artificial satellite of the planet.

In all cases, gravity has pulled the shell toward the center of the planet at the same acceleration. But at the extreme ranges, you must take into consideration the fact that the planet is spherical and curving away from the shell as quickly as the shell is falling toward it.

On earth, if you could build a gun to shoot an artillery shell up to 7,600 meters per second, you not only have a gun with infinite range, you also have a satellite launching vehicle.

It's impractical to build a gun barrel long enough to shoot an ordinary artillery shell more than about a hundred kilometers (sixty-two miles). In order to contain the expanding gases of the burning gun propellant and continue to accelerate the artillery shell to the proper high velocity, the gun barrel would have to be a kilometer or more in length. The impracticality of building a gun barrel that long as well as strong enough to withstand the extremely high pressures of all the required gun propellant led to the development of a new kind of artillery: rocket-propelled ballistic missiles.

However, some types of artillery shells carry a "booster charge," which is a built-in rocket whose thrusting, after such a shell leaves the gun, continues to accelerate the shell and extend the shell's range.

But a gun barrel does more than provide a cylinder in which the "piston" that is the shell can be accelerated by the expanding gases of the burning gun propellant. A gun barrel provides the guidance for an artillery shell. The direction in which the gun barrel is pointed determines the path the shell follows on its flight to the target. On the other hand, since it doesn't use a gun barrel, a ballistic missile must be self-guiding if it is to hit its target.

Therefore, a ballistic missile not only is self-propelled but must be guided either by external means or internal devices.

Again, the ballistic missile is not unique in possessing self-guiding characteristics. Many modern artillery shells and gravity bombs known as "smart" weapons carry their own target-seeking and terminal guidance systems to ensure pinpoint accuracy when they impact their targets. But these smart weapons are either shot from gun barrels or dropped from aircraft.

The limits of ordinary cannon technology were reached in the early twentieth century with the development of 16-inch (406.4-millimeter) and 18-inch (457.2-millimeter) rifled cannon mounted on seagoing battleships. These huge guns could fire shells weighing several tons to a range of fifty kilometers. These shells had no self-guidance. And they carried high explosive warheads.

When a technology reaches the point where an enormous amount of effort can produce only a small increment of improved performance, it's time to go looking for a new technology.

In the case of the ballistic missile, the new technology was already there in its crude, early, infant form when the limits of gun artillery were reached.

But it wasn't embraced because of military need.

And it had been discarded at an earlier time because it couldn't compete with gun technology.

# The Rockets' Red Glare

Weapons are generally grouped into two categories: shock weapons and missile weapons.

The club was the first shock weapon.

The initial missile weapon was the rock that a warrior or hunter hurled against the enemy or the prey.

We still see displays of prowess in these two weapon categories in the Olympic games every four years. Fencing is the modern equivalent of club bashing because the sword and its derivatives were developed from the primitive club. The Olympic javelin throw and shot put are two field sports that are examples of the ancient art of human-launched missile weapons. David's biblical sling was another missile weapon. Slings were developed to throw stones to a greater distance and with more force than was possible by arm power alone. The development of the bow permitted the javelin or spear to be launched to greater ranges with more accuracy and more penetrating power, and the sport of archery is directly descended from the development of this missile weapon.

The invention of blackpowder created a new category of missile weapon: the gun. Blackpowder is an early and primitive form of gunpowder. As slower-burning gunpowders were developed as gun propellants, blackpowder itself gave way to corned or pelleted blackpowder, which was eclipsed in the nineteenth century by the development of other gun propellants such as smokeless powder.

Gun propellants are explosives but not "high explosives" such as dynamite, TNT, and other chemical compounds. Gun propellants are "low explosives" that actually burn progressively by a process called "deflagration." On the other hand, high explosives convert almost instantaneously from solid form to gaseous form as the result of a compressive shock wave being transmitted through them by the initiation of the explosive, which is in turn started by a physical shock from a detonating blasting cap or initiator.

High explosives are useful in warheads but not as gun propellants because they act too quickly. All gun propellants and ballistic missile propellants are low explosives.

It's important to recognize this basic difference in explosive materials at the start. Ballistic missiles became practical because of the development of better low explosives that could be used as rocket propellants. ICBMs became practical with the development of the ultimate in high explosives, the thermonuclear explosive that could create a great deal of warhead damage from a very small and relatively lightweight warhead.

Blackpowder was invented by the Chinese sometime before the thirteenth century A.D. The first mention of its use was as a rocket propellant in a weapon. Reports from the Battle of Kai-Feng-Fu near Beijing in China in 1260 A.D. mentioned the use of "flying arrows of fire." The Chinese troops had attached small blackpowder rockets to the sides of arrows to extend their range and possibly also create a severe fire hazard when they landed.

Blackpowder became generally known in Europe in the fourteenth century. Francis Bacon is credited with introducing blackpowder to Europe. Bacon got his information from merchants who had traveled to Arabia. At first blackpowder was used in Europe to propel rounded stones from short, conical guns made in the shape of an apothecary's grinding mortar.

Until the nineteenth century the accuracy and range of both cannons and handguns were limited to about 500 meters. A few very heavy long-range cannons were developed, but they were difficult to make, difficult to move, difficult to aim, and dangerous to use. Cannons were used primarily as siege weapons to reduce the walls of a fortress or a city by simply pounding these targets to rubble by firing large stones or iron cannonballs against them. They were used as infantry support weapons on the battlefield where they fired solid shot, air-burst rounds, or shotgunlike "grapeshot," among other specialized projectiles.

Development of artillery proceeded until the creation of the large-caliber naval guns of the early twentieth century and, most important to our story, the legendary Paris gun.

The Paris gun was not the original "Big Bertha." That name was given to the 18-inch (460-millimeter) German siege mortars used to destroy the forts at Liège, Namur, and Antwerp in 1914. These huge guns were named after the ample lady who had recently inherited the house of Krupp although they were made by the Skoda Werk in Austria-Hungary (now in Czechoslovakia). However, the Allied press borrowed the name "Big Bertha" and applied it to the Paris gun.

The Paris gun—seven of them were made and used—had a bore of 8.26 inches (210 millimeters). The barrel was 117 feet long, and the entire piece weighed 142 tons. It fired a shell weighing 264 pounds, only 23 pounds of which were high explosive, to a range of 130 kilometers (about 80 miles). Emplaced in the forests of Crépy, the guns began firing on Paris on March 23, 1918, and kept it up for 140 days, killing 256 people in Paris. When the Allies finally figured out where the shells were coming from, the Paris guns were forced out of action by counterbattery fire from French guns much closer to them than Paris.

In a strange way, the Paris gun played a major role in the development of the ICBM.

However, the ancestors of the ballistic missile were also making their appearance. Pyrotechnic skyrockets had found their way to Europe from China, and it didn't take long before someone realized that these display rockets might be converted into artillery weapons. In 1668, Col. Christoph Friedrich von Geissler did some early work on war rockets for the Elector of Saxony and the King of Poland. Von Geissler built some experimental war rockets weighing 50 pounds and 120 pounds.

However, the military need for ballistic missiles made itself known to the British when they came up against the rocket troops of Hydar Ali, Prince of Mysore in India, in the battles of Seringapatam in 1792 and 1799. The Indian war rockets were 6-pound and 12-pound units with 10-foot bamboo stabilizing poles. They had a range of between 1,700 and 2,500 yards. Their accuracy was terrible, but their psychological effect on the British troops was devastating. The rocket troops of Hydar Ali not only launched the rockets on ballistic flight paths through the air but fired them along the ground at the British troops.

This stimulated the work of the man known as the father of the war rocket, Col. (later Sir) William Congreve of Great Britain. Working under the patronage of the Prince Regent and with the assistance of the Earl of Mulgrave, Master General of Ordnance, Congreve began experiments that culminated in the British development of a Rocket Corps to supplement the Royal Artillery. Congreve developed an arsenal of ten different ballistic rockets ranging in weight from 6 pounds to 300 pounds with ranges up to 3,000 yards. They were the first rockets to use iron bodies, but they were still stabilized by long guidance poles like skyrockets.

The accuracy of the Congreve rockets was terrible, but they were very useful in barrage fire because a few soldiers could launch a hundred of them in a salvo, then quickly line up more rockets for another salvo.

Congreve developed a complete weapons system to use his rockets on land by cavalry, artillery, and infantry troops and at sea aboard vessels of the Royal Navy. Congreve rockets could be launched from special launching racks, by laying them against a sloping embankment, or actually throwing the smaller units toward the enemy lines.

The British Royal Navy burned the Danish city of Copenhagen to the ground in 1807 using Congreve rockets launched from ships.

The British use of Congreve rockets in the Battle of Leipzig on October 16–19, 1813, was credited with destroying Napoleon Bonaparte's war-making abilities in Europe.

The British launched Congreve rockets from ships in Baltimore harbor against Fort McHenry in September 1814, leading Francis Scott Key to pen the phrase in the American national anthem, "the rockets' red glare."

Congreve rockets and other early ballistic missiles were widely used in the war with Mexico in 1848 and during the Civil War.

It seemed that the ballistic missile had finally come of age. But the basic inaccuracy and unreliability of the Congreve rockets made them useful only as barrage weapons. They were not pinpoint target seekers. In artillery terms, they had too much dispersion.

Of course, the same could be said for the cannons of the day. But the Congreve rockets were so much easier to carry, load, and fire. The only reason why Congreve rockets continued to be used at all was because of the inaccuracies, weight, and difficulty of using the field artillery pieces of the day. This didn't last because rifled guns and improved technology during the nineteenth century improved cannons far more than rockets.

In the first half of the nineteenth century, many experimenters attempted to improve upon the Congreve rockets. The first step was to get rid of the long, heavy stabilizing stick that was basically dead weight. Another Britisher, William Hale, developed a spin-stabilized war rocket that didn't need a stabilizing stick.

By the end of the nineteenth century, rifled, breech-loading artillery guns had so outstripped rockets in terms of range, reliability, accuracy, and ease of storage and use that the war rocket went into eclipse. It looked like the era of the rocket-propelled ballistic missile was at an end.

However, fertile minds found all sorts of other uses for ballistic missiles. The basic designs were put to work at sea as line-carrying rescue rockets, for example.

It was now the turn of rifled artillery to dominate the ballistic missile. And no one expected the ballistic missile to make a comeback.

# The Legacy of Versailles

Germany has been a central European power since the division of Charlemagne's Frankish Empire between his three grandsons in A.D. 843. Germany has existed under various names since then, often in a condition of fragmentation. The situation of a divided Germany or one fragmented into small political units seemed to make other Europeans happy. The German culture has always been a militant one that has on numerous occasions attempted to conquer and thus unify Europe by military means. Time after time, Germany has been beaten in its attempts to unify Europe under the German banner. These defeats have always brought fragmentation or division as the victors attempted to break up this fearsome central European culture. But for more than a thousand years, the Germans have always managed to reunite.

When the German Empire was defeated in World War I, the German government, now a democracy minus its imperial Kaiser, was forced to sign the Treaty of Versailles in 1919. The politicians and diplomats who drafted that treaty were as inept and unprepared as their military counterparts had been during World War I.

The Treaty of Versailles didn't attempt to break up Germany. However, it deprived the country of some of its borderlands and created a future trouble spot by giving Poland a corridor to the Baltic Sea. This took away some of the Prussian heartland of Germany, and the Germans didn't like that.

The Germans also didn't like the crushing burden of war reparation payments imposed on them by the treaty. This shortsighted effort by the Allies to get the Germans to "pay" for the war backfired by bankrupting Germany and perhaps even adding fuel to the fires of the worldwide economic depression ten years later. Twenty years later, the economic conditions of the treaty were seen as being among the causes of World War II.

The biggest mistake of the Treaty of Versailles was the attempt to demilitarize Germany. Twice within a hundred years, the Germans had crossed the Rhine River into France. Germany had defeated France in the Franco-Prussian War of 1870, and the French were unhappy about this and wanted revanche. They got the chance when Europe blundered into World War I.

World War I bled Europe white and destroyed a generation of young men. The effect of the new weapons of war had not been reckoned on by military leaders. The machine gun and the heavy artillery gun rendered unarmored infantry assaults deadly. More than 50 percent of the 65 million mobilized troops became casualties. Germany and the other Central Powers suffered far fewer casualties than the Allies. Therefore, the victorious Allies were determined to end German militarism and make World War I truly the "war to end all wars." They'd had enough of German saber-rattling and intimidation prior to the war. And they'd come out of the war with a respectful dread of Germany's industrial and military capabilities in aviation, submarines, and long-range heavy artillery.

Under the provisions of the treaty, the German army was cut to 100,000 men. A German general staff was not permitted. A maximum of only 1,000 officers was permitted for this truncated army. No navy or air force was permitted.

To further hobble the German armaments industry, Krupp, the famous German gunmaker, was forbidden to make any gun with a bore larger than 170 millimeters (about 6.7 inches).

The Treaty of Versailles had many other provisions, but these are the major ones that affected the history of the ICBM.

The treaty sowed the seeds of the next war because the Germans didn't like it and were forced to sign it. They had no choice. Their army was defeated, and their navy lay scuttled at the bottom of

Scapa Flow in Scotland. The terms of the Treaty of Versailles were so onerous and crushing that the Germans secretly vowed to somehow, some day, get out from under it. The only way they knew to do that was to become a strong military and industrial nation again. However, since the victorious Allied nations had observers looking over the shoulders of the Germans, that was a difficult goal to achieve. Be that as it may, the Germans weren't about to sit there and take it on the chin for decades to come. So they began to plan for the next war even as they signed the treaty under protest.

Therefore, in the midst of national economic and political chaos during the 1920s, the Germans began to circumvent the treaty in secret or to search for means to do things the treaty had not prohibited.

It's no secret that during the 1920s the Germans had an unannounced protocol or agreement with the Soviet Union to train officers and to test and develop weapons in a clandestine fashion in the USSR. The Soviets came to rue that protocol in 1941.

Because the treaty limited artillery to 170-millimeter guns, Krupp naturally continued development of a 1917 design, the 150-millimeter K16. Krupp also increased the gun's size to the treaty limit, producing the *17 cm. K in Moser Lafette* (17-centimeter gun on howitzer carriage). It had a maximum range of about 27,400 meters (17 miles).

Even though the primitive motor vehicles and tanks of World War I could travel at the speed of a marching column of troops, 17 miles is a distance that can be covered in a little over five hours during a march. Having no artillery that could range beyond a day's march put definite restrictions on the tactical doctrine the German army could use. They needed some way to hit the enemy's rear echelons.

With no navy to provide a source of large-caliber guns capable of being modified as land-based guns, no air force capable of bombing deep behind the enemy lines, and no legal ability to build any field gun larger than 170 millimeters, the German army lacked what is known today as a "deep tactical strike capability."

Enter again the artillerists.

In 1929, Fritz Lang at Ufa Films released a motion picture about a trip to the Moon, *Frau im Mond (The Woman in the Moon)*. It was one of the most accurate science-fiction movies of its time and still stands as a landmark in the film industry. It was as accurately done from the scientific and technical standpoints as was possible with what was known at the time. Lang acquired the consulting services of Professor Hermann Oberth, a Romanian schoolteacher who had published a classic book on space travel. Also working as technical advisers for the film were members of the Verein für Raumschiffahrt (Society for Space Travel) such as Dr. Willy Ley. The film was a huge success in Germany.

The film caused Hauptman (Captain) Karl Becker, Ph.D., of the German Heereswaffenamt Prüfwesen (Army Weapons Testing Office) to take a renewed interest in the possibility of using rocket propulsion for military purposes.

The reason was simple: *The Treaty of Versailles said absolutely nothing whatsoever about rockets.* Germany was free to pursue rocket technology without restriction.

This is an excellent example of the conduct of technological warfare.

It should also be a lesson for those people who believe that technology can be "controlled" or technical development prohibited. Often a politician or bureaucrat will attempt to control or bottle up technology by trying to get it "firmly in hand." This is done either to prevent some imagined misuse or to deny technological transfer to another country. However, technology has a disturbing tendency to squirt out between the restrictions and go off in a totally new and unsuspected direction. Conversely, perhaps it can be said that if one wishes to encourage the development of new technology, one should place legal prohibitions or limitations on existing technology. In either case, such a restriction usually serves only to stimulate engineers, technicians, and inventors to discover and perfect technologies that aren't prohibited or limited by political or bureaucratic edict.

The first major player in the ICBM story now comes on stage.

In 1930, Capt. Walter R. Dornberger graduated from the Technischen Hochschule in Berlin with a Master's degree in mechanical engineering. Most professional German military officers of that time were also engineers with advanced degrees, and Dornberger was no exception. He was an artillery officer with no artillery branch to which he could be posted. So he was assigned to Capt. Karl Becker's Ballistics Section in the *Heereswaffenamt Prüfwesen,* where he was given responsibility for rocket research.

Although Dornberger may have been dismayed at this assignment because he knew little if anything about rockets, he could have consoled himself with the knowledge that no one else in Germany did either.

However, Captain Becker, his commanding officer, may have been thinking about rocket-propelled weapons for some time. He and Dr. Carl Crantz had written the classic and monumental *Lehrbuch der Ballistik (Handbook on Ballistics),* which is still a standard work in the field. Part 2 of Volume 2 of this work contains a section dealing with the ballistics or flight of rockets.

Although Dornberger reported to Capt. Ritter von Horstig—a man whose name appears briefly in the history between 1930 and 1932 and then disappears along with any biographical material, which is not unusual considering the quantity of records and documents that perished at the end of World War II—he was given a simple but direct order by Becker: *"Develop in military facilities a liquid-fuel rocket, the range of which should surpass that of any existing gun and the production of which would be carried out by industry. Secrecy of the development is paramount."*

This direct order from Captain Becker to Captain Dornberger marks the real starting point of the development of the intercontinental ballistic missile.

# The Army and the Inventors

As Capt. Walter Dornberger began his task of developing a long-range liquid-fuel ballistic missile, he first had to find a place to do it.

The Heereswaffenamt Prüfwesen had established a small rocket proving ground between two artillery firing ranges at Kummersdorf, a suburb located about 27 kilometers south of Berlin. Here at Versuchsstelle Kummersdorf-West, Captains Becker and von Horstig had built a small facility for static testing solid-propellant rockets of the Congreve and Hale type.

A static test stand is a facility where a rocket motor is tied down in a frame so it can't go anywhere while it's being operated. Various measurement devices or sensors are attached to it so that the performance parameters of the rocket can be measured during its operation. Devices such as strain gauges, thermocouples, and pressure sensors detect and measure factors such as thrust or force, temperature, and pressure inside the rocket chamber. This information is recorded for later study and analysis. The early static test stands at Kummersdorf were primitive affairs compared with their descendants that are in use all over the world now to test rocket motors and engines ranging in size from little model rocket units to those propelling the NASA Space Shuttle.

In 1930, Becker was developing a short-range (6 to 7 kilometers) solid fuel rocket bombardment weapon that could be fired in large numbers. The memories of the Congreve rockets were fresh in the minds of some of the older German generals because such rockets were in use by the German army as late as 1864. Solid propellant rockets still offered military advantages. They did not need heavy and expensive guns. In theory, they could shoot farther than guns. Unlike airplanes, they couldn't be attacked en route to the target. All that was needed was to make solid-fuel rockets safe and reliable. That's an engineering job. Properly trained and educated people can be hired and put to work doing such a thing.

Dornberger was given command of Kummersdorf-West. His first task was to turn it into a rocket testing ground. During the winter of 1930, he saw to the construction of a small office, a workshop, and a U-shaped bay in which to set up the static test stand for solid-fuel rockets. Over the next few months, the first scientific tests on all available types of domestic fireworks rockets in this test stand showed conclusively that they had neither the repeatability nor reliability to serve as military weapons.

In this regard, it may be said parenthetically that nothing has changed with fireworks in general since then. Skyrockets, bottle rockets, and other rocket products of the classical fireworks industry everywhere in the world remain unreliable and nonrepeatable because of a lack of scientific testing and modern quality control, which was pioneered by the aerospace industry. Fireworks of all sorts remain highly unreliable today in comparison to other forms of pyrotechnics. The fireworks industry has not taken advantage of the technology developed since 1930 in professional rocketry. On the other hand, the hobby/sport of model rocketry has and would not have survived if it hadn't.

And professional rocketry would never have gotten the ICBM off the ground if it hadn't been for the principles and procedures developed by Dornberger and his colleagues starting at Kummersdorf-West in 1930.

Beyond the monumental task of setting up the first modern testing station for solid-fuel rockets at Kummersdorf-West, Dornberger and von Horstig found themselves operating in a total vacuum when it came to liquid-fuel rocket technology. No one in the German academic institutions or industry was interested in liquid-fuel rockets. The year 1930 was the height of the worldwide depression, and most companies were struggling simply to stay alive. In the academic world, rocket technology was ignored because of something we now call the "NIH Factor." NIH is an acronym for "Not Invented Here." It describes an attitude created by the fact that an idea, device, or procedure wasn't created or thought of in the particular institution that suffers from said Factor. Therefore, since it wasn't invented there, it is of no interest or is of trivial importance.

Dornberger began to get in touch with the many private rocket research organizations in Germany. Most of these had been started as a result of a 1923 book on space travel, *Die Rakete zu den Planetenräumen (The Rocket into Planetary Space)*, written by a German-speaking Romanian schoolteacher, Hermann Oberth. The Fritz Lang film *Frau im Mond* had given additional incentive and impetus to rocket experimentation. These experimental rocket groups were run by one or more gifted amateurs. Some of them were lone inventors with a couple of assistants. One of them was the *Gesellschaft für Raketenforschung (Society for Rocket Research)* or GfR in Hanover formed by Albert Püllenberg and Albert Löw. But the biggest rocket society in Germany was the *Verein für Raum-schiffahrt (Society for Space Travel)* or VfR in Berlin with 870 members.

Most of the rocket inventors were either enamored of their own pet ideas which had very little scientific or technical basis, or were tinkerers with no real knowledge of how to make things work. In order to make a living and support their experimentation, most of them had to resort to giving publicity demonstrations (for which some of them charged an admission fee) or writing sensationalistic newspaper and magazine articles. This behavior led to opposition from university professors and degreed scientists because of the NIH Factor and the refusal of the inventors to play by the established rules of scientific endeavor, publication of results, and peer review. The inventors not only distrusted the academicians and scientists who they believed might steal their ideas but also maintained on-going feuds with all other inventors who took an interest in rockets.

Although some of the inventors and organizations were actually building, operating, and flying liquid-fuel rockets (and creating loud, energetic explosions when these contraptions didn't work), no one and no organization was doing any real scientific research and development. There were no records showing thrust, propellant consumption, pressures, and other technical factors. Everything was done by cut and try with the philosophy, "When in total ignorance, do anything and you'll be less ignorant."

However, Dornberger did find some individuals and groups such as the GfR and VfR who appeared to be serious about rocket research. Some of them appeared to lack the funds to buy or make the measuring equipment required. Others appeared to have ideas of real merit. So Dornberger arranged for study contracts to promising individuals and groups, thus giving them some financial support. He then had to await results.

The results began to come in, and Dornberger was dismayed. There were no real data. The findings were unscientific and unreliable. At the end of two years, no real progress had been made.

And because of the way that most inventors and rocket societies had operated in the past, depending upon the glare of publicity when they could get it, the Army Weapons Department became extremely uneasy. They were afraid that thoughtless shoptalk as well as beer-hall bragging on the part of their wildly individualistic rocket contractors might break the secrecy behind the army's support of rocket research. Although the Treaty of Versailles was still very much in force in 1932, Dornberger and his superiors didn't want to take the chance that the German government might be accused of breaking it. Dornberger remembered his orders: "Secrecy of the development is paramount."

Furthermore, the study contract results weren't what the army was looking for. Dornberger made it clear in his 1954 memoirs, *V-2:*

> *We wanted to have done once and for all with theory, unproved claims, and boastful fantasy, and to arrive at conclusions based on sound scientific foundation. We were tired of imaginative projects concerning space travel. The value of the sixth decimal place in the calculation of a trajectory to Venus inter-*

*ested us as little as the problem of heating and air regeneration in the pressurized cabin of a Mars ship. We wanted to advance the practice of rocket building with scientific thoroughness. We wanted thrust-time curves of the performance of rocket motors. We wanted to know what fuel consumption per second we had to allow for, what fuel mixture would be best, how to deal with the temperatures occurring in the process, what types of combustion-chamber shape and exhaust nozzle would yield the best performance. We intended to establish the fundamentals, create the necessary tools, and study the basic conditions. First and foremost came the propulsion unit.*

By 1932, Dornberger convinced his superior officers that the only solution was to do it themselves. He recommended that Kummersdorf-West be expanded to handle liquid-propellant rocket research. Furthermore, he wanted to staff it with civil servants who were educated, bright, motivated, and paid to produce the sort of results he wanted. This would also provide the necessary secrecy. By 1932, the Germans had become extremely adept at secret military activities in Germany and abroad. They were supporting weapon development in Sweden, Switzerland, and Spain. Under a secret treaty with the Soviet Union, the German army was training cadres of Panzer and parachute troops in the Soviet Union. Military aircraft were being designed, built, and flown in the guise of racing aircraft and airline transports.

Dornberger wanted to start with the most promising amateur rocket groups as the core of his civilian rocket R&D staff.

So Colonel Dornberger, General d'Aubigny, and Colonel Becker paid a casual visit in civilian clothes to the testing ground of the VfR known as the *Raketenflugplatz* (Rocket Flying Field) near Berlin. As Dornberger had anticipated, the experimental work done by Rudolph Nebel, Klaus Riedel, Willy Ley, Kurt Heinisch, and a young student named Wernher von Braun was impressive and probably the most advanced in Germany at the time. These members of the VfR had built and flown, with mixed success, several liquid-fuel rockets called Repulsors and Miraks, none of which flew very high, if at all. The propellants had been gasoline and liquid oxygen. But the rockets had gotten off the ground.

However, the army officers were still appalled by the total lack of meaningful data on any of this work. The only measurements made by the VfR during static testing of their liquid fuel motors were thrust and firing duration. But that was more than anyone else had measured except on the solid propellant rocket test stand at Kummersdorf.

As a result of this visit, the VfR was given a contract for 1,000 reichsmarks to build a liquid-fuel Repulsor rocket for a flight demonstration at Kummersdorf.

# Enter Wernher von Braun

Early on a beautiful July morning in 1932, the members of the VfR loaded their silver-painted rocket called Mirak II and its launching rack atop one of their two available cars and put the liquid oxygen, gasoline, and tools in the other. They set out from the Raketenflugplatz to Kummersdorf, meeting Dornberger at the army testing station about 5:00 A.M. Dornberger led them through the woods to an isolated part of the artillery range.

The VfR members were astonished at what they saw. The army had set up a truly formidable array of phototheodolites, ballistic cameras, and other artillery measuring instruments, some of which they hadn't even known about. It was obvious that the Army Weapons Office wasn't just paying for a show; it wanted any and all data that could be gotten from the launch. If the VfR couldn't take data, the army could and would.

The Mirak II was erected and fueled by 2:00 P.M. and was ignited shortly thereafter. It got off the ground. It rose to an altitude of about 60 meters where it turned into horizontal flight and impacted the ground before its parachute could open.

Dornberger later recalled, "The failure of this demonstration brought home to us in the Army Weapons Department how many scientific and technical questions needed answering before we could hope to construct a rocket that could fly efficiently."

But if Dornberger and Becker weren't impressed by the performance of the Mirak II, it was a different matter when it came to one of the members of the VfR. Dornberger was struck by "the energy and shrewdness with which a tall, fair young student with the broad, massive chin went to work, and by his astounding theoretical knowledge."

He put the young technical student, Wernher von Braun, first on his list of proposed technical assistants.

Born in 1912, Wernher von Braun was the second of three sons raised on an ancestral estate in Silesia by Baron and Baroness Magnus Freiherr von Braun. In school, Wernher scored high marks in music appreciation and languages (he spoke several fluently). But he got poor marks in mathematics. Hoping to stimulate Wernher's scientific interests, his mother, who was an amateur astronomer, gave him a unique present upon his confirmation. He later wrote, "I didn't get a watch and my first pair of long pants like other Lutheran boys. I got a telescope. My mother thought it would make the best gift."

He too became an avid amateur astronomer, but his math grades didn't improve. Then and throughout his life, Wernher von Braun was a dreamer at heart. But it was an article in an amateur astronomy magazine that fired the dream to which he would thereafter dedicate his life. He later said, "I don't remember the name of the magazine or the author, but the article described an imaginary trip to the moon. It filled me with a romantic urge. Interplanetary travel! Here was a task worth devoting one's life to! Not just to stare through a telescope at the moon and the planets, but to soar through the heavens and actually explore the mysterious universe!"

Wernher von Braun's early life would take him in a different direction, but eventually he made the dream of a flight to the moon possible in his final years.

Personally, Wernher von Braun was not only a consummate diplomat but also one of the best engineers I've ever known. I liked the man and will make no excuses for it. He was a role model. A man with dreams _and_ academic credentials, a person who could theorize _and_ design, an individual whose charisma was so powerful that he could instantly dominate any assemblage of people by his mere presence _and_ who was also warm and friendly, he was also a practical person who knew how to work with his hands.

When von Braun was 12 years old, he read about the exploits of a German daredevil, Max Valier, with a rocket-propelled car. So he lashed six big skyrockets to a coaster wagon, got aboard, and lit the rockets. "I was ecstatic! The wagon was wholly out of control and trailing a comet's tail of fire, but my rockets were performing beyond my wildest dreams. Finally, they burned themselves out with a magnificent thunderclap and the vehicle rolled to a halt. The police took me into custody very quickly. Fortunately, no one had been injured, so I was released in charge of the Minister of Agriculture— who was my father." He thereafter made and launched a number of his own solid-fuel skyrockets. (It gave me great pleasure in the 1960s to send him a complete model rocket setup with launcher, model, and premanufactured rocket motors "for your son, Peter." I had no doubts what he would do with it or that he wouldn't build it and operate it with careful, consuming care and safety.) He tried to build his own homemade auto. He was always at home with technology.

Wernher von Braun continued to obtain and devour everything he could read about space flight. Then in 1925 after his family moved to Berlin, he saw an ad for Hermann Oberth's classic book. "When the precious volume arrived, I carried it to my room. Opening it I was aghast. Its pages were a hash of mathematical formulas. It was gibberish. I rushed to my math teacher. How can I understand what this man is saying? He told me to study mathematics and physics, my two worst courses."

Wernher von Braun not only was motivated to pass his courses in physics and math with honors but went on to study at the Charlottenburg Institute of Technology, equivalent to America's Cal Tech or MIT. His intimate knowledge of actual hands-on technology was reinforced because he was in a course of study known today as a "co-op program." He was apprenticed to the Borsig Works. There, an old foreman handed von Braun a chunk of iron about as large as a child's head. He also gave von Braun a file and pointed to a bench vise. "Here are your tools. Make this into a perfect cube. Make every angle a right angle, every face perfectly smooth, and every side equal." Five weeks later, his hands and fingers raw, von Braun had filed the chunk of iron into the required perfect cube which was now the size of a walnut. Borsig then put him to work on a lathe, on a shaper, in the foundry, in the forging plant, and finally in the locomotive assembly sheds. When he was finished six months later, von Braun recalled, he had gotten more insight into practical engineering than he had in any semester at the university.

Except for his early, youthful experiments with solid-fuel rockets, Wernher von Braun's entry into the world of rocketry occurred when he looked up the author of a space travel book he'd read, Dr. Willy Ley, the same man whose books inspired me to become involved in space twenty years later. As Ley wrote:

> *One day in the fall of 1929, I came through my front door to hear Beethoven's "Moonlight Sonata" being played on the piano. The musician was a visitor whom my aunt had admitted, a very polite young man who introduced himself as Wernher von Braun. He told me that he had just graduated from high school, intended to become an engineer, had heard of our experimenting in the VfR of which I was one of the seven founding members. This young man concluded by saying that he had read my book and wanted some advice.*

(When I met Willy Ley in 1953, he was playing the "Moonlight Sonata" on Isaac Asimov's piano.)

Through Ley's efforts, von Braun met Hermann Oberth and became involved in the VfR experimental liquid-fuel rocket program at the Raketenflugplatz.

And that is where Col. Walter Dornberger found him in 1932.

Colonel Becker called von Braun to the Army Weapons Office and made a proposition to him. Dornberger wanted him to work for the army. Becker further proposed that they allow von Braun to study for an advanced degree at the University of Berlin under physics professor Erich Schumann who was also in charge of the research section of the Ordnance Department of the Army Weapons Office. Von Braun would be allowed to use army facilities at Kummersdorf for the experimental work necessary for his doctoral thesis whose subject would deal with liquid-fuel rocket motors.

Von Braun hesitated. He knew he'd be working toward making the rocket a weapon of war, not devoting his efforts toward the achievement of space travel. "It is, perhaps, apropos to mention that at the time none of us [in the VfR] thought of the havoc which rockets would eventually wreak as weapons of war," he admitted in later years. "We were very much in the position of aviation pioneers when the airplane could be developed because of its military value."

Von Braun's road to space was via the military. He saw that and had to accept it. Whether or not it was to be evaluated as good or bad in later years, it was the only way open. What von Braun's decision did in the long run was not only to take men to the moon but to establish the principle of government monopoly in rocket research, development, construction, and operation. Even though this work would be carried on in later years in America under a civilian government agency, it was the first step in establishing the principle that space is the exclusive domain of governments, that only government rocket programs can lead to space access, and that space programs under government funding and control are the only space programs. Half a century later, it was beginning to dawn on rocket enthusiasts and space advocates that this might not be the only or the best way to do it. But, in 1932, it *was* the only way. The fault lies in those who continued to support it as the only way long after it was no longer such.

Wernher von Braun, then only 21 years old, accepted Becker's offer but not without some reluctance.

On October 1, 1932, Wernher von Braun became a civilian employee of the German army.

# The Kummersdorf Team

Col. Walter Dornberger and his civilian expert, Wernher von Braun, quickly ramped-up the activities at Kummersdorf. Their initial objective was to design, build, and successfully test a liquid-fueled rocket motor producing 300 kilograms of thrust using liquid oxygen and gasoline. In order to do this, they had to expand the meager facilities at Kummersdorf. Although backed by the German army, they had to operate in secrecy and therefore with a low budget. Everything in those days operated with a low budget. Not only was the entire world reeling in the depths of the Great Depression, but Germany was still overtly (but not covertly) operating within the military limitations of the Treaty of Versailles.

So Kummersdorf was a shoestring operation. It had to be built slowly. The winter of 1932–1933 was one of political turmoil as well. Adolf Hitler and the Nazi party were not yet totally in control of Germany. That wouldn't occur until February 1, 1933, when Hitler became Chancellor.

So Dornberger had to resort to extreme measures to obtain even the most mundane supplies for the fledgling rocket testing facility. The budget monitors kept a sharp eye on Kummersdorf and wouldn't permit Dornberger to order either machine tools or office equipment. What Dornberger, von Braun, and their colleagues learned that winter has since become standard operating procedure in American aerospace circles and elsewhere as engineers and managers discovered it.

"We learned in a hard school to get everything we wanted," Dornberger wrote.

*We acquired things "as per sample." For instance, even the keenest budget bureau official could not suspect that "Appliance for milling wooden dowels up to 10 millimeters in diameter as per sample" meant a pencil sharpener, or the "Instrument for recording test data with a rotating roller as per sample" meant a typewriter . . . And if there was nothing else to do, we entrenched ourselves behind the magic word "secret." There, the budget bureau was powerless.*

Dornberger quickly hired as many rocket engineers and technicians as he could. From the VfR's Raketenflugplatz came the expert mechanic, Heinrich Grünow. From the Association for the Utilization of Industrial Gases came Walter Riedel (no relation to the Klaus Riedel of the VfR) and Arthur Rudolph.

However, Rudolph Nebel and several other VfR members from the Raketenflugplatz were not hired. Nebel, a World War I fighter pilot, was apprehensive about any military support of the VfR's rocket work. He was concerned about bumblings, delays, and potential attempts at restrictive control inherent in any military-funded project. A little bit of spite was probably also present because Dornberger had hired the young von Braun and not him. Nebel continued to work at the Raketenflugplatz with Klaus Riedel on the development of a liquid motor to produce between 100 and 350 kilograms of thrust. Nebel's general attitude was that no one except those at the Raketenflugplatz knew anything about liquid-fuel rockets, and the army would therefore have to make a deal with the VfR to finance the Raketenflugplatz on Nebel's terms. However, Nebel and the others didn't count on the Gestapo, the new Luftwaffe, or a huge utilities bill from the city.

First, the Luftwaffe showed up in powder-blue uniforms in the spring of 1933 and announced that the land used by the Raketenflugplatz was now their drill ground. Then a city representative handed Nebel a water bill for 1,600 marks; numerous leaky faucets in all the buildings, some of them never used, had dripped away, silently running up this bill from September 1930. The VfR and Nebel couldn't pay the bill of course. The final blow landed when the Gestapo showed up to confiscate documents and equipment because, once Hitler had come to power, all non-government rocket research became *verboten.*

Even government rocket research wasn't really sanctioned by the Nazi government at first. But the Army Weapons Office continued to find a little money here and there. Slowly, the Kummersdorf facilities grew in number and size. An officers' mess was built, and this dwelling also served as home for both Wernher von Braun and Arthur Rudolph.

Rudolph admitted, "We didn't like to get up early; we liked to work late at night instead. At midnight, von Braun had his best ideas. He would expound them on a sketch pad and his ideas led to one thing: space travel."

But the Kummersdorf team, the beginning of the famous von Braun team of later days that got mankind to the moon, developed its first liquid-propellant rocket motor using ethyl alcohol and liquid oxygen.

On the night of December 21, 1932, the Kummersdorf team made ready for the first static firing of this motor.

Dornberger was very proud of this primitive creation, which was a small, pear-shaped aluminum combustion chamber only 50.8 centimeters long. It was suspended in the middle of a test cell and illuminated by floodlights. Behind concrete walls 4 meters high topped by a tar paper and wood roof stood Walter Riedel with his hands on two valves that would control the flow of alcohol and liquid oxygen (LOX) to the chamber. Nearby was Heinrich Grünow watching a pressure gauge and controlling the valve that pressurized the propellant tanks. In the open end of the test bay stood von Braun, gingerly holding a 4-meter wooden pole with a can of flaming gasoline at its end, the igniter.

Dornberger snuggled up to a fir tree 10 meters from the open end of the test stand, taking "cover" behind its tree trunk only 100 millimeters in diameter.

Although the modern "countdown" was first used in Fritz Lang's

*Frau im Mond* movie which had originally motivated everyone there, a countdown wasn't used in this test. The sequence was a series of shouted orders: *"Feuer!—Benzin!—Sauerstoff!"* (Fire! Gasoline! Oxygen!)

Von Braun held the flaming can of gasoline under the rocket nozzle.

Riedel opened the propellant valves in order.

According to Dornberger's later recollection, a round white cloud appeared out of the nozzle and sank slowly to the ground. It was followed by a trickle of clear alcohol. It contacted the flames from the bucket of gasoline on the pole.

According to Dornberger,

> *There was a swoosh, a hiss, and—crash!*
>
> *Clouds of smoke arose. A single flame darted briefly upward and vanished. Cables, boards, metal sheeting, fragments of steel and aluminum flew whistling through the air. The searchlights went out.*
>
> *Silence.*
>
> *In the suddenly dark pit of the testing room a milky, slimy mixture of alcohol and oxygen burned spasmodically with flames of different shapes and sizes, occasionally crackling and detonating like fireworks. Steam hissed. Cables were on fire in a hundred places. Thick, black, stinging fumes of burning rubber filled the air. Von Braun and I stared at each other wide-eyed. We were uninjured.*
>
> *The test stand had been wrecked. Steel girders and pillars were bent and twisted. The metal doors had been torn off their hinges. Immediately above our heads sharp, jagged splinters of steel were stuck in the brown bark of the trees. Riedel and Grünow came running up, agitated and full of concern. Then we had to laugh.*

They had experienced something American rocket engineers now call a "hard start." Hard indeed. I have seen one hard start, and one was enough; it demolished a test stand at White Sands in 1955 and killed two men. Hard starts still occur. The Space Services, Inc.

Percheron rocket suffered a hard start during a test firing on Matagorda Island, Texas, in 1981. Starting a liquid-propellant rocket engine is like playing with the devil, and it's still an empirical feat. Timing is critical.

It was the first of many failures, fires, explosions, and other disasters that would dog their efforts for a decade in Germany and for thirty years thereafter in America.

"The mistakes we made then may, of course, cause smiles now, but we trod with fine freedom of ignorance in a new field of technology and learned from failure and bitter experience," Dornberger wrote.

Three weeks after the test stand explosion, the first rocket motor design was ignited and burned successfully. "Burned" is the literal description of what happened. After a few seconds, a dazzling white light appeared in the bluish-red rocket exhaust and grew brighter. The combustion chamber had been made of aluminum and was on fire. The Kummersdorf team had encountered its first cooling problem.

But because of Dornberger's insistence on careful engineering development and testing, they began to make slow progress. At first, it was one disaster after another on the test stand. They designed and tried out new combustion chambers. They designed and tested new propellant injection systems.

Getting both the fuel and the oxidizer into the combustion chamber at the right place and in the proper amounts to create a smooth combustion instead of a sooty flame or an explosion requires an injector. It is somewhat like the fuel injector in a modern auto engine and very much like a shower head in the bathroom. However, a liquid rocket injector has to deliver both a fuel (something to burn) and an oxidizer (something for the fuel to burn with). Injector design is still a black art, not a science. It's cut-and-try, true empirical experimentation.

Finally, after months of work, failure, success, and failure again, Dornberger's group had developed a rocket motor giving 300 kilograms of thrust consistently. They weren't very happy with it, however, because it had very low efficiency in terms of exhaust velocity—

"only" 1,900 meters per second (6,200 feet per second or about 4,225 miles per hour)!

But now they were making measurements of flame temperature and sampling the rocket exhaust. They were controlling propellant flows and mixture ratios. They tried different propellant combinations. They were doing the first real rocket engineering.

At Kummersdorf, they were far ahead of everyone else in the world at that point. Even the German rocket inventors couldn't come up with a rocket motor that was as good as that first Kummersdorf model, and Dornberger kept looking in hopes of finding someone with more expertise. It didn't exist except at Kummersdorf in 1933–1935.

It was now time to move ahead, and that meant that Dornberger had to demonstrate a liquid-propellant rocket vehicle that could not only fly but hold to a prescribed flight trajectory.

It was time to get to work on the first *aggregat* or "assembly."

# The First Assemblies

Col. Walter R. Dornberger knew he had his hands full of problems and was standing on the lone edge of technology when it came to building a stable liquid-propellant rocket that would fly in a reliable manner.

A militarily acceptable long-range artillery shell had to go where it was aimed and perform in a highly predictable fashion. Congreve-type solid-propellant rockets didn't, but their dispersion was compensated for by the sheer volume of rockets launched. Solid-propellant tactical rockets could be considered like the pellets of a shotgun shell: Fire enough of them at once in a salvo, and perhaps a few might hit the target or come close enough to do the job. This was not what Dornberger was working for.

The requirements of very long-range rocket artillery based on liquid-fuel rockets meant that the missiles had to be self-stabilizing and even guided toward their targets. Dornberger realized that no one knew how to do that yet. All the rocket experimenters and inventors had subordinated stability and flight reliability to the overwhelming technical task of simply getting a liquid-propellant rocket motor to work well enough to propel the vehicle in the first place. No one had tackled the stability and trajectory problems yet. And it was absolutely necessary that this be done now that the Kummersdorf team had a liquid-fuel rocket motor in which they could place some confidence. Dornberger and von Braun recalled only too well the July 1932 flight of the Mirak II at Kummersdorf.

Perhaps Dornberger, von Braun, Riedel, and Grünow thought about simply putting aerodynamic fins on their first *aggregat* vehicles. Feather-fletched arrows had been flying in a quite stable and predictable manner for centuries. No one remembers why the team didn't try this first. But they didn't. Basically, it was because Dornberger was a modern artillery officer, not an archer.

"We were still too much influenced by the traditional ways of thinking expressed in the ballistic reports of the department," Dornberger admitted. "We were still unable to shake ourselves quite free of the idea that what was valid for shells must also be valid for rockets."

Dornberger's notion was that their first rocket, *Aggregat.1* or A.1, should be stabilized by spinning it around its long axis like a bullet or artillery shell.

But this would present some serious engineering problems. The rocket would have to rotate but not the liquid propellant tanks. Otherwise, the liquids would be plastered against the walls of the tanks by centrifugal force, and this would create very serious and perhaps insoluble propellant feeding problems. How would they get the liquids out of the spinning tanks into the combustion chamber?

Dornberger suggested that only part of the rocket should rotate to provide gyroscopic stabilizing forces.

The A.1 was designed with a rotating nose section weighing 38.6 kilograms that also held the payload. The A.1 itself was 1.4 meters long and 30 centimeters in diameter. It held 38 kilograms of alcohol and liquid oxygen in two tanks. These propellants were forced into the rocket combustion chamber by pressurized nitrogen carried in yet a third tank. With a takeoff weight of 150 kilograms and a motor thrust of 300 kilograms, the A.1 could lift off with a 1g acceleration. The rotating section would be the rotor of an electric motor that was brought up to speed before launching.

The purpose of the rotating section was not to provide a gyroscopic reference to a guidance system that would operate servomechanisms to move air vanes on fins or swivel the rocket motor to provide steering. The rotating section *was* the guidance and stabilization system. Its job was to keep the rocket going straight by its own brute-force gyroscopic forces.

The A.1 never flew. It turned out to be too nose heavy for the likes of the Kummersdorf team. In terms of what we know today about rocket stability, this seems rather unusual until one realizes that they didn't know anything about rocket flight stability then.

Rather than attempt to rebuild the A.1, Dornberger told his team to leap to the next stage of development and proceed with the design of the A.2.

The *Aggregat.2* used a new rocket motor design perfected by the Kummersdorf team in the months between the decision to build the A.1 and the realization that the A.1 was nonflyable. This had been done in the new test stand they'd built for higher-thrust motors. The Kummersdorf team was also planning a third stand in which they could test complete vehicles. It was obvious that they intended to build bigger rockets. The little A.1 and A.2 rockets were just test vehicles. To produce a long-range ballistic missile or a rocket capable of probing space, the Kummersdorf team realized they'd need much bigger rockets than had ever existed before.

It was Dornberger who kept his team's energies concentrated on the practical development of rockets for military purposes even though he'd grown to share their dreams of space travel. Arthur Rudolph later admitted, "We didn't want to build weapons; we wanted to go into space. Building weapons was a stepping-stone. What else was there to do but join the War Department? Elsewhere there was no money."

The new rocket motor would deliver 1,000 kilograms of thrust, and they planned for the A.2 rocket to have a burning time of 45 seconds instead of the 16 seconds of the abortive A.1 with the 300-kilogram motor. Otherwise, the A.2 had the same dimensions as the A.1.

The other important difference between the two assemblies was the location of the rotating gyroscopic section. Von Braun moved it from the nose to the midsection between the two propellant tanks. As in the A.1, the rocket combustion chamber was recessed into the alcohol tank. Only one drawing of the A.2 survives.

Two A.2 rockets were designed, built, and ground tested at Kummersdorf. They were named Max and Moritz after the two mischievous boys in the comic strip known in the United States as *The Katzenjammer Kids;* in America, the kids were called Hans and Fritz.

Kummersdorf didn't have enough room to launch the A.2 rockets, so von Braun took them to the island of Borkum in the East Frisian Islands off the delta of the River Elbe in the North Sea. In December 1934, the two rockets didn't live up to their troublemaking namesakes. A few days before Christmas, both Max and Moritz were launched and flew to an altitude of about 2 kilometers.

Max and Moritz weren't the first liquid-fuel rockets to fly, of course. Dr. Robert H. Goddard flew the first one near Auburn, Massachusetts, on March 16, 1926. The VfR and other German experimenters had gotten liquid-fuel rockets into the air since then. And the first Soviet liquid-fuel rocket, the OR-1, was flown near Moscow in 1933.

Nor were they the first liquid-propellant rockets whose flight was gyroscopically controlled. That had been accomplished by Dr. Robert H. Goddard with one of his *Nell* rockets near Roswell, New Mexico, in 1934.

But the A.2 rockets are oft-forgotten milestones in rocket research and development. Their success allowed Dornberger, von Braun, and the Kummersdorf team to get the funding to go far beyond what Goddard was doing in the United States. They showed the German army that Dornberger and his team were indeed making substantial and visible progress in developing the rocket as a practical and desirable long-range artillery weapon.

Even as Max and Moritz were being planned, built, and flown, Riedel and his motor team were perfecting a more powerful motor with a thrust of 1,500 kilograms. This allowed von Braun to begin design work on a larger, more powerful rocket known as the A.3.

According to Dornberger, the A.3 was intended to be "a purely experimental apparatus to test liquid-fueled rocket propulsion for missilelike bodies and for trials of the guidance system." Although the heavy rotating section of the A.2 rockets had stabilized them, von Braun wanted something smaller and lighter.

Von Braun got in touch with the Kreiselgeräte G.m.b.H., a gyroscope company at Breitz near Berlin, and spoke with a former Austrian naval officer, a man named Boykow who had become obsessed with the subject of naval torpedoes and their gyros. Boykow had secured hundreds of patents relating to gyros in compasses and stabilized fire-control devices.

When von Braun told Boykow what he wanted, the gyro expert answered with a smile, "I've been expecting a call like yours for many years and I've prepared for it."

He told Dornberger and von Braun that he could design and build a gyro stabilizing system for the A.3, pointing out that it wasn't enough to use the gyro to correct deflections of the rocket from its intended attitude but to stop the initial tendency to deviate. Only if an immediate action was taken to counter the deviation could a divergent trend in oscillations be stopped. In short, the gyro stabilizer had to sense not only a change in attitude but the *rate of change* of attitude. A stabilizing guidance system would have to be sensitive not only to position but to acceleration. Boykow's gyro stabilizing system for the A.3 would do just that, he said.

On top of that, the stability and "dynamic stability" of the rocket's shape had an effect on the tendency to oscillate in flight. It became clear to von Braun and his colleagues that a ballistic missile stabilized by fins would possess "arrow stability" that would in turn give Boykow's gyro stabilizing system less work to do. But according to the standard text on ballistics written by Colonel Becker and Carl Crantz, it was impossible for fin-stabilized bodies to remain stable in supersonic flight. However, no one had actually tested fin-stabilized ballistic vehicles in a wind tunnel, much less in flight. Supersonic speeds would be achieved by any long-range ballistic missile. In fact, a ballistic missile would have to remain stable from very low subsonic velocity to supersonic speeds. Dornberger would have to find the money to build a supersonic wind tunnel. He did.

Another problem involved how to control a rocket over such a wide speed range and from air at sea level density up to the near-vacuum of extremely high altitudes of 100 kilometers or more. Von Braun and his group considered swinging or gymballing the rocket motor—which was impossible in the A.3 because the motor was still surrounded by the alcohol tank—as well as using air rudders on the stabilizing fins—which wouldn't work at near-zero air speeds at launch—to using control vanes in the rocket jet—if a material could be found that would withstand the heat and forces inside the jet. They decided to use molybdenum vanes in the rocket exhaust jet.

By October 1937, all design, construction, and static tests of the A.3 were completed. Three A.3 rockets were taken to the island of Greifswalder Oie north of the towns of Wolgast and Zinnowitz on the Baltic Sea in an area that was to see the launch of many more rockets in the years to come. In December 1937, von Braun's team was ready to launch them in terrible weather and under the most primitive conditions. No central range control facilities existed yet, and days were spent waiting while everyone got into position and ready—radio operators, recovery aircraft, divers. However, all three A.3 rockets were launched from a simple concrete pad without a launch tower. All of them malfunctioned. The first A.3 deployed its recovery parachute 5 seconds into the flight and went unstable. The parachute was omitted from the second A.3, but it, too, tumbled and crashed. Von Braun waited until the wind was absolutely calm before launching the third rocket, but it went unstable as well.

Because von Braun and his team had little knowledge about gyros and had hesitated to question the competency of Boykow, the great gyro expert, they hadn't paid much attention to the gyro system. Now the gyros took all the blame. Boykow never built another rocket gyro system. Von Braun and his team now understood that they would have to develop their own expertise in gyro systems and build their own stabilizing system. Since it would take an estimated 18 months for the new system to be designed and tested to von Braun's own specifications, his team used the time to correct several of the shortcomings of the assemblies they'd designed and built thus far. These would be incorporated into another test missile, the A.5.

The designation A.4 had already been assigned to a far more ambitious project that they hoped would follow the A.3.

# Good Duck-Hunting Country

The development of the long-range ballistic missile didn't proceed in an orderly fashion from a bright idea through a logical series of development steps on a PERT chart to the final finished weapon. As with every other development in technology, a lot of different things were going on simultaneously, even in Germany.

The flights of the A.2 vehicles—Max and Moritz—resulted in a loosening of the budgetary purse strings at the Army Weapons Office. The two A.2 rockets convinced the general officers in the Army Ordnance Department that rocket technology could produce a practical and desirable long-range artillery weapon.

As had happened in the past and would happen again in the future, this additional support came just in time.

Dornberger and his rocketeers were outgrowing the limitations of Kummersdorf. They didn't have enough room to build a test stand capable of handling rocket motors with thrust levels of 2,000 kilograms and more—and they were definitely planning for larger motors to propel larger vehicles. They had no room at Kummersdorf to flight-test even the small A.2 rockets, much less the A.3; both vehicle types had to be tested elsewhere. Also, Kummersdorf couldn't be expanded; it was too close to Berlin and the German capital's densely populated environs. This also made the rocket work at Kummersdorf more difficult to keep secret; when a 1,500 kilogram rocket motor was test fired, it could be heard for kilometers. And by 1935, the work force had grown to more than 80 people.

German rocketry had outgrown its cradle.

The German rocketeers wanted to build their own test center on a grand scale. They had started to plan for large production facilities, and they had no desire to see these put up in the style of "Unit Model 78, Old Type," right out of the army construction manuals. Dornberger, von Braun, and their architects were fascinated by the beauty and style of the new Luftwaffe buildings. But to build their new test center, they needed a site and they needed money.

According to Dornberger, "Again and again we tried the old dodge that nearly always works in matters of weapon development— demonstrating our wares in front of the prominent people who sit on the money bags." Dornberger and von Braun learned how to do this very well, indeed. And in later days, they taught the managers and engineers of the American aerospace industry how to do it, too. So if this procedure sounds familiar even today, readers will know that the Germans taught the Americans about things other than rocket technology.

In March 1938, Dornberger persuaded Major General Wernher von Fritsch, commander in chief of the Reichswehr, to visit Kummersdorf with his staff. Dornberger and von Braun presented brief but thorough lectures with colored charts and many diagrams. Wernher von Braun was a charismatic personality. When he gave a lecture or a briefing, he was a consummate actor, reaching out to his audience and pulling them in, making them hang on his every word. He could and did repeatedly mesmerize generals, financiers, diplomats, politicians, and world leaders. He was *good* at this sort of thing.

Then, in a carefully orchestrated production, they took the General and his staff out to the rocket test stands and demonstrated the 300-kilogram, 1,000-kilogram, and 1,500-kilogram liquid-rocket motors they had developed.

Watching the flight of a large liquid-propellant rocket is transient. The brief few seconds full of a lot of fire and smoke and thunder end quickly when the rocket is first launched; then it is up and gone out of sight. However, a static test of a rocket motor is awesome. The fire, the smoke, and the deafening thunder are there for as much as a minute. They assault the senses up to the threshold of pain in some cases. The fiery demon doesn't go anywhere. Static tests have been known to cause strong men to tremble or run. Time after time, witnesses have admitted, "I kept telling myself it can't go on. It must not go on. It must stop. But it just kept on and on and on until I thought the world would come apart."

When the last test of the 1,500-kilogram motor was over, the fire had gone away, the thunder was still echoing off the surrounding hills, and the smoke was quietly rising from the hot flame pits, General von Fritsch said the one thing Dornberger and von Braun wanted to hear: "How much money do you want?"

Yet this statement of full and complete backing made Dornberger feel uncomfortable. He had a new idea about how to develop weapons.

> We wanted to investigate and develop on a single site everything that seemed essential to the effective employment of such a new and powerful weapon. We wanted to develop, not only the rocket itself, but also the necessary ground handling and testing equipment, and to study all its implications in the most diverse branches of technology and science. We wanted to start with applied research and end up with a fully developed article ready for production in the factories. In short, we wished to put through on our own account a complete program. We needed a research and development site fully equipped with all the latest resources of science and technology. And that cost money.

Dornberger's estimate seemed to be an impossible sum running into seven figures.

Dornberger sat down and established the criteria for a center that would develop and test the very large rockets of the future as they moved from the drawing boards to the field. He was the first person to do this. His criteria are still followed today in the development and flight of ballistic missiles and, unfortunately, also space launch vehicles.

A rocket development and testing center, Dornberger wrote, should be located on a seacoast where large rockets could be launched in a direction away from the base itself. The line of flight should be parallel to a long stretch of coastline so that the entire trajectory could be observed and documented by camera and by radio means (later radar). The facility site itself should be flat. It should be large enough to accommodate a long airfield runway to be used in rocket-assisted takeoff and rocket-propelled aircraft research. Finally, the site should be in a remote location for reasons of both safety and security. In short, Dornberger's criteria describe the ultimate artillery range for long-range artillery shells. Since land in Germany for this sort of range was largely unavailable, Dornberger specified a seacoast location. However, large tracts of desert land were available in other parts of the world, and similar large-rocket artillery ranges were established there within the next twenty years. The ultimate testing range for very long-range artillery rockets, of course, would have to be located on a seacoast for flight safety reasons.

We are still wedded to the Dornberger requirements today, even for space transportation, because space transportation vehicles were developed the easy way from ballistic missiles.

Wernher von Braun stumbled on the ultimate site for German rocket research.

During a visit to the family estate in Aklam, Silesia, at Christmas 1935, von Braun told his mother all about his new work and happened to mention that he was looking for an out-of-the-way place on the seacoast where it would be possible to fire rockets for long distances along the shore.

"Wernher," the Baroness von Braun told her son, "speaking of out-of-the-way places, your father used to go duck hunting on the island of Usedom up near Peenemünde . . ."

Von Braun went to Usedom for a look. Then he brought Dornberger up for a tour of what he'd discovered.

Usedom is one of two islands that separate the Bay of Stettin from the Baltic Sea. Wollin is the other. The channel separating the two is the Swine at whose seaward end is the village of Swinemünde. The channel on the west separating Usedom from the mainland is the Peene and near its mouth was a small village called Peenemünde, literally "the Mouth of the Peene." One takes the railway to Wolgast, the ferry to Usedom, and one is at Peenemünde.

The place was far away from large towns and traffic. Usedom consisted of sand dunes and marshland overgrown with oak and pine trees. Deer roamed these forests. The reedy marshlands along the Peene and the Baltic were home to swarms of ducks, grebes, coots, and swans. In 1935, nothing disturbed the peace and quiet but the cry of birds and the occasional report of a hunter's shotgun. It was great duck-hunting country.

The island was owned by the city of Wolgast on the mainland. Dornberger approved of the site.

Back in Berlin in late 1935, the Wehrmacht had begun a cooperative rocket research program with the fledgling Luftwaffe. Dornberger's counterpart in the Luftwaffe was Major Wolfram von Richthofen, past commander of the German Condor Legion in the Spanish Civil War and cousin of the Red Baron, the legendary Baron Manfred Freiherr von Richthofen of World War I.

The Luftwaffe was interested in rocket propulsion for aircraft and rocket-assisted takeoff of heavily loaded bombers. Although airplanes were not the army's area of interest, the Kummersdorf team had strapped one of its 300-kilogram motors to the belly of a Junkers A.50 "Junior" all-metal light plane, and von Braun himself test-flew it.

At a joint Wehrmacht–Luftwaffe meeting in Berlin in April 1936, Gen. Albert Kesselring, chief of aircraft construction, in what Dornberger later wrote as "an attack of acute generosity," approved of the purchase of the island of Usedom. He agreed that the Luftwaffe would build the test station at Peenemünde and that there would be a Luftwaffe section, Peenemünde-West, and a Wehrmacht section, Peenemünde-East. The two services would share operating expenses. He sent the Ministerial Councilor of the Air Ministry to Wolgast the next day and bought the island from the city for 750,000 reichsmarks.

The acute generosity of the higher authorities continued. To expedite the development of rocket motors for aircraft and in a thinly veiled attempt to monopolize all rocket research by wooing

Dornberger's team to the Luftwaffe, Major von Richthofen authorized 5 million reichsmarks for the construction at Peenemünde.

The Wehrmacht countered immediately. General Becker, now Chief of Army Ordnance, was wrathfully indignant at the impertinence of the upstart junior Luftwaffe. At a meeting quickly called in Berlin, Becker told Dornberger and von Horstig that the Luftwaffe was going to find itself the junior partner in the rocket business. Becker snapped testily, "I intend to appropriate six million reichsmarks on top of von Richthofen's five!"

Interservice rivalry in ballistic missile technology is therefore nothing new.

The rocketeers had really learned how to tap the government till to pay for their rocket research!

And they taught others how to do it and kept it up for the next fifty years.

# The Genesis of Assembly Four

The development of the Aggregat.4 began before the A.3s were flown. The proposed A.4 was originally to be a larger version of the A.3 and would be capable of carrying a payload.

But in spite of the fact that the purse strings had been loosened as a result of the March 1936 visit of General von Fritsch to Kummersdorf, it had been made clear to Dornberger long before the visit that he was expected to show something as a result of the research and development. Becker and his superiors were expecting a return on their investment. The army wanted a rocket that would be capable of throwing a very big payload over a very long range with an excellent prospect of hitting the target.

Although none of the records survive, it's possible that the German General Staff was even at that time developing war plans for German *Lebensraum* expansion into the Soviet Union. Bombers were at that time limited in range and bomb-carrying capability. Bombers were vulnerable to interception on their way to and from their targets. Bombers had to be flown by crews that required expensive training and even more expensive ground support facilities at airfields. And bombing was the Luftwaffe's role and mission. The Wehrmacht wanted its own long-range equivalent for delivering explosives on a target. Although the provisions of the Treaty of Versailles had been thrown out and ignored by the German government a short time after Hitler's acquisition of power, long-range artillery had its limits insofar as effective range was concerned: about

50 kilometers for railway-mounted naval guns.

In retrospect, it may be possible to speculate that the Wehrmacht wanted long-range ballistic missiles because the German General Staff knew they might be called upon to conduct military operations in the vast expanses of the Soviet Union that lay to the east. Deep penetration by artillery meant one thing in western Europe, but it was a different story when facing the USSR and the thousands of kilometers of steppe and tundra that stretched across Asia to the shores of the Pacific Ocean.

Dornberger was told by the Army Weapons Office that the initial windfall of funding from von Fritsch and von Richthofen probably couldn't be maintained unless his team could begin the development of a useful rocket weapon.

Therefore when Dornberger met with von Braun and Riedel a few days after the visit of General von Fritsch in March 1936, he immediately squashed the euphoria of his two associates who now saw that the road to space was suddenly open to them at last.

Dornberger told them that they were being paid to develop a long-range artillery weapon, not a spaceship. Therefore, the A.4 rocket would be designed at the outset to meet certain military specifications.

Dornberger was an officer-engineer who had specialized in heavy long-range artillery. He knew that artillery's highest achievement to that time was the Paris Gun. As we have seen, it had fired a 120-kilogram shell containing 10.45 kilograms of explosive to a range of 130 kilometers. Needing to start somewhere, Dornberger told von Braun and Riedel that they would proceed to develop the A.4 against the following military specifications:

1. The A.4 would have a range of 260 kilometers, twice that of the Paris Gun.
2. The A.4 would deliver a warhead weighing 1,000 kilograms (one metric ton), roughly a hundred times the weight of the explosive charge of the shell fired from the Paris Gun.
3. The A.4's dispersion—the distribution of 50 percent of the impact points around the target point—would be 2 to 3 mils,

half that of conventional artillery. In artillery jargon, this means that for every thousand meters of range, a deviation of 2 to 3 meters longitudinally or laterally was acceptable.

4. The A.4 would be capable of being transported on any road or railway in Germany; this meant that its size would be determined and limited by the size of the tunnels and the amount of curvature permitted in the German railway system as well as the clearances on German roads and through the streets of towns and villages.

With these marching orders handed down by Dornberger, von Braun, Riedel, Rudolph, and the other members of the team realized they had to march. So they did. Now they had a firm set of specifications against which to design a rocket. They wouldn't be able to continue to do experimentation for experimentation's sake. Any experimentation they carried out would have to be experimentation to gain a goal.

Earlier, I remarked that von Braun was an outstanding engineer. When given this engineering job to do, he exercised his leadership talents as well as his technical talents. But Dornberger had given the primary responsibility for the design of the A.4 to Walter Riedel; von Braun continued to be the civilian team leader, the coordinator, the project manager. This didn't keep von Braun out of the design process, however.

Within a few weeks von Braun and Riedel had come up with the general design of the A.4.

In order to carry a one-ton warhead to 260 kilometers, the rocket would have to attain a maximum velocity of 2,050 meters per second (3,350 miles per hour). The rocket would therefore be traveling at roughly three times the speed of sound, making it the largest man-made object ever to achieve supersonic flight.

The thrust and total impulse of the liquid-propellant rocket motor necessary to achieve that velocity was determined by using the technical and performance data from the rocket motors developed thus far at Kummersdorf. Those motors showed that a rocket exhaust velocity of 2,134 meters per second (7,000 feet per second) was attainable with the technology they had already developed and with the familiar propellants, liquid oxygen and alcohol. Assuming this exhaust velocity and "specific impulse" (the amount of thrust produced by burning a given weight of propellant per second), and working with the same conservative ratio of propellant weight to takeoff weight, von Braun and Riedel knew the A.4 would need a rocket motor capable of producing 25 tons of thrust for 65 seconds. At least 8,000 kilograms of propellants—liquid oxygen and alcohol— would be needed. This meant that the A.4 would weigh about 12 tons at takeoff.

This was probably the first time in history that a rocket was specifically designed to meet an established set of specifications and requirements. Prior to that time, a rocket was built and then flown to determine its performance. Thus, Dornberger, von Braun, and Riedel laid the basic foundations not only for the ICBM and other ballistic missiles but also for the early space launch vehicles that came from their development work in Germany.

The mobility restrictions established by Dornberger meant that the A.4 couldn't be long and skinny or it wouldn't be able to negotiate the curves of German roads and railways. It couldn't be short and fat or it wouldn't be able to go through the railway tunnels. To carry the needed propellant volume and not exceed the maximum dimension of 3.5 meters that would allow it to pass through railway tunnels, it would have to be more than 14 meters long. By a method of mathematical calculation known as reiteration, von Braun and Riedel determined that the A.4 would need to have a body diameter of about 1.5 meters (about 5 feet). The span over the fins, of course, could not exceed the 3.5-meter maximum dimension that would allow it to go through railway tunnels.

It was quickly apparent to Dornberger, von Braun, and Riedel that the A.4 was an extremely ambitious project, given the state of the art of rocket technology at the time. Today, the term used to describe the project would be "high risk."

"We were a bit uneasy," Dornberger recalled later, "for we were up against a mass of new problems and quite aware that the step was really a little too ambitious. We suspected that it might take years to work out the best shape for the missile, which would have to exceed all the usual speeds of aircraft and projectiles."

They would have to conduct aerodynamic research in subsonic and supersonic wind tunnels. No subsonic tunnels existed that could accept a vehicle the size of the A.4; scale models would have to be tested instead. No supersonic wind tunnels existed that would come near achieving the supersonic speeds the A.4 would attain in flight.

A new rocket motor would have to be developed, one that was far larger than any yet built. The step from a 3-ton motor to a 25-ton motor was a large one. Neither von Braun nor Riedel knew how to scale up a rocket motor, but they did know from their past experience that it wasn't a simple matter. Scaling a liquid-propellant rocket motor *still* isn't a simple matter more than sixty years later because there are no neat scaling equations; it is a matter of empirical, cut-and-try development accompanied by a lot of static testing and failures. A new test stand would have to be built because the biggest Kummersdorf test stand was capable of handling only the 3-ton motor. Von Braun wanted to build a test stand that would handle motors up to 100 tons so they wouldn't have to build a new test stand every few years as the size of motors and missiles increased. No one had ever built a rocket test stand that large before, and von Braun knew it would have to be different from the open bays that had worked well for the Kummersdorf motors.

The A.4 would require a drastic change from the existing system of delivering the propellants to the combustion chamber. The first three *aggregat* designs had used pressurized tanks to force the propellants into the motor against the internal combustion pressure produced by burning the propellants. The weight of tanks large enough to hold the required volume of A.4 propellant would be too great if the pressurized feed system was used. Therefore, pump feeding would be required. Yet no pumps were known that would be light enough or capable of handling liquid oxygen at −185 degrees Celsius. And how were the pumps to be driven? By gas turbine? If so, should the turbine be fed with exhaust gas from the combustion chamber or in some other way? They knew that Dr. Goddard in the United States was building some of the first pump-fed liquid-propellant rockets, but they didn't know the details.

In order to achieve the accuracy specified by Dornberger, von Braun and Riedel knew they would have to develop a system for shutting down the rocket motor within a fraction of a second once the required velocity was attained. At *Brennschluss*—literally, "all burnt," equivalent to the modern term "burnout," which has nothing whatsoever to do with the rocket motor burning through some portion of its combustion chamber—the A.4 would be moving at nearly 2 kilometers per second, and any small deviation from the required final velocity would either shorten or lengthen the longitudinal range. And yet another system would have to be developed to control the lateral dispersion of the missile.

These were major technical problems, and the A.4 and all subsequent ballistic missiles would face them in one way or another.

The Dornberger team set out to find the answers.

Contrary to popular current belief among most Americans, fueled mostly by national patriotism, most of the German rocket research and development did not depend on ideas "stolen" from Goddard's work or patents. Von Braun and his team developed their solutions independently. This is a rather commonplace phenomenon in science, technology, and engineering. When engineers in different companies or countries are faced with similar problems to solve, the solutions they come up with are usually similar as well. The universe is the same for everyone everywhere; the only "differences" are in each individual's varying *perceptions* of the universe.

# Cross-Fertilization
# and Serendipity

From 1936 through 1939, the new rocket test station at Peene-münde was built and the Kummersdorf work was slowly transferred there. However, not all research on the A.4 was carried on by the Dornberger team, although Dornberger and von Braun continued to build their team by bringing in people who were not only the best in their fields but highly motivated as well.

One of these was Dr. Walter Thiel, a fair-skinned man with dark eyes behind black horn-rim glasses, fair hair brushed straight back in the fashion of the day, and a strong chin. Thiel was a hardworking, conscientious, and systematic research worker, extremely Teutonic in his approach and behavior. Thiel was ambitious and had a very large ego. He adopted a superior attitude and demanded total devotion from his colleagues. He wasn't an easy man for even the diplomatic and charismatic von Braun to work with, and Dornberger's management skills were used to the utmost in reducing friction between Thiel and the rest of the team.

Thiel was put in charge of the development of the 25-ton rocket motor. Although Dornberger, von Braun, and Riedel continued to contribute to motor design by means of brainstorming sessions with Thiel and his motor development group, it was Thiel who took the bright ideas, worked them into practical applications, and tested them. Thiel developed new methods of injecting propellant into the combustion chamber. He also reduced the length of the A.3 combustion chamber and increased its exhaust velocity by 5 percent because of improved propellant mixing after injection. This reduced the propellant use rate and thus increased the specific impulse, which is a measure of the efficiency of a rocket motor. Dornberger suggested that the injectors be recessed away from the combustion chamber itself to prevent them from being burned by the increased combustion temperature, and Dr. Thiel perfected this using the working and well-documented 1.5-ton motor as a test bed to examine such improvements.

Thiel then developed a 4.5-ton motor by increasing the size and clustering three of the proven injector heads.

But rocket motors still burned through at the most critical point, the narrow throat of the nozzle. Thiel's engineering colleague, Pöhlmann, suggested injecting a thin layer of alcohol through the nozzle wall at critical points, thus creating a sort of insulating layer between the heat of the combustion gases and the nozzle wall. This "film cooling" technique not only worked but was used in many subsequent rocket motors. A large number of small holes were drilled at the endangered areas to allow alcohol from the double-walled cooling system to bleed into the nozzle where it was instantly vaporized. After drilling, the holes were plugged with Woods metal, a material with a low melting point, that quickly melted out once the motor was started and the flame formed.

As a result of these innovations, full reliability of liquid-propellant rocket motors was achieved at Kummersdorf for the first time anywhere.

Thiel stayed at Kummersdorf when most of the other members of the group were moved to Peenemünde in May 1937. He continued development of the 25-ton motor. Thiel did not come to Peenemünde until the summer of 1940.

Von Braun made the critical suggestion that allowed the construction of the 25-ton motor. Injection systems were then, as now, the biggest problem in scaling up a rocket motor. Thiel had a working injector for the 1.5-ton motor, which he'd clustered successfully for the 4.5-ton motor. Von Braun suggested that Thiel place 18 of these proven injectors at the front of the combustion chamber arranged in two concentric circles. Those first big chambers were ready for testing by early 1939. Except for the usual engineering glitches and tweakings that accompany the development of any new device, the 25-ton motor worked.

Von Braun stumbled onto the solution to the propellant pump problem. To anyone who didn't specialize in pumps, then and now, the pump problems would sound insoluble—light weight, simple construction, quick reaction, and high-volume delivery at a constant pressure. Von Braun visited a pump factory and, with some trepidation, described the propellant pump requirements to the engineering staff. When he finished, he was prepared to listen to protests that these requirements were impossible. But the pump experts said, "No problem. What you want is a fire-fighting pump. We make lots of them." Fire pumps must deliver a large volume of water. The delivery pressure must be steady and constant so that firefighters can hold the nozzles steady. They must be simple, lightweight, easy to use, and quick to respond. Thus, the design of the A.4's propellant pump—and all subsequent liquid-propellant rocket pumps—was based on existing fire-fighting equipment. Von Braun had unknowingly looked into other existing technologies to find an answer to his high-tech problem . . . and found it. Today, this is known as "technological cross-fertilization."

The power source for the pump was found in the technology developed for some of the liquid-fuel aircraft rocket motors being developed at Kummersdorf and several industrial firms. These units used the rapid decomposition of high-strength hydrogen peroxide, which was just becoming available in Germany. By bringing hydrogen peroxide together with a permanganate solution, high temperature, high pressure steam could be generated. This could be used to drive a steam turbine of the sort in everyday use in turbogenerating equipment for electrical power plants. Again, technological cross-fertilization kept the rocket engineers from having to "reinvent the square wheel," as the saying goes today.

The solutions to the problems of ballistic missile aerodynamics weren't as easy. Dornberger had placed a straitjacket on the A.4 design by his dimensional restrictions created in turn by the dimension of roads, railway cars, and railway tunnels.

Dr. Rudolph Hermann was the assistant to the aerodynamics chair at the Technical University of Aachen. Later, he would join the team at Peenemünde to run the wind tunnels there. At the request of von Braun, Hermann had made some tests of the A.3 configuration in the supersonic wind tunnel at Aachen. The test section in this tunnel, the largest supersonic test facility in the world at the time, was only 10 centimeters by 10 centimeters (3.97 inches by 3.97 inches). He carefully explained to Dornberger and von Braun the difficulties of finding the proper shape for a fin-stabilized missile in supersonic flight.

Dr. Hermann found the cause of the A.3 flight stability problems as a result of his wind tunnel tests. The sharply swept back fins and the stabilizing ring fin used on the A.3 not only would be subjected to extreme heating from the rocket jet plume if they were used on the A.4 as planned, but they also would make the missile very sensitive to wind effects. Any fin-stabilized missile—rocket or arrow—tends to turn into any wind that blows sideways against it during launch and while in flight. In the case of the A.3 where three failures in a row almost brought the German ballistic missile program to a halt, Hermann determined that a wind of as little as 4 meters per second (about 8 miles per hour) would create such strong aerodynamic turning forces on the A.3 that the gyroscopic control system would be overpowered and unable to right the rocket.

This convinced Dornberger and von Braun that they would have to have wind tunnel facilities at Peenemünde to reduce the time spent in cut-and-try development with expensive rocket flight test vehicles. But the price was staggering. Von Braun estimated the cost at 300,000 deutschmarks. "I had had enough experience with building to know that there wasn't the least chance of the cost remaining at that figure, especially with von Braun about," Dornberger said. He estimated the cost at about a million deutschmarks. When he mentioned that figure to General Becker, he got a grave look but an agreement to fund the supersonic wind tunnel under one condition: At least one other division within the Army Weapons Department had to show interest in it and agree to make use of it.

To Dornberger, it was intuitively obvious that such a wind tunnel could be used to improve the shape of artillery shells and perhaps increase the range of an ordinary gun by as much as 20 percent. But even the Ballistics and Munitions Department saw no value in a wind tunnel. Dornberger had exhausted every avenue and finally approached a friend who was in charge of the antiaircraft division. The possibility of increasing the altitude to which an antiaircraft gun could shoot at a high-flying bomber was enough to get Dornberger the endorsement he needed.

Thus, the supersonic wind tunnel for the first ballistic missile was partly justified by, again, the artillery officers to meet the needs of improved long-range artillery.

The tail fins that were used on the A.5 test vehicle and later on the A.4 ballistic missile had no stabilizing ring fin. They were wider. The trailing edges curved outward to keep them out of the rocket exhaust plume which aerodynamic research said would widen out into a bell shape at high altitudes where the surrounding air was only a fraction of its sea level density. This new fin design was first tested in the subsonic tunnels at the Zeppelin Aircraft Works and then in the supersonic tunnel at Aachen. It was incorporated into the first A.5 test vehicles that were built in the Peenemünde shops in 1938.

The tests that clinched the design were not made in a wind tunnel or with flight test vehicles. At that time, even the Aachen supersonic tunnel couldn't take measurements at supersonic speeds but only determine whether or not a body would remain stable. And no fin-stabilized body had maintained stability in flight at supersonic speeds without breaking up.

The first A.5 tests were made with models dropped from Heinkel He-111 bombers at 20,000 feet. Some of these were solid iron models about 200 millimeters in diameter and 1.5 meters long, weighing about 250 kilograms. They were equipped with fins of various shapes. All carried smoke generators and flares. When dropped from an He-111 at 20,000 feet altitude, their falling trajectory was tracked by camera telescopes called cinetheodolites. At about 3,000 feet above the ground, these "bombs" reached a speed of about 800 miles per hour, thus exceeding the speed of sound. And they remained stable, wobbling only about 5 degrees, a diversion easily handled by control systems of reasonable size and weight.

Controlling the A.5 and A.4 in flight could thus be carried out with a properly designed gyro-stabilized autopilot which sent signals to servomotors used to turn both air vanes on the fins and jet vanes in the rocket exhaust. A newly hired technical draftsman at Kummersdorf suggested using graphite vanes instead of molybdenum units. This reduced the price of a jet vane by a factor of 100 to 1.5 deutschmarks. Graphite jet vanes were thus adopted for the A.5 and A.4.

It looked to Dornberger and von Braun that perhaps the most difficult technical problems had been solved. Little technical problems continued to crop up during the development program. But they were as nothing compared with the nontechnical problems that grew up around the first ballistic missile.

# Hitler's Rockets

Adolph Hitler was never very much interested in rockets.

In the first place, he didn't understand them. It's apparent that the sum total of his military expertise came from his experience as a soldier in World War I, a conflict in which long-range ballistic artillery rockets weren't used.

But Colonel Dornberger and Dr. von Braun knew that without Hitler's support they wouldn't be able to continue very long.

Hitler never saw the rocket research center at Peenemünde. And he never saw a ballistic missile launched. His sole contact with rocket research in Germany came during a visit to Kummersdorf on March 23, 1939, when he showed up with the army chief of staff, Gen. Walther von Brauchitsch, and the chief of Army Ordnance, Gen. Karl Becker. He and his entourage were met at the gate by Colonel Dornberger and von Braun.

Standing behind a protective wall 10 meters away, he witnessed a horizontal static test of a 300 kilogram motor. The pale-blue exhaust jet with its standing shock diamonds drew not a single word from *der Führer*. Nor did the vertical test of a 1,000 kilogram motor.

Von Braun then gave Hitler a careful, simplified presentation on liquid-propellant rockets using a cutaway model of the A.5 test vehicle. Von Braun had heard of Hitler's fascination with modern technology and intricate machinery. So he gave *der Führer* an enthusiastic and detailed briefing.

Hitler asked von Braun a few questions, wanting to know how the camera film payload was recovered from the A.5 and why two propellants were needed. Von Braun became worried lest he make *der Führer* look silly by explaining the basics of rocketry to him.

But as from the moment he entered Kummersdorf, Hitler's face remained passive and his attitude was one of general disinterest as if his thoughts were far away on other matters.

Hitler finally asked, "How much payload will it carry?"

To which von Braun had to answer that the A.5 was an experimental test vehicle that would lead to the A.4 which would carry a one-ton warhead.

Hitler wanted to know if the rockets could be made from steel instead of aluminum which was allocated for airplanes. Dornberger said that it could be but that the redesign would take more time. It was apparent from the questions he asked that Hitler was trying to fit the long-range ballistic missile into his own grandiose plans. He asked how long it would take to develop the A.4. Von Braun let Dornberger field that question as a military man; besides, it would give Dornberger a chance to plug for more development money.

The grand finale was a vertical static test of an entire A.5 rocket suspended in a test stand. Dornberger and von Braun felt that such a Wagnerian production would certainly provoke a response from Hitler. But unlike others who had watched and would later watch rocket-motor static tests, *der Führer* remained impassive. It's difficult even today for rocket engineers to understand this because a static test is a highly emotional experience. Hitler had always shown immense enthusiasm for all new weapons and found no tank or gun or airplane too difficult to understand. When new guns had been demonstrated to him, he could hardly be induced to leave and wanted all the technical details explained in depth. Yet Hitler never showed any enthusiasm for rockets during that enigmatic Kummersdorf visit.

Dornberger wrote, "Why that brain, equipped, so far as all questions of armament were concerned, with a positively staggering memory for figures, could not take in the true significance of our rockets remained a mystery to me."

During lunch Hitler made one comment about what he had seen that morning, and it is even today somewhat enigmatic. He is quoted as saying, *"Es war doch gewaltig!"* This has been translated many times as, "Well, it was grand!" But, as Willy Ley pointed out, *gewaltig* also means "enormous," "impressive," or "imposing." In any event, it was praise of a sort. The rocketeers, expecting more, didn't think so at the time.

Von Braun later said he knew then that they could have trouble in the future without Hitler's enthusiastic support. *Der Führer* told his cronies what his thoughts were about everything. And Hitler's "infallible judgment" was accepted as the gospel truth and passed down the party line. In many respects, von Braun's premonition was right. In others, it wasn't. Even today, no one can really say what motivated the madman who was to loose on Europe the most destructive war in history.

Hitler's statement can perhaps be understood better when it isn't taken as a sound bite and the following conversation is taken into account. Hitler went on to say that he had known the rocket enthusiast Max Valier, who had gotten a lot of publicity in the late 1920s by attaching solid-propellant rockets to a racing car. Valier had spoken with Hitler in Munich about the rocket's prospects for space travel. Hitler told the Kummersdorf rocketeers that Valier had been a dreamer. Dornberger, trying hard not to contradict *der Führer* who couldn't stand contradiction, replied that they were only in the early days of rocket development as aviation had been in the late nineteenth century with Lilienthal and his gliders and Zeppelin with his airships.

Hitler stated that he did not believe the Zeppelin airship to be a great invention. When Dornberger asked if he had ever been up in one, Hitler replied without hesitation, "No. Nor shall I ever get into an airship. The whole thing always seemed to me like an inventor who claims to have discovered a cheap new kind of floor covering which looks marvelous, shines forever, and never wears out. But he adds that there is one disadvantage. It must not be walked on with nailed shoes and nothing hard must ever be dropped on it because, unfortunately, it's made of high explosive."

Was rocket technology simply too new and alien for Hitler to understand?

*Der Führer* left with thanks to all, but Dornberger didn't know whether he was pleased or not. Even Dornberger was unsure of himself on that count. However, General von Brauchitsch, the army chief of staff, gave an honest and unqualified expression of admiration and approval for what Dornberger and his team had accomplished in such a short time. General Becker likewise heaped praise on the Dornberger team, but he might only have been trying to maintain morale, his own included, because he'd backed Dornberger from the start ten years before.

When Reichsmarschall Hermann Göring was given the same dog and pony show at Kummersdorf a few weeks later, the impulsive and easily excited chief of the Luftwaffe and Hitler's Number Two man could scarcely contain his enthusiasm. He hugged Dornberger, yelling "This is colossal! We must fire one at the first postwar Nuremberg Party rally!" Göring immediately forecast all sorts of future applications of rocket technology for air travel, shipbuilding, railroads, automobiles, and other uses which could never happen. Göring named everything but space travel. And he completely missed the point that the rocket was being developed primarily as a long-range artillery shell that could make his beloved Luftwaffe bombers obsolete.

Hitler came to give his total and enthusiastic support to the A.4 and long-range ballistic missiles only when it was too late.

Official support and funding for Dornberger's rocket research and development vacillated. By 1940, when most of the activity and personnel had been transferred from Kummersdorf to Peenemünde, the priority for the long-range rocket program was stricken. Hitler had conquered Poland and western Europe. It was up to Göring's Luftwaffe to finish off England. The need for the A.4 and subsequent ballistic missiles no longer existed, or so thought Hitler's high officials. In August 1940, the high priority was restored. Then in October, it was revoked again. It was only through the continual support and connivance of Field Marshal von Brauchitsch that the program continued.

On January 8, 1943, Dornberger was told by Albert Speer, then Minister of Munitions, "The Führer cannot give your project higher priority yet. He is still not convinced that your plan will succeed!"

In March 1943, Dornberger received an amazing message from Army headquarters: *"Der Führer* has dreamed that no A.4 will ever reach England."

On May 26, 1943, Peenemünde was visited by the Long Range Bombardment Commission headed by Speer and including Air Marshal Milch of the Luftwaffe, Admiral Dönitz, and a host of VIPs from various ministries and high commands. In a private conversation with Dornberger, Speer told him, "I never knew, I never even dreamed you'd got so far! I see now that the rocket will be used after all! You have convinced me. From now on I shall be one hundred percent behind you. I shall help you wherever I can." Speer was going far out on a limb because Hitler had no confidence in the Peenemünde work. Later, in his memoirs, Speer denounced the long-range ballistic missile program.

Hitler's conversion to a true believer did not occur until July 7, 1943, when Dornberger, von Braun, and guidance expert Dr. Ernst Steinhoff were suddenly summoned to Hitler's headquarters, Wolfsschanze (Wolf's Lair) at Raustenberg in East Prussia. Von Braun showed a color motion picture of the first successful A.4 launch and how the missile would be used in the field. For the first time, Hitler showed real interest. When Dornberger finished explaining how the A.4 would be deployed and used against England where no German bomber could now fly, Hitler said, "I thank you. Why was it I could not believe in the success of your work? If we had had these rockets in 1939 we should never have had this war . . . Europe and the world will be too small now to contain a war. With such weapons humanity will be unable to endure it."

When the briefing was over and just as he was leaving the room, Hitler turned and came back to Dornberger. Quietly, he remarked, "I have had to apologize to only two men in my life. The first was Field Marshal von Brauchitsch. I did not listen to him when he told me again and again how important your research was. The second man is yourself. I never believed that your work would be successful."

And Hitler left the room.

When the A.4s began to fall on England, the British press called them "Hitler's rockets." They weren't. Nor were they the products of the Luftwaffe, which had tried and failed to shatter England's defenses. They were the products of German army artillery officers and civilian engineers who had developed rockets not as devices for space travel but as better long-range artillery shells.

# First Failures and Flights

By 1942 the A.4 rocket was ready for flight testing.

Nearly all Wehrmacht rocket test operations had been transferred from Kummersdorf to the Heersversuchsstelle Peenemünde (HVP, "Army Research Center Peenemünde"). The Wehrmacht had put more than 300 million deutschmarks (about $70 million) into the HVP, and by 1942 Dornberger was in command of more than 1,960 scientists, engineers, and technicians as well as 3,852 support people. The annual HVP payroll was almost 13 million deutschmarks.

Thousands of other people were working under Wehrmacht contracts at universities, research centers, and factories throughout Germany. In fact, Dornberger and von Braun had convened a three-day conference back in September 1939 to which were invited scientists and researchers from among the German universities. The academic community was presented with the engineering and technical problems facing the researchers at Peenemünde, and von Braun stressed that he was looking only for solutions, and within two years at that. This was a boon to the professors who were suffering from conscription and needed some justification for keeping themselves and their brightest students from being drafted into the armed forces as cannon fodder. Peenemünde established an important rapport with the German academic community as a result and also obtained fresh and intelligent new inputs and technically valid data to help solve problems. Furthermore, when the Nazis attempted to "organize" all research and development in Germany when the war began to go badly, the professors could respectfully decline to fill out the long forms and cooperate with the loudmouthed and heavy-handed Party men by pointing out that they were fully occupied and committed with secret high-priority work for Peenemünde.

The Luftwaffe was conducting tests on its Feiseler Fi-103 un-manned cruise missile, later called the V-1, at Peenemünde-West. In addition, the Wehrmacht rocketeers had developed several take-off assist rocket motors for bombers.

Various flights of the A.5 test vehicle had been made to prove out the basics of the A.4 systems—the gyroscopic guidance system, the jet vanes, the aerodynamic shape, and the launch facilities. Dr. Hermann had a 1-meter by 1-meter supersonic wind tunnel operat-ing, providing the world's first opportunity to test and make mea-surements of aerodynamic shapes at supersonic speeds. Dr. Walter Thiel and his motor development team had gotten the 25-ton motor working repeatedly and reliably. Dr. Ernst Steinhoff had joined the team as the guidance expert.

Steinhoff became as vitally important to the development of the ballistic missile as Dornberger, von Braun, Thiel, and Riedel. Von Braun had met him at a conference in the spring of 1939, invited him to come up to Peenemünde to look around, and smuggled him into a static test of the 25-ton A.4 motor. After that shattering experience, he ran over to Dornberger who had just arrived at the test stand, seized his hands, and enthusiastically exclaimed, "Sir, you must take me! I'm all yours! I want to stay!" When Dornberger realized this was yet another one of von Braun's surprises, Steinhoff stayed. He contributed to the vital guidance system technology of ballistic missiles, later came to America, participated in the White Sands operations where I met him, retired to Alamogordo, New Mexico, and passed away there.

In the spring of 1942 the first complete A.4 was ready. But it never flew. Official records and historical research say that it ex-ploded during a static test. In 1953, while I was at White Sands, I learned what really happened when Konrad K. Dannenberg told me about it in a private conversation, in a lecture presented at White Sands on February 25, 1953, and in an article about it in a now-forgotten local American Rocket Society section's magazine which I still have in my archives:

*The first A.4 missile was a hand-made job. Motor tests preceding a first flight were to be carried out in a huge, mobile test stand which held the entire missile. However, this first A.4 never flew. It found its end in that test stand. In order to clamp the missile into the stand without attaching the thrust mounts to the missile structure, a large steel corset was built. Unfortunately, the builders of this corset did not take into account the shrinkage of the missile components when the frigid liquid oxygen was pumped aboard. The first A.4 shrank, dropped out of the corset, and was a total wash-out.*

This, then, was the cause of the explosion reported in Kennedy's "Vengeance Weapon 2" published in 1983 by the National Air and Space Museum of the Smithsonian Institution.

The next attempt to launch an A.4 occurred on June 13, 1942. Everyone who could be there was, some with the flimsiest of excuses. Again, this became a standard practice in ballistic missile testing from that time onward. They stood at distances from the rocket proportional to their belief in the A.4's designers or in inverse proportion to their ignorance of what could go wrong. Some were within 250 meters of the vehicle. As the years went by and people learned that ballistic missiles were guided by mechanical brains that often had minds of their own, only the foolhardy, the news media, or the official photographers who were paid to be there ever stood closer than 500 meters.

Test Flight 001 took off normally, but a slight rolling motion was seen as it disappeared into the low clouds. A few seconds later the missile reappeared, tumbling back through the cloud deck to crash in the Baltic Sea about a kilometer away with a huge splash.

No one really knew what had happened. The technology of telemetry—measuring performance parameters of a remotely located device and sending the results to a ground station by radio—was in its infancy.

Undaunted, the Peenemünde rocketeers tried again with A.4 002 on August 16, 1942. The sky was clear that day. Ordway and Sharpe say it climbed to an altitude of 11.72 kilometers and exploded. Willy Ley reports that the nose broke off. Eric Bergaust writes that it began to oscillate 45 seconds into the flight and broke apart. At an altitude of nearly 12 kilometers (7.5 miles), it would have been difficult to actually see what was happening, and even the photographic theodolites available then would not have shown much. The reported accident time of 45 seconds into the flight is not consistent with the other reports. However, clearly something went wrong because the vehicle splashed into the Baltic 9 kilometers away. This was not a good time to have a flight failure, either. Among the spectators were the armaments chiefs of the three services: Field Marshal Edward Milch of the Luftwaffe, Adm. Karl Witzell of the Kriegsmarine, and Col. Gen. Friedrich Fromm of the Heer.

Three spectacular failures. Some people would think it was an inauspicious start for a new program. But as the rocketeers at the VfR and Kummersdorf had learned from hard experience, this seemed to be the way rocket development progressed. It took the German rocket team twenty years to learn how to overcome this sort of start-up failure series. Many start-up American rocket teams still have to learn it the hard way although the experienced groups have profited greatly from the German experience. But this sort of failure pattern would dog ballistic missile development for a long time to come.

A.4 Number 003—officially 003 although actually 004—was launched on October 3, 1942.

It was a complete success. The A.4 could be seen through its powered flight of 63 seconds during which it rose to an altitude of 85 kilometers and achieved a speed of 1,500 meters per second, about 5 times the speed of sound. It had remained stable through the subsonic, transonic, and supersonic flight regimes, and it was the largest man-made vehicle ever to have broken the sound barrier at that time. It had also flown higher than any man-made vehicle to date.

The warhead had been loaded with green dye so that its impact point in the Baltic Sea could be spotted. Steinhoff took off in a

Messerschmitt Bf-110 to locate the impact point, which he estimated to be about 200 kilometers away. He located the impact point 192 kilometers away only 2.5 kilometers from the aiming line.

The man whose 1923 book had started it all, Dr. Hermann Oberth, was there to witness it. He shook Dornberger's hand and said words that were highly uncharacteristic of him, "That is something only the Germans could achieve! I would never have been able to do it!"

Dornberger is also reported to have exclaimed enthusiastically to his colleagues, "Do you know what we have done? Today we have invented the space ship!"

What Dornberger *did* say was recorded during his little speech at a dinner celebration held that night during which von Braun was awarded the *Kriegsverdienstkreuz I Klasse mit Schwertern* (the War Service Cross, First Class, with Swords), Germany's highest civilian decoration.

Dornberger's words on this occasion concerning the use of rockets in space travel have been widely quoted in many places. What is often forgotten is some of the rest of his congratulatory speech:

> *The history of technology will record that for the first time a machine of human construction, a five-and-a-half-ton missile, covered a distance of a hundred and ninety-two kilometers with a lateral deflection of only two and a half kilometers from the target. Your names, my friends and colleagues, are associated with this achievement. We did it with automatic control. From the artilleryman's point of view, the creation of the rocket as a weapon solves the problem of heavy guns. We are the first to have given a rocket built on the principles of aircraft construction a speed of fifteen hundred meters per second by means of rocket propulsion. Acceleration throughout the period of propulsion was no more than five times that of gravity, perfectly normal for maneuvering of aircraft. We have thus proved that it is quite possible to build piloted missiles or aircraft to fly at supersonic speed, given the right form and suitable propulsion. Our automatically controlled and stabilized rocket has reached heights*

*never touched by any man-made machine. Since the tilt was not carried to completion our rocket today reached a height of nearly eighty-five kilometers. We have thus broken the world altitude record of forty kilometers held by a shell fired from the now almost legendary Paris Gun.*

He concluded, "So long as the war lasts, our most urgent task can only be the rapid perfecting of the rocket as a weapon. The development of possibilities we cannot yet envisage will be a peacetime task."

# The A.4 Becomes the V-2

As a result of the successful first flight of the A.4 on October 3, 1942, and the meeting at Wolfsschanze on July 7, 1943, Hitler ordered the A.4 into production at a rate of 2,000 per month.

*Der Führer* also demanded that the warhead weight be increased from 1 ton to 10 tons and became furious when he was told by Dornberger that it was not possible with the A.4 but would require the design and development of a totally new ballistic missile.

The story of the production and deployment of the A.4 rocket as a weapon is a long and complex one. However, anyone involved in the development of any new device or system that involves new technology and pushes the "state of the art" should read Dornberger's book, *V-2*. To an outsider, the unraveling story might sound like some sort of black comedy. But it will be all too familiar to those people who were involved in later ballistic missile development as well as those who are today toiling on the leading edge of technology in both military and commercial arenas.

Since Dornberger, von Braun, and the rest of the Peenemünde team believed they knew more about the A.4 than anyone else, they also believed they should be in charge of both the production and the field deployment of the missile. Of course, this is the same sort of mistake that is made even today.

Development people are not production people. Development engineers are interested in constantly perfecting the product to the ultimate performance possible with the state of the art. To them, every development prototype must be as nearly perfect as possible.

Production engineers, on the other hand, are concerned with "punching out product," knowing full well that the "Gaussian distribution" or bell-shaped curve of statistics means that a certain percentage of the output won't meet specs and must be either rejected or reworked until it does. They're also interested in simplifying the system to make it easier, cheaper, and quicker to produce. Production people often do not get along well with development people. Later at White Sands Proving Ground in New Mexico, America's first large rocket launching range, this came to be exemplified by the apocryphal statement made by acceptance testing and troop training engineers, "Get them scientists away from that rocket and *shoot it!*"

Production engineers, in turn, are not the same as field engineers or technical representatives who have to worry about how the production version is shipped, stored, handled, tested, and used by the ultimate consumers. If production engineers are prone to find bugs and glitches in preproduction prototypes released for production, field engineers are also quick to discover bugs and glitches in the final product, things that the production engineers never even thought about. There's a long list of products that can be quickly and easily assembled on a production line yet cannot be even partially disassembled for cleaning, maintenance, or repair. For example, in the 1970s Detroit produced an automobile that required its engine be removed in order to change the spark plugs. It's only on rare occasions that development, production, and field engineers work closely together to produce a truly superior product from all points of view.

The A.4 was not a prime example of that.

Dornberger had erected a preproduction plant, Peenemünde-South, which he believed would be able to produce A.4s at a rate that he had determined, as an artillery officer, suitable for a totally new weapon being integrated into the existing tactics and doctrine. He intended to control as much of the A.4 production as possible for as long as possible.

But von Braun and the other civilian engineers—some of them who had been drafted into the army from industry, then quickly reassigned to Peenemünde where they ended up supervising officers many ranks above them—had concentrated on the A.4 vehicle and paid little attention to how to transport and handle it in the field. As a result, it took over a year to develop the ground support equipment (GSE) such as the erector-transporter, the various propellant vehicles, the control and launching vehicle, and the equipment that could be used to perform final checks and tests on a vehicle that, when erected, stood more than 16 meters (55 feet) high on its launching table.

The A.4 went into production with a lot of bugs in it. In the first place, it hadn't been designed for mass production. It was an experimental long-range ballistic missile, the very first of its kind. As a result, each A.4 was hand-built. Individual engineering changes and modifications had been incorporated into each rocket based on a long-range program of continuous development. Each A.4 rocket contained an estimated 90,000 individual parts and components. Between the time that the A.4's design was "frozen" for full-scale mass production and the end of the war in 1945, more than 60,000 engineering change orders were issued against the design *while it was supposedly in mass production!*

In spite of the fabled teutonic efficiency, Germany made some incredible blunders in the production and deployment of the A.4 rocket.

Over the objections of Dornberger, a development engineer who had picked his own engineer for the production job so he could maintain control, Speer gave the responsibility for the production of the A.4 to Gerhard Dengenkolb on January 8, 1943.

Gerhard Dengenkolb comes across in all the memoirs of the Peenemünde team and in most history books as an insensitive, stupid, overbearing, impetuous slob. This is precisely the way most development engineers view production engineers who are assigned to take a pet experimental prototype and turn it into a production item that can be punched out by the thousands. And they in turn really don't like the field engineers and reps who continually uncover nasty little discrepancies in the product that make the development engineer appear to have done a bad job. The development engineers' dislike and distrust of marketing and sales personnel are even greater.

The development engineers want to make "just a few more minor modifications" before freezing the design for production, and the marketing people often peddle the gadget in a way that seems absurd and dishonest, stressing the benefits and saying nothing about the shortcomings. In the case of the German A.4 development and deployment, substitute the Ministry of Propaganda and the Nazi politicians for the marketing and sales personnel.

Dornberger didn't like Dengenkolb because the locomotive czar had been linked in 1940 with the transfer of all the responsibilities of the Army Weapons Department to the Minister of Munitions. That had led to the suicide of Gen. Karl Becker, Dornberger's longtime friend and supporter. Internal politics within the Third Reich were beginning to run wild following Hitler's initial military successes in Europe, and they really began to fester when it became generally known, if unvoiced, that Germany had lost the war after the setbacks of 1943 when Hitler canned his experienced military men and took supreme command himself. People in high places grabbed what they could while the grabbing was good, hoping to stash away enough of it to tide them over through the inevitable defeat they sensed with great foreboding as being only a few years away (although it meant a concentration camp and death to say so aloud).

For all the bad publicity and negative comments about his appearance and lifestyle, Dengenkolb was a successful production engineering manager. He was assigned to the A.4 mass production project, *Sonderausschuss A.4* (Special Committee A.4) following his chairmanship of the Locomotives Special Committee. In 1941, Krupp and Henschel had produced only 1,900 railway locomotives using traditional craft techniques. Dengenkolb had taken over, standardized on a few locomotive designs, instituted true mass production techniques, and increased production to 5,500 locomotives in 1943. A steam locomotive is an incredibly large and complex device even though it incorporates old or "low" technology. The Peenemünde team believed that their beloved A.4 on which they had expended so much skull sweat and time couldn't possibly be put into mass production by a mere locomotive production engineer. In the long run they were wrong. And they didn't help the situation because the record clearly shows that they "cooperated" in the same manner as a cat who has been disciplined to do something it doesn't like: just barely.

Be that as it may, Dengenkolb made plans for the production of 300 A.4s in October 1943 rising to 900 per month in December. The Peenemünde preproduction works, never intended to produce more than a few hundred A.4s for development and proving tests, was included in a scheme that involved the Zeppelin Works and the Henschel-Rax Works. When Hitler finally gave his approval of the program in July 1943, a fantastic production schedule of 6,000 A.4s per month was set up by Dengenkolb.

But Allied bombing raids were demolishing the German industrial base by 1943, including the Zeppelin Works near Lake Constance and the Henschel Works at Wiener-Neustadt outside Vienna. Therefore, the main production plant for the A.4 was established in a series of underground tunnels called the Mittelwerke near Nordhausen in the Harz Mountains. A state-owned corporation, Mittelwerke G.m.b.H., was set up and a purchase order (still in existence) was issued by the Army High Command for 12,000 A.4 rockets at a unit price of 40,000 reichsmarks.

Shortages of parts and propellants plagued the A.4 production program for the rest of the war. Liquid oxygen could be made by liquefying air, and many LOX plants were set up. The A.4 didn't use enough concentrated hydrogen peroxide to really matter. The real shortage was the fuel: ethyl alcohol. As Soviet troops overran the grain-producing areas in the east, the shortage of alcohol became acute. Another big problem was that Germans to this day drink far more schnapps than Coca Cola, and it was necessary to place a denaturing agent in the ethyl alcohol used both at Peenemünde and in the field. Many technicians were killed drinking the denatured alcohol, and skilled technicians were at a premium. Therefore, the deadly denaturing compound was replaced by a powerful purgative; any of the development crews or missile launching troops who sampled the rocket's alcohol supply were only temporarily indisposed by a very intense version of the most common soldier's malady.

As the A.4 program picked up momentum, many people tried to gain control of it. For example, proposals were put forth to turn Peenemünde into a capital stock company controlled by Siemens, the big German electrical firm. Dornberger successfully fought off all of these while he tried vainly to maintain control of production and deployment of the A.4. He thought he had some control over the production and a lot more control over the deployment than history has subsequently shown to be the case.

Heinrich Himmler and his Schütz Staffel (SS) became more interested and involved when a severe shortage of production workers at Mittelwerke became critical. Soviet POWs and other concentration camp workers were moved into the Nordhausen region and put to work in the Mittelwerke. At the peak of production at Mittelwerke, 15,000 concentration camp inmates and POWs under SS control worked along with 2,000 engineers. Conditions were abominable; more than 250 slave laborers and POWs died weekly, most of them being starved to death while the rest perished from communicable diseases and exposure. Himmler tried to take over the Peenemünde and Mittelwerke operations first by attempting to co-opt von Braun (whom he later had thrown in jail for several days on trumped-up charges that the man had not been producing weapons at all but had concentrated on rockets disguised as spaceships). Himmler finally succeeded in placing one of his henchmen, SS Brigadeführer Major General Hans Kammler, in charge of providing slave labor, and finally seeing to it that Kammler was in de facto total command of the A.4 program. Dornberger could do nothing against such political clout.

Because of a combination of problems—trying to mass-produce a device never designed to be mass-produced, a growing shortage of parts, materials, and propellants, the constant problem of finding knowledgeable and trainable personnel, and a bizarre series of mad attempts to gain control of the program that now resembled a Keystone Cops comedy of errors—the A.4 rocket wasn't launched against England until the first round was fired from the vicinity of The Hague on the morning of September 8, 1944.

From that point on, the *Aggregat.4* was renamed by the Ministry of Propaganda under Dr. Joseph Goebbels.

The Luftwaffe's Fi-103 flying bomb, the first cruise missile, was proclaimed *Vergeltungswaffe 1* (Vengeance Weapon Number One) or V-1. The A.4 rocket therefore became *Vergeltungswaffe 2* (Vengeance Weapon Number 2) or V-2.

And it is as the V-2 that the first long-range ballistic rocket was henceforth known in the history books.

But it was too late. As Dwight D. Eisenhower later wrote in his book, *Crusade in Europe:*

"It seemed likely that, if the German had succeeded in perfecting and using these new weapons six months earlier than he did, our invasion of Europe would have proved exceedingly difficult, perhaps impossible. I feel sure that if he had succeeded in using these weapons over a six-month period, and particularly if he had made the Portsmouth-Southampton area one of his principal targets, Overlord might have been written off."

# Perfecting the First Production Ballistic Missile

Although the V-2 (A.4) missile went to war on September 8, 1944, the V-2 was far from being an operational field weapon. (When we're talking about the A.4 as a ballistic missile weapon rather than as a development vehicle, it will be referred to as the V-2.) In fact, it was still being tested not only at Peenemünde but also at a new operational testing and training site.

Early in the summer of 1944 large-scale operational testing of the V-2 was begun. Many preproduction and Mittelwerke production V-2s were now available to determine the actual reliability of the ballistic missile.

Problems were legion.

They weren't helped by the fact that the Allies began to suspect something unusual was happening along the Baltic coast. When a reconnaissance Spitfire pilot happened to shoot a few extra high-altitude photos of the Peenemünde area on a flight elsewhere and an RAF photo interpreter, Constance Babington Smith, happened to spot the shape of an A.4 rocket lying on its transporter next to one of the test stands, British interest grew rapidly. The RAF sent a force of 597 heavy bombers against Peenemünde on the night of August 16–17, 1943. The raid destroyed much of the housing area, killing Dr. Walter Thiel and his family. This was a definite signal that the Allies knew about the German ballistic missile program at last. Steps therefore had to be taken to establish underground production plants such as Mittelwerke and to set up a new firing range at an ex-SS training camp, Heidelager, near Blizna in southeast Poland.

The V-2 had far too many problems for an operational field weapon. The steering mechanism using carbon vanes in the rocket exhaust and small air vanes on the fins was unreliable. If the V-2 rolled in flight, the liquid propellants tended to slosh away from the pipes in the bottom of the tanks and thus starve the motor. The gyros in the guidance system had an unacceptably high degree of drift. Combustion vibration was a constant headache (and was to continue to be so even until the flight of the last V-2 at White Sands on September 17, 1952) because it loosened some of the many pipe fittings and connections. Structural integrity was a constant worry because V-2s kept losing their fins and breaking up during re-entry shortly before impact. The warhead fusing problem was never solved.

Adolph Hitler was the first to spot the potential fuse problem during the famous presentation at Wolfsschanze on July 7, 1943. Von Braun told Hitler during the presentation, "The bird will carry a ton of TNT in her nose. But it will hit the ground at a speed of over one thousand meters per second and the shattering force of impact will multiply the destructive effect."

Hitler replied to the man upon whom he had just conferred a professorial title, "Professor, I don't accept that thesis. It seems to me that the sole consequence of that high impact velocity is that you will need an extremely sensitive fuse so that the warhead explodes at the precise instant of impact. Otherwise the warhead will bury itself in the ground and the explosive force will merely throw up a lot of dirt."

"I'll be damned if he didn't turn out to be absolutely right. Hitler may have been a bad man but he certainly wasn't stupid," von Braun later admitted. A new fusing system was developed, but it was never totally successful; many V-2s buried themselves deeply before the warhead exploded.

Actually, if German wartime nuclear research had been able to perfect a nuclear warhead, things would have been quite different. This will be discussed shortly.

The Peenemünde team had to fire a lot of V-2s in order to determine the causes of many problems. Today, when a ballistic missile is launched, thousands of measurements are radioed back to the ground with a technology called radio telemetry. In 1968 when the first Saturn 5 moon rocket was launched at Cape Kennedy, 3,552 separate data channels were radioed to the ground in flight; at Peenemünde, the state of the art was so primitive that only four data channels were available. And not all of them always worked right. So an enormous number of experimental rockets had to be fired, each one incorporating one little change that the engineers hoped would solve a particular problem. For example, it took 20 flights of A.4 rockets before the propellant valve designs were perfected. When the third production V-2 from the Mittelwerke was launched at Peenemünde and blew up just three seconds after ignition, chief test engineer Hartmut Küchen remarked to another test engineer, Willie Muenz, "We just blew a million marks in order to guess what could have been reported accurately by an instrument probably worth the price of a small motorcycle!"

Ground-based flight test instruments—accurate tracking radar and tracking telescopes with motion picture cameras on them, for example—didn't exist yet. (Many of them were developed and perfected later at White Sands.) The biggest problem faced during the production flight testing of the V-2 was the breakup of the missile during re-entry a few seconds before it impacted the target. This breakup was enough to destroy the accuracy of the V-2 and often resulted in the failure of the warhead fusing system to explode the warhead.

When a V-2/A.4 was launched at Peenemünde, its intended impact point was in the Baltic Sea, where it couldn't be recovered for post-flight analysis of the wreckage. In addition, Peenemünde was vulnerable to RAF and USAF bomber attacks at any time. Therefore, many flight tests were conducted near Blizna in Poland. These were carried out concurrently with launches by Wehrmacht rocket troops in their training program. On the average, about ten missiles with live warheads were launched daily at Blizna during the summer of 1944.

Because the Blizna V-2s were impacting on land, it was possible to assess the missiles' accuracy and the destructive effect of the one-ton warheads. The general impact area was well instrumented with observation posts, sound-tracking facilities, and tracking sites.

As forecast by Hitler, the warhead buried itself deep in the ground before the fuses—there were two of them—initiated the high-explosive Amatol.

By the end of the war, the fusing system was never improved. There wasn't time.

Another problem reared its head: The training batteries were reporting that almost 60 percent of the V-2s were breaking up in the air before impact at an altitude of about two kilometers.

Von Braun left Peenemünde with an observation crew to find out if he could determine the cause of the breakups. At Dornberger's suggestion, he established his observation post exactly on the bull's-eye in the impact area. "It was Dornberger's tongue-in-cheek reasoning that this would certainly be the safest spot," von Braun recalled. When he arrived, he found Dornberger already there.

Wernher von Braun was certainly a cool character because he stood in the open in the impact area after learning by telephone that a V-2 had been launched. He watched for the telltale incoming vapor trail and then watched the re-entry of the V-2 with binoculars. However, he recalled one incident where his own rocket design almost got him. He was standing as usual in the middle of the field watching for a missile that was due to arrive in the impact area.

> *Imagine my horror when I glanced up in the direction from which it was expected, to see a thin contrail moving toward me! There was barely enough time to fall flat on the ground before I was hurled high into the air by a thunderous explosion, to land unhurt in a neighboring ditch. The impact had taken place a scant hundred meters away and it was a miracle that the exploding warhead did not grind me to powder.*

From this series of observations and examinations of the recovered debris of V-2 rounds that had broken up in midair, von Braun discovered a weakness in the missile's structure just behind the control compartment and in the forward portion of the shell covering the alcohol tank. When the thickness of the steel skin in that area was increased from one millimeter to two millimeters, the V-2s no longer broke up in midair.

The V-2 used very little aluminum, a scarcity. In accordance with Hitler's suggestion, the final production models were fabricated with steel formers and longerons over which a sheet steel skin was spot-welded. This was standard aircraft structural procedure. But it produced a missile that looked positively decrepit with a wrinkled surface that wasn't as smooth and slick as one would expect on a vehicle that would travel at five times the speed of sound.

In spite of the fact that the V-2 was an experimental rocket that was subjected to continual engineering change orders up to the day the war ended and in spite of the fact that RAF and USAF air raids effectively put the preproduction plant at Peenemünde-South out of production as well as disrupting the German industrial base in general, V-2 production was maintained until the final days of the war in 1945. Several hundred experimental preproduction prototypes were assembled at Peenemünde-South. It is estimated that more than 6,000 V-2s were produced in the Mittelwerke. Each V-2 required only 13,000 man-hours to produce, and the unit cost of the final lots dropped to 38,000 Reichsmarks per missile. The V-2 did not use any critical materials such as aluminum or scarce aviation jet fuels. Considering that the first successful flight of this complex ballistic weapon had taken place less than three years before the end of the war, this production and deployment effort stands as a monumental achievement even today.

# The First Missile War

It is perhaps ironic that the V-2 ballistic missile—a device whose specifications had been determined from the legendary Paris gun—had as its first target the city of Paris. Early on the morning of September 8, 1944, two missiles were launched by the 1st and 2nd batteries of the 444th Artillery Abteilung. One missile failed, and the other hit near the Porte d'Italie in Paris 292 kilometers from the firing point. No one was killed, and the explosion was not reported as a missile hit until later.

Later that day, 1st and 2nd batteries of the 485th Artillery Abteilung, firing from road crossings between The Hague and Wassenaar in the Netherlands, launched two V-2 rockets toward London. Their aiming point was 1,000 meters east of Waterloo Station.

The two launchings, the first at 6:39 P.M. London time, were witnessed by 14-year-old Hans von Wouw Koeleman. When the V-2s were launched simultaneously, he saw them rise up and form contrails as they went through the stratosphere. "The thunder of the rocket engines was tremendous," he reported.

Five minutes later, 64-year-old Robert Stubbs, caretaker of the Staveley Road School in the west London suburb of Chiswick, was walking across the school's playing field to finish up a few chores. At 6:44 P.M., he was picked up and hurled 20 feet across the field by a tremendous blast that occurred without warning. Getting to his feet, he saw houses on both sides of the road demolished. He was lucky. Two people were killed, and 20 others were injured; 11 houses were totally destroyed, and another 27 were seriously damaged and had to be evacuated.

The second V-2 hit near Epping 16 seconds later, causing no casualties.

When newspaper reporters showed up at Chiswick soon thereafter and asked a local Civil Defense man if the sudden explosion could have been caused by some new kind of robot bomb—several hundred V-1 or Fi-103 flying bombs called "doodlebugs" were being launched against London every day, but you could hear them coming—the CD man replied, "We can't tell you what it was. It might have been a gas main explosion."

All over London people heard the two explosions. The man who had been appointed to head the special War Office Intelligence Branch commission on long-range rockets, Duncan Sandys, the 35-year-old son-in-law of Prime Minister Winston Churchill, heard the two bangs but also something else ignored by most Londoners: the sound of a heavy object rushing through the air which was the rumbling of the V-2 reentry. The supersonic V-2 had outrun its own noise. Sandys knew at once what had caused the two explosions.

The V-2 had been anticipated by the British.

And they knew there was no way to stop it.

The V-1 flying bombs could be defended against by belts of fighter interceptors, barrage balloons, and antiaircraft guns. Of the 6,725 V-1 flying bombs launched against England, only 2,790 had gotten through those defenses. Those that hit London and its environs killed 5,500 people, injured 18,000, and destroyed 23,000 dwellings. Although antiaircraft defenses could reduce the number of V-1 flying bombs that got through, Sandys and the rest of the British government knew that the only way to stop the doodlebugs entirely was to destroy or capture the launching sites in the Pas de Calais area of occupied France.

The V-2 was another matter.

A ballistic missile *can* be intercepted and destroyed in flight, but it took more than 25 years for engineers to develop the technology to do it.

The British knew a surprising amount about the V-2 thanks to an outstanding intelligence network and good engineering analysis. The German rocket activity at Peenemünde on the Baltic had been reported since 1939, when the British naval attaché in Oslo received a three-inch-thick report in the classical plain brown envelope containing the note, "From a German well-wisher." To this day no one knows where that report came from, but it was the first information the British had about some sort of secret weapon research going on at an obscure place on the Baltic Sea called Peenemünde. Nothing more was heard until the British got some photo-reconnaissance aircraft with enough range to penetrate that deeply into German airspace. Constance Babington Smith, head of the Aircraft Section of the Central Interpretation Unit, saw the photos indicating construction and unusual facilities at Peenemünde but was unable to identify what she was seeing. Her unit finally identified two A.4 rockets on their transporter trailers at the Peenemünde Test Stand VII. The first RAF raid on Peenemünde followed.

By 1944, the British also had photo-recon evidence of the V-2 testing at Blizna. At that point they began to get their hands on V-2 hardware.

The Polish underground, in the form of the Armia Krajowa (AK), began to pay more attention to the Blizna SS training camp in the autumn of 1943. Security was so tight, however, that they didn't manage to get one of their members into the compound for several months. The AK did manage to buy a map of the Blizna compound from a German soldier. By January 1944, they noted that the rate of rocket launchings had increased. By the simple expedient of eavesdropping on radio communications between the Blizna launch control and pilots of recovery aircraft, the AK learned of the impact points of the V-2s. In most cases, they got to the sites before the Germans and were able to recover a large number of relatively undamaged parts. The AK also got the cooperation of the local farmers. As a result, by May 1944 thousands of V-2 parts were hidden in potato sacks and haystacks in the area. In mid-May 1944 the AK found an almost complete V-2 rocket motor in the soft mud of a riverbank. On May 20, 1944, an entire V-2 impacted in soft marshland with relatively little damage. The AK promptly rolled it into the nearby river and arranged for a farmer to drive his cows into the water to stir up the mud. When the German recovery team arrived, all it could find was a herd of watering cows.

The AK then transported the V-2 to a nearby barn where it was stripped down into smaller parts. Photographs and drawings were made, and the AK stood ready to smuggle an entire V-2 rocket out of Poland to England.

The acquisition of an intact V-2 was quickly reported to London. Photos and drawings accompanied the report. But this information was put on the bottom of someone's "In" basket because all available personnel were assigned to duties in support of Operation Overlord, the Normandy invasion. Nothing was done until an A.4 test missile happened to land in Sweden on June 13, 1944.

On that date, A.4 Number V89 was launched from Peenemünde carrying an experimental radio guidance system intended for the *Wasserfall* antiaircraft missile also being developed by the Dornberger team. Dr. Ernst Steinhoff, the missile guidance expert, had trained an engineer to steer the missile by means of a joystick on the ground. When the missile was in the air, the guidance commands seemed to work exactly opposite to the way they were supposed to. It turned out that the guidance system had been wired incorrectly so that the signs were reversed. In spite of the fact that last-moment efforts were made to ensure that the missile impacted in the Baltic instead of in Sweden, where it was headed, it ended up scattered in and around the village of Knivingaryd, not far from Kalmar in southern Sweden.

Steinhoff didn't know exactly where it had landed, so he took off in an airplane to find the impact point. While he was airborne, General Dornberger, who had by that time heard of the flight and seen some of the early tracking data, radioed to ask, "Steinhoff, did you fire into Sweden?"

To which Steinhoff answered lamely, "I must have."

The circumstances in which this happened are fascinating because of their great similarity to the only occasion on which a ballistic missile launched from the United States landed on foreign soil, impacting in Juarez, Mexico, on May 29, 1947. It was also a

How to shoot a cannon around the world. If you shoot from the top of a high mountain (and there is no air resistance) with a small powder charge, the cannon shell will travel only a short distance. If you increase the powder charge and thus the muzzle velocity of the shell, the shell will travel to a greater distance before it strikes the ground. If you put in even more powder so that the shell goes most of the way around the world, you have an Intercontinental Cannon Shell (ICCS). Finally, if you put enough powder in, the cannon will shoot the shell all the way around the world and you've got an Orbital Cannon Ball Satellite (OCBS).

An historic photo of some of the German rocket pioneers taken on August 5, 1930, after the successful test of a liquid-propellant rocket motor at the Chemisch-Technische Reichanstalt near Berlin. *Left to right:* Rudolph Nebel, Dr. Franz Hermann Karl Ritter, Hans Bermüller, Kurt Heinisch, unknown, Dr. Hermann Oberth, unknown, Klaus Riedel in white coat holding a Mirak I, Wernher von Braun, and a foreman of the Institute. The rocket is the partly finished Oberth model built to publicize the film *Frau im Mond.*

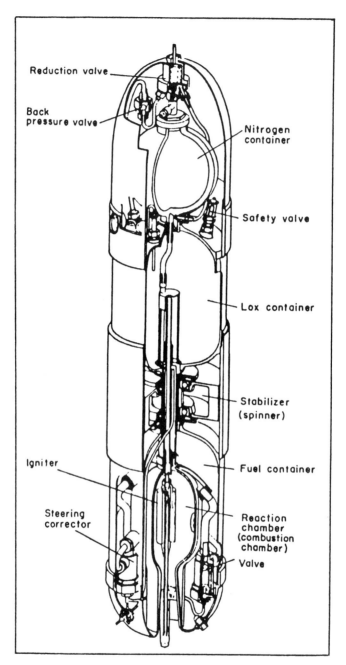

Reduction valve

Back
pressure valve

Nitrogen
container

Safety valve

Lox container

Stabilizer
(spinner)

Igniter

Fuel container

Steering
corrector

Reaction
chamber
(combustion
chamber)

Valve

Cutaway drawing of the interior arrangement of the *Aggregat.2*, the first successful liquid-propellant rocket built by Dornberger and von Braun at Kummersdorf-West.

The A.3 test vehicle on the test stand ready for a static test at Kummersdorf sometime in 1936.

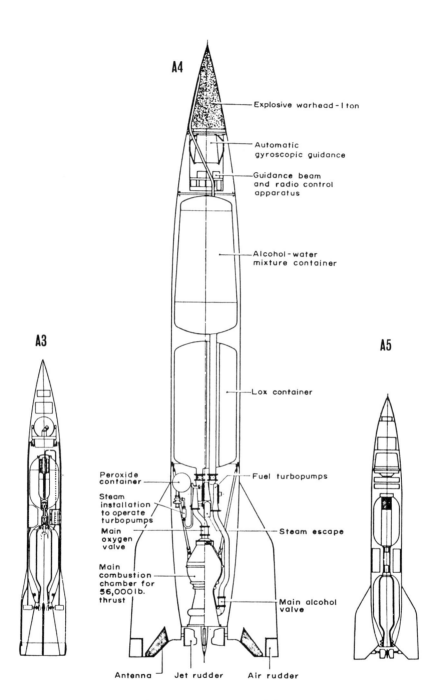

A4

Explosive warhead - I ton

Automatic
gyroscopic guidance

Guidance beam
and radio control
apparatus

Alcohol-water
mixture container

A3

A5

Lox container

Peroxide
container

Fuel turbopumps

Steam
installation
to operate
turbopumps

Main
oxygen
valve

Steam escape

Main
combustion
chamber for
56,000 lb.
thrust

Main alcohol
valve

Antenna    Jet rudder    Air rudder

The relative sizes and interior arrangement of the German A.3, A.4, and A.5
rocket vehicles.

## Die wichtigsten Maße des A4

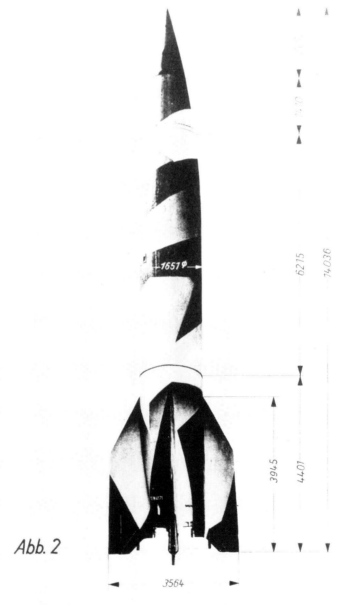

Abb. 2

Vom 1. 2. 45

A dimensioned photograph of the A.4 rocket taken from the field firing manual in the possession of the author.

## Das Gerät A 4

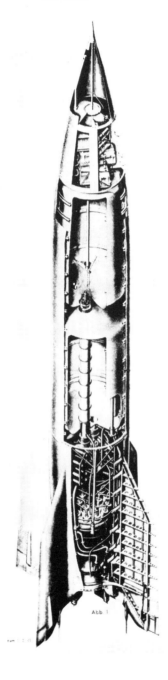

Abb. 1

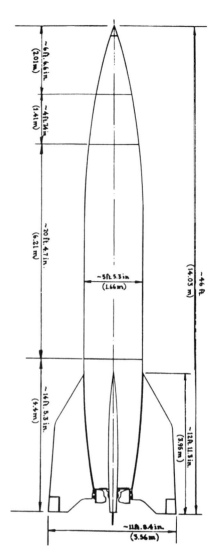

A dimensioned outline drawing of the German A.4 rocket.

Cutaway drawing of the A.4 rocket taken from the field firing manual in the possession of the author.

Dr. Wernher von Braun near the Saturn-Ib launch pad at Cape Kennedy, Florida, in about 1965.

German V-2 White Sands Round 2 photographed under preflight preparation in the Army Launch Area at White Sands Proving Ground, New Mexico. The view looks west. The date is April 15, 1946.

The gas generator that produced high-temperature high-pressure steam to drive the V-2 turbopump. The generator used 75 percent hydrogen peroxide decomposed by liquid potassium permanganate. Photo taken by the author at White Sands Proving Ground in 1954.

Cutaway of the turbopump of the German V-2 rocket engine as it was displayed in the open at White Sands Proving Ground in 1954. Photo taken by the author.

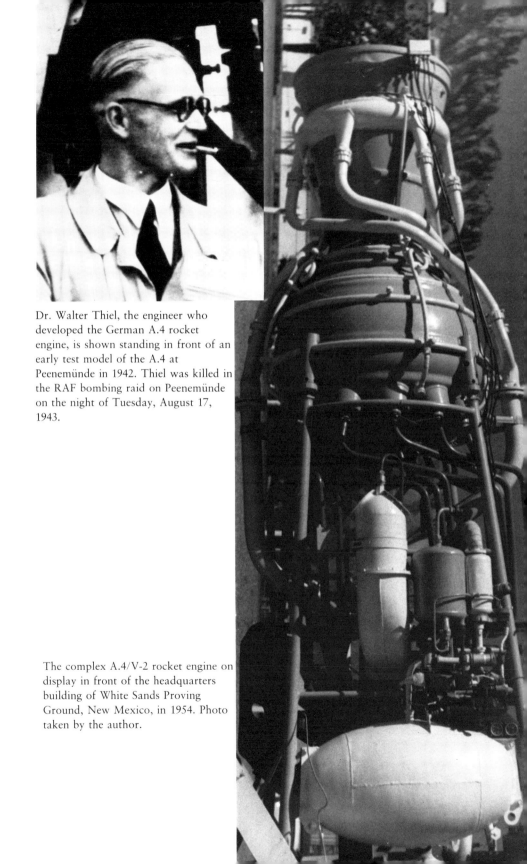

Dr. Walter Thiel, the engineer who
developed the German A.4 rocket
engine, is shown standing in front of an
early test model of the A.4 at
Peenemünde in 1942. Thiel was killed in
the RAF bombing raid on Peenemünde
on the night of Tuesday, August 17,
1943.

The complex A.4/V-2 rocket engine on
display in front of the headquarters
building of White Sands Proving
Ground, New Mexico, in 1954. Photo
taken by the author.

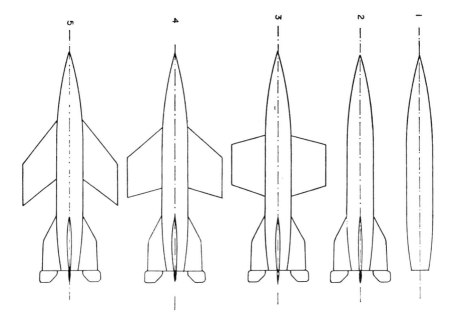

The various configurations tested in the Peenemünde wind tunnel to determine the proper shape for the gliding wings fitted to the A.4b and, hopefully, later to the A.9.

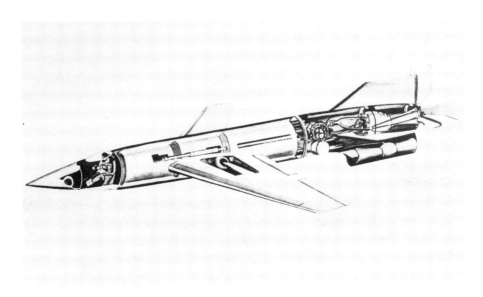

The only known German drawing of the manned A.9 transatlantic bomber, which was to be launched as a second stage from the A.10 booster. Note the retracted landing gear in the wings.

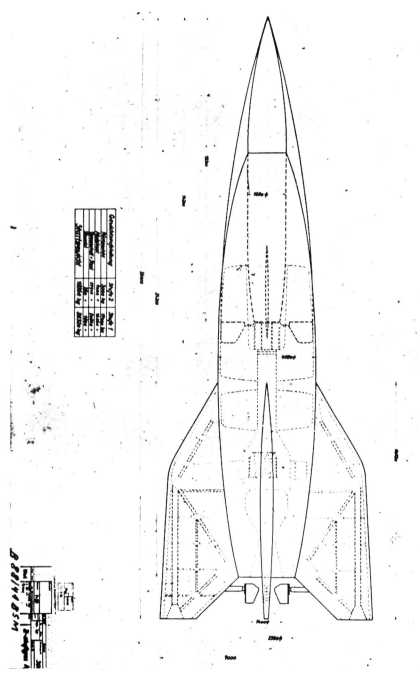

One of the few surviving blueprints of the first ICBM proposal, the two-stage German A.9/A.10 with the arrow-winged A.9 nested inside the nose of the A.10 booster. The overall length was to be 26 meters with a fin span of 9 meters and a body diameter of 6.07 meters.

The Hermes II ("Roman Two"), a German V-2 at White Sands Proving Ground in the late 1940s showing the mounting of the lenticular supersonic ramjets at the base of the nose control compartment and tiny canard elevators for ramjet vehicle stabilization. The V-2 was to lift and accelerate the ramjet-powered nose section to supersonic speeds, and the nose section was to separate and fly under its own power. The flight was a "partial success."

The Hermes A-1 Missile #2 on the launch pad at White Sands Proving Ground's Army Launch Area on September 14, 1950.

The GE Hermes A-3AE2 (RV-A-8) on the launch pad at White Sands Proving Ground's Army Launch Area in 1952. Contrary to several statements in other works, this missile did fly. The author was there and saw it.

The GE Hermes A-3B (XSSM-A-16) at White Sands Proving Ground's Army Launch Area. This was the last of the GE Hermes designs to fly.

The Convair MX-774 "Hi-Roc" (RTV-A-2) Missile #3 on the launch pad at the White Sands Proving Ground's Army Launch Area on December 2, 1948.

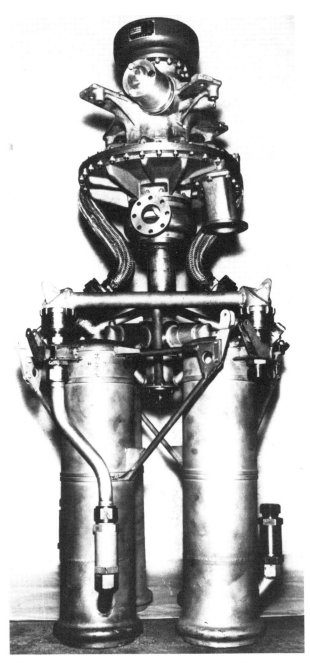

The four-chamber Reaction Motors, Inc. 6,000-pound thrust liquid-propellant turbopump-fed rocket engine used in the Convair MX-774 (RTV-A-2).

V-2. It was launched from White Sands in south-central New Mexico. It carried an experimental guidance system for another rocket project. Because of cross-wiring in the guidance system, the V-2 turned south instead of north. Dr. Ernst Steinhoff was the project officer who was responsible for the error. And to the time of his death, he was too arrogant to own up to either mistake.

Swedish authorities gathered up about 2 tons of fragments and sent them to Stockholm. Within a week, a British intelligence report from Sweden contained enough information for a preliminary description of the V-2. Negotiations for the transfer of the V-2 parts from Sweden to the Royal Aircraft Establishment at Farnborough were completed within a short time, and by mid-July 1944 the parts were arriving at Farnborough. This gave British Intelligence the first real data on the V-2, but they mistakenly believed the V-2 was radio-guided because the one they recovered from Sweden was an experimental missile for testing a radio-guided antiaircraft missile.

The complete V-2 from Poland was another matter, and if the British had paid more attention to it and acted faster, they would have known that the V-2 used a self-contained gyro-stabilized inertial guidance system. The Polish underground, cooperating with their counterparts in London, developed Operation Wildhorn III, a plan for flying the V-2 parts out of Poland to England. It was done using a Douglas C-47 "Gooney Bird" flown in secretly from Brindisi, Italy, to a farm field at Zaborow near Tarnow. The mixed crew was told nothing about the mission other than it was a "Polish trip." The pilot was RAF Flight Lieutenant Standley George Culliford who was assisted by a Polish copilot, Kazimiera Szajer, an English navigator, and an unknown Welsh radioman. They were to take the unarmed transport across the enemy-patrolled Adriatic, across Yugoslavia, up along the Hungarian-Romanian border, through eastern Czechoslovakia, and into southern Poland. The return route was to be the same.

They took off after dark on July 25, 1944, and arrived after midnight, landing on a field illuminated by flares held by partisans. The C-47 lost hydraulic pressure, and they were unable to retract the landing gear for the return flight. Although they spotted several

German aircraft on the return flight in daylight, they landed the crippled but loaded C-47 in a crosswind at Brindisi on a runway under construction. This heroic effort has received little if any attention over the years because of the Swedish recovery of the V-2.

Once the Allies had enough recovered V-2 parts, they knew that there was only one way to stop the ballistic missile: Capture the launch sites. This wasn't easy to do because unlike the V-1 doodle-bugs that were launched from fixed ramps, the V-2 could be launched within two hours from any open field or road. So the answer to stopping the V-2 assault on England was to push the Germans back into Germany and out of range.

This, of course, is exactly what happened. But before it occurred, the V-2 was used against the Belgian port of Antwerp and fired in an attempt to prevent the Allied seizure of the bridge across the Rhine River at Remagen.

The first ballistic missile war ended only when Germany was defeated, not because the Allies discovered and developed a counter-measure or a counter-weapon against the ballistic missile.

# What Might Have Been

In his 1954 book *V-2*, and in several papers presented before professional societies after World War II, Gen. Walter Dornberger took pains to point out the A.4/V-2 was merely the first ballistic missile design, that it had not received the support he believed was necessary to turn it into a truly decisive weapon, and that many statements from people such as Albert Speer and others that the V-2 had diverted important German resources were basically excuses. In a 1962 paper delivered before the American Association for the Advancement of Science in Philadelphia, Dornberger wrote:

> *The historical facts are these:*
> *(1) Hitler did not support Peenemünde at all, not until it was too late (July 1943). American aircraft production at that time could never have been rivaled by Germany's aircraft production. It was only a question of time before the Allies would have air superiority over Europe and Africa.*
> *(2) Up until the end of the war it was not aircraft production that caused the Germans trouble. Underground factories in aircraft production ran full blast right up to the final days. What was lacking was fuel, not airplanes. Germany could not protect the oil fields under its control nor the factories producing synthetic gasoline. They were destroyed by bombing from the air. . . .*
> *(3) The V-2 was developed as an artillery weapon with high*

*accuracy to surpass the range of long-range guns. In 1940 and 1941 when a German bomber could not fly over England more than three times before being shot down, the question of whether such a weapon as the V-2 could take over some of the tasks of the bombers became urgent. The advantage of a big long-range rocket costing only about $38,000 became evident when compared with the $1,250,000 cost of a bomber, not to mention the loss of its crew.*

*(4) What would have happened if, starting in 1942, the Germans had fired such long-range rockets against England in increasing number, with greater range and accuracy; or if the German High Command had followed our advice to develop and mass-produce anti-aircraft guided missiles in sufficient quantities so that they could go into action in 1942? It can be assumed that the outcome of the war would have been quite different; at least, there would not have been the devastating bombing of German cities, industries, and the synthetic gasoline generating plants. Germany would have kept air supremacy over Europe not with fighters and bombers but with anti-aircraft guided missiles and long-range missiles. Under their protection a new, powerful bomber fleet could have been built up in order to carry the war over enemy territory.*

Dornberger's postwar critique does contain some truth. Much of what he says in his last point was later shown to be substantially correct over Hanoi and Haiphong during the war in southeast Asia when Soviet SAM missiles made bombing a very expensive proposition for the United States.

He was also right about aircraft and fuel production. The advanced German jet fighters sat hidden in hard stands, unable to fly in 1945 because they didn't have fuel; these jet interceptors such as the Me-262 could outfly even the vaunted P-51 Mustang. They would have been available earlier if Hitler had not decreed that this effective interceptor be used as a tactical bomber, a task for which it hadn't been designed. Fuel for every sort of engine—ordinary internal combustion, Diesel, and jet—became difficult to get in

Germany from 1944 onward, as Gen. George S. Patton stated when he pointed out that the Germans had had to fall back on horse-drawn military vehicles in order to conserve fuel for the Panzers and aircraft.

Where Dornberger was possibly wrong was in his evaluation of the German capability to develop a long-range strategic bomber and build it in sufficient numbers to make a difference. It had taken the United States over a decade to develop the strategic bomber, and even the B-17 Flying Fortress and the B-24 Liberator had significant shortcomings. The only true strategic bomber to emerge from World War II was the Boeing B-29 Superfortress, whose technology was beyond the Germans' capabilities. The German jet bombers, while fast, suffered from high fuel consumption and lack of range sufficient for them to be used in the strategic bombing role although their high speed might have made them difficult for propeller-driven interceptors to shoot down.

Dornberger was correct in his perception of the A.4/V-2 as a long-range artillery weapon. He also knew its shortcomings and knew that it had been introduced into operational service long before the technology was ready.

The Dornberger team at Peenemünde was definitely thinking beyond the A.4 even as the first test vehicles were flying.

Very little has been written about these other *aggregat* models.

The A.4 was labor-intensive to build and to operate in the field. It used volatile liquid oxygen which was difficult to transport and handle.

It turns out upon reflection on the Peenemünde planning documents that fell into Allied hands in 1945 that the Dornberger team considered the A.4 to be only an intermediary step in the development of more effective, more efficient, field-compatible, longer-range ballistic missiles culminating in the first intercontinental ballistic missile. The ICBM had its genesis at Peenemünde.

The Peenemünde rocket team members who emigrated to the United States after World War II and became American citizens did not like to talk about their development plans for ballistic missiles and ICBMs, preferring to concentrate their discussions on the use of rockets for space flight. This is understandable. To them, weapons were a means to an end: space. The use of the unmanned V-1 and V-2 missiles against London and other targets aroused a great deal of emotional ire and animosity among Britishers and Americans who had been the targets of those "inhuman" weapons against which there was little if any defense and which killed, maimed, and destroyed, without selectivity, both military and civilian targets. The black humor of the time reflects this in such statements as "von Braun aimed for the stars and sometimes hit London." And when they came to the United States, it was under contract to the military establishment for the development of advanced ballistic missiles. What they developed, it turns out, was what they'd been planning as future missiles at Peenemünde.

The A.6 ballistic missile was a design study. It was an A.4 modified to use so-called "storable" liquid propellants: nitric acid and kerosene. These liquids do not have the volatility of liquid oxygen and also have the capability of being "hypergolic"—i.e., they do not need an igniter to initiate combustion, but undergo spontaneous combustion upon contact with one another. Nitric acid is not easy to handle in the field, and hypergolic propellants create a higher degree of hazard than LOX-alcohol. But the combination does simplify battlefield logistics.

The A.7 was a test missile, essentially an A.5 with wings intended to develop the aerodynamics and control systems for a winged supersonic missile launched vertically and then utilizing a glide to extend its range. Several nonpropulsive models were built, and unpowered drop tests from aircraft were made in 1943.

The A.8 was a little A.4 of reduced payload and range that utilized storable propellants and would have had a range of 135 kilometers. A missile similar to the A.8 was designed, built, and fielded by the U.S. Army Ordnance Corps in the 1945–1955 period. It was called the Corporal.

The A.9 was a much-improved A.4 using LOX-alcohol but with sharply swept wings to extend its range. No A.9 vehicles were ever built. But both wind tunnel and flight tests were conducted on A.9 configurations using the A.4 project as a cover to ensure availability of funding. The tests were done as the A.4b project which, according to Dornberger, stood for "A.4 bastard."

Three A.4 rockets were modified to the A.4b configuration by attaching swept wings with 5.5-meter span to the center section of an A.4. The first A.4b was launched from Peenemünde on December 27, 1944, but the guidance system failed at an altitude of 50 meters. We have no record of the launch of the second vehicle. The third A.4b was launched on January 24, 1945, went through Mach 1, attained a final velocity of 1,207 meters per second, but failed to achieve its planned range of 435 kilometers when a wing broke off during the gliding phase of flight.

The Peenemünde rocket men emphasized that the A.9 was not meant to operate all by itself but was intended to be the upper stage of a huge booster rocket, the A.10. This rocket would have been 26 meters long and 4.1 meters in diameter with a fin span of 9 meters. Using a cluster of 6 A.4-type rocket motors burning nitric acid and kerosene with a total thrust of 182 tons for 50 seconds—this was the source of the later Saturn method of clustering individual rocket motor chambers—the A.10 was intended to boost the A.9 as an upper stage. Thus it was planned that the A.9/A.10 two-stage combination would permit the delivery of a 1-ton payload at a range of more than 4,800 kilometers.

The A.9/A.10 was the first ICBM concept.

This 85-ton vehicle was never built because the war brought development to a halt. But a 250-ton test stand was on the drawing boards at Peenemünde.

A version of the A.9 was designed with retracting landing gear and a pilot compartment in place of the warhead.

The A.11 was visualized as a third stage under the A.9/A.10 combination. This would have been able to place the manned A.9 vehicle into low earth orbit. The A.12 was projected as an even larger booster with 1.4 million kilograms (about 2.5 million pounds) of thrust capable of putting the A.10 into orbit as a 30-ton space station module. The genesis of von Braun's three-stage orbital spaceship proposed in the 1952 _Collier's_ magazine derives from this. Although this vehicle served as the paper prototype of the Saturn 5 moon rocket, the Soviet Union did indeed build and deploy something like the A.9/A.10/A.11 concept as its Fractional Orbital Bombardment System (FOBS).

Which leads to the question, Why develop these expensive rockets just to deliver ordinary high-explosive warheads?

The answer remained buried in the historical records because of two factors: (1) the Peenemünde team didn't want to talk about more energetic warheads, and (2) the Peenemünde team had little or no control over the deployment or strategic doctrine actually developed for their advanced projects.

It wasn't until the publication in England of Philip Henshall's *Hitler's Rocket Sites* in 1985 that the story began to fall together. Henshall became fascinated with the possibility that some of the concrete launching bunkers for the V-2 rockets might still exist in the Pas de Calais and Cherbourg peninsula regions of France. He visited those sites and found more than he expected. He discovered concrete underground missile silos for V-2s and A.9s but also others large enough to hold the A.9/A.10 combination. Further research into documents and records in various archives and war museums in England and Germany revealed the following:

1. The Peenemünde team had virtually no say over the ultimate strategy or deployment of the ballistic missiles they were developing or planning.
2. The German high command expected to be able to develop a nuclear warhead for the Peenemünde ballistic missiles or, barring that, utilize chemical or biological warheads.
3. Silos would provide protection for ballistic missiles against bombing raids.
4. The V-2/A.9 silos would be used to hold Britain at bay while Germany occupied the Soviet Union.
5. The A.9/A.10 silos would house ICBMs capable of reaching the United States; these missiles would be used to keep the United States out of the European war and hold America at bay once England capitulated or an armistice had been arranged.

It was only Hitler's belief in 1941 that he could win a short war against the Soviet Union that kept the long-range strategic planners of the German high command from implementing this first doctrine for the deployment of the ICBM. As with the development of the assault rifle and several other high-tech German weapons of World War II, the high command had found ways to get around Hitler's dreams and preconceptions. What they failed to do was overcome the madman's predilection to bleed the German nation white and take it into a suicide pact with him when he failed. Knowing now what we know about German long-range plans for the deployment of ICBMs, we can be profoundly thankful that Hitler was not assassinated, a coup that would have allowed the German high command to proceed with the Peenemünde ICBM.

But another European power led by a dictator would do that.

# Backfires and Russians

When the Third Reich collapsed, Allied intelligence teams were already spreading over those parts of Europe not occupied by the Soviets. These teams were looking for whatever they could find out about specific German developments—high-speed aerodynamics, turbojet engines, nuclear energy, chemical weapons and nerve gases, tanks, infantry weapons such as the new assault rifles, electronics, radar, and rockets. In most cases the United States and Great Britain were already developing their own versions of many of these things. But the Americans and British knew that any information they could round up about German work in these areas would help prevent them from "reinventing the wheel."

An additional motivation drove these teams very hard: The Soviets were rapidly occupying eastern Europe, and most of the German research centers in the Soviet-conquered zones were shut off from the western Allies by the Soviets. True, the Soviet Union was an ally in the war against Germany. But many Americans and Britishers simply didn't trust the Russians at all. Several attempts at joint military operations during World War II had been badly disrupted by typical Russian attitudes and approaches. The Russians had a different way of fighting a war, much of which their ancestors had learned from Genghis Khan and the Golden Horde.

The Red Army had occupied what was left of Peenemünde and, as of the time of this writing, 45 years later, no one from the west has set foot on the former German rocket base. Furthermore, the

Soviets were scheduled to take over that portion of Germany where the Mittelwerke V-2 production factory was located near Nordhausen in the Harz Mountains. This was formerly part of the German Democratic Republic, and no one from the west was allowed to visit the site since 1945. In spite of the unification of Germany, no one has yet visited it.

The British teams were operated under the War Office jurisdiction and not British Intelligence. The make-up of the American intelligence-gathering teams was unique and quite American, being a combination of military officers, civilian scientists, and a corporate contractor.

On November 15, 1944, the General Electric Company in the United States was given a contract to conduct research and development in all phases of guided missiles. This was the beginning of Project Hermes which was the first American long-range ballistic missile program. Practically unknown today, Project Hermes laid the foundations for the American ICBM programs.

General Electric was and still is an unusual corporation. Founded in 1900 by inventor Thomas Alva Edison and financier John Pierpont Morgan, GE has found itself on the forefront of high technology ever since. In many cases, GE was in there first and later opted out for reasons known only to its outstanding marketing people and board of directors. Because of GE's expertise in designing and building high-temperature steam turbines for electric generating plants, it became involved in the development of turbosuperchargers for aircraft engines following World War I. When the War Department received its first example of a British Whittle turbojet aircraft engine, GE got the contract to build it in America, and it has been building turbojet and turbofan aircraft engines ever since, again because of their early expertise in turbines.

Whether or not it was because the V-2 rocket motor used a steam turbine to drive the propellant pumps, GE got involved in liquid-propellant rocketry in 1944. Dr. Richard W. Porter headed the GE Project Hermes team that went into western Europe along with military personnel from the U.S. Army Ordnance Corps, the U.S. Army Air Forces, and the U.S. Navy as the Combined Intelligence

Operations Subcommittee (CIOS). Their objectives: (1) Find, interview, and offer employment to as many members of the German rocket team as possible and (2) round up as many V-2 rockets as possible and ship them immediately to the United States.

This was a monumental task because of the utter chaos of the collapse of Germany in April and May of 1945. Because so many technical intelligence teams poured into Germany literally on the heels of the advancing troops and because there was so little coordination between them, a lot of duplication was inevitable. Even a lot of artifacts were overlooked and many German personnel not interrogated by qualified experts. On the American team, the acronym CIOS was quickly corrupted to CHAOS.

The Peenemünde team under Dornberger and von Braun surrendered to the American 44th Division on May 2, 1945. They were taken to Garmisch-Partenkirchen for interrogation. Eventually, some 400 members of the Peenemünde team and the Mittelwerke production group were located and brought there. This story has been told in great detail elsewhere.

Finding the V-2 rockets was something else.

From the best estimates arrived at by studying the records, 6,240 A.4/V-2 rockets were produced in Germany. About 240 of these were made and tested at the Peenemünde-South preproduction works. Another 6,000 were produced at the Mittelwerke. The breakdown of their disposition is as follows:

> V-2s reaching the United Kingdom—1,115
> V-2s reaching European targets (Paris, Antwerp, Remagen)—1,775
> Failures—700
> Expended in tests and training at Peenemünde and Blizna—300
> Number in field storage, May 1945—2,100
> Number at Mittelwerke when occupied by the U.S. Army—250

Half the V-2s in storage were in the Soviet occupation zone. About a thousand were scattered in the western portions of Germany. Of these, 515 were developmental models, rockets that had failed to pass systems testing, or V-2s that were consigned to be parted out or scrapped.

The competition among the western Allies—the United States, Great Britain, and France—for V-2s was so intense that Supreme Headquarters, Allied Expeditionary Forces (SHAEF) issued orders on May 4, 1945, that all missile hardware in Europe was to be reported and left where it was until questions of allocating this technical treasure trove could be worked out. The British wanted 150 V-2s. The United States wanted as many as it could get its hands on for the Hermes Project.

But the luxury of time to do this wasn't available. The Soviets were scheduled to take over the portion of Germany that included the Mittelwerke. At Yalta, Stalin had demanded reparations of $20 billion from Germany once the war was over. The Soviets didn't wait, however. As they advanced through Poland and eastern Germany, special shock troops of the *Vsesoyuznyi institut aviatsionnykh materialov* (All-Union Institute of Aviation Materials) dressed in Soviet army uniforms deliberately stripped factories of all sorts, whether or not these plants had had anything to do with war or aviation production. The U.S. commissioner of the Allied War Reparation Commission reported to Secretary of State James F. Byrnes, "What we saw amounts to organized vandalism directed not alone against Germany but against the US Forces of occupation." The Soviets looted equipment belonging to American companies because the plants were German subsidiaries of such firms as Anaconda Copper, IBM, Ford Motor Company, National Cash Register, General Electric, and Paramount Pictures.

Fortunately for the United States, the old army axiom that "there's always someone who doesn't get the word" saved the contents of the Mittelwerke for the United States. When word of the American capture of the Mittelwerke reached Paris on April 11, 1944, then-Colonel Holger N. Toftoy, chief of U.S. Army Ordnance Technical Intelligence in Europe, organized Special Mission V-2 on his own and issued specific orders: Go to the Mittelwerke, get enough V-2 components to make up 100 rounds, and ship them to the United States. Less than a month before, he had received a request from the Pentagon for 100 operational V-2s for firing at the Army's new White Sands Proving Grounds in New Mexico. Then-Major James P. Hamill, later to be instrumental in the operation of White Sands, was designated by Toftoy to transport the V-2s from the Mittelwerke to Antwerp, then by ship to New Orleans, and then by rail to El Paso, Texas, and by road to White Sands.

In spite of great confusion and a total lack of authorization or orders to utilize the German railways, Hamill cleaned out the Mittelwerke by May 31, 1945, and had enough parts for about 100 V-2s on their way to America.

Other U.S. Army Ordnance officers located nearly all the Peenemünde and Mittelwerke documents, drawings, reports, and written material that had been hidden by von Braun's team near the Mittelwerke and in Bavaria.

In the meantime, the British were busily at work implementing Operation BACKFIRE under the Special Projectile Operations Group (SPOG). The objective was to round up completed ready-to-launch V-2s, which would be fired by German rocket troops while they could still be found and their training was fresh. It proved impossible to find ready-to-launch V-2s, and the British were forced to expend nearly 200,000 man-hours during the summer of 1945 in the search for enough working V-2 parts to assemble and fire a few rockets. All the available V-2s and associated material had been left out in the open for months, deteriorating in the weather and being pilfered by troops and souvenir hunters. By September 1945 German rocket troops had assembled 5 V-2s for launch from the Krupp Naval Gun Testing Ground at Altenwalde near Cuxhaven on the North Sea.

The first BACKFIRE V-2 was launched by German personnel on October 2, 1945. This was the first time Allied personnel had witnessed the launch of a large rocket at close range, and it was thoroughly documented by various cameras and tracked in flight by Allied radars.

The second launch, on October 4, 1945, suffered from a variety of problems. When the firing command was given, the power plugs did not separate and the motor did not ignite although the pyrotechnic _Zündkreuz_ or "fire cross" fired. A technician was sent out to install a new igniter amidst a drizzle of alcohol from the motor chamber. When he didn't return promptly, it is reported that other technicians were sent out to the rocket to learn why and discovered a very inebriated technician intoxicated by the alcohol fumes. When the V-2 was finally launched, it suffered a premature thrust failure and crashed into the North Sea.

The third launch, on October 15, 1945, was a VIP affair for invited spectators from the United States, France, the press, and the Soviet Union.

The names of three Soviets had been submitted by Moscow. Five showed up.

The three listed were: Col. Yuri Aleksandrovich Pobedonostsev, one of the founders of rocket research in the Soviet Union; Col. Valentin P. Glushko who was the Chief Engine Designer of the Soviet Union and was already testing captured V-2 motors at Lehesten; and a general who might have been Sergey Leonidovich Sokolov, later the first deputy minister of defense for the USSR. One of the other unlisted Soviets remains unknown, but he was probably an NKVD agent assigned to guard the other unlisted man who was at that time serving a life sentence for treason in Special Prison Number 4, where a group of engineers was working under Glushko on liquid-propellant rockets. The prisoner was dressed as a captain and was chief of the Soviet Special Commission in charge of re-starting the V-2 production lines at Mittelwerke. His name was Sergei Pavlovich Korolev, and we will hear more about him.

The three listed Soviets were permitted inside the compound, but Korolev and his guard were forced to watch the launching from just outside the gate. After the successful launch, the Soviets were denied permission to tour the assembly area and launching bunker.

Afterward, Lt. M. S. Hochmuth, who was later to serve on the staff at White Sands, spoke with Pobedonostsev, who knew he'd been at Mittelwerke and had helped strip it. The Soviet engineer also knew what was going on at White Sands, which was supposed to be secret at that time. When Hochmuth asked him about the Mittelwerke, Pobedonostsev said they were having a difficult time because the Americans had cleaned it out. He offered to let the Americans see Peenemünde if they could see White Sands.

The Americans said no, turning down the chance to see the late enemy's rocket research center in exchange for letting the Soviets see hundreds of square miles of what was then nothing but barren desert.

Among the Americans present at BACKFIRE was a man wearing a hearing aid and the rumpled uniform of a colonel. Like many other civilian scientists at BACKFIRE, he was obviously in costume for the occasion, just like most of the Soviets. He was Dr. Theodore von Kármán, the world's foremost fluid dynamics scientist, director of the Jet Propulsion Laboratory (JPL) of the California Institute of Technology, and a founder of Aerojet, the second American rocket company. So was Dr. William H. Pickering, also of JPL. And a legitimate naval officer, Lt. Comm. Grayson P. Merrill.

After the BACKFIRE launchings, Merrill wrote in his report that rockets probably could be launched from ships at sea, not knowing that experiments doing just that had already been carried out at Peenemünde. Merrill later recalled, "I feel the Cuxhaven launchings had a definite bearing on the genesis of the now famous Polaris program."

None of the victorious Allies really got anything of value from Operation BACKFIRE. But it affected a lot of people. (When I first saw the motion pictures of the BACKFIRE launchings as a college sophomore in 1947, I knew what I wanted to do as my life's work.) Richard S. Lewis of *Stars & Stripes* wrote in his 1968 book, *Appointment on the Moon*, "That demonstration marked a transition point in the development of rocket technology in the West. That was the last V-2 fired in Germany. The engineering science which the weapon represented was carried off by the victors as spoils of war."

In the official British report of Operation BACKFIRE, Maj. Gen. A. M. Cameron wrote, "No nation can afford to allow the development of long-range rockets to jog along as a matter of routine. There is a need of all the imagination, drive, and brains that can be mustered. For the sake of their very existence, Britain and the United States must be masters of this weapon of the future."

One of them wouldn't, and the other one would be dragged into it by the threat of annihilation.

# Antipathy in the West

The British never did make much of their share of the V-2 loot from Germany. They couldn't. Two major wars had bled Britain white, exhausted the Exchequer, and robbed the country of yet another generation of young men. Winston Churchill and his coalition government didn't even survive the end of the European portion of World War II. The best the British could do was analyze the long-range ballistic missile that had targeted their country, come to the conclusion that they didn't need a ballistic missile with a range of 200 miles to fight France, decide that they couldn't do anything to stop a ballistic missile attack anyway, and then sit back and do exactly nothing. In retrospect, what else could they do? Britain was broke, losing its empire, and trying to make some sort of a dent in the postwar international market for jet airplanes, especially jet transports. Britain did have a lead in turbojet engine technology, but didn't keep it as an exclusive national technology hoard for very long.

The Americans had the atomic bomb and thought they had an exclusive on that technology. The United States was also tired of war, although the country had been at war for only four years. People wanted new cars, new houses, and new everything to replace the gadgets that had worn out. In 1946 the United States was the grandest seller's market in history, and people had lots of money to spend because they hadn't been able to spend it on anything during the war.

Furthermore, the United States not only had the fearsome atomic bomb but also had a way to deliver it to a target nearly anywhere on earth: the long-range manned strategic bomber. No one had been able to match that technology during World War II. The Boeing B-29 and the improved Boeing B-50 were supreme. But they were soon to be relegated to the backseat by the huge Convair B-36, which had been under design during the war. The B-29 and the B-36 could carry the atomic bomb nearly anywhere in the world with the help of aerial refueling, which was perfected by the United States shortly after the war, using a tanker version of the B-50, the KC-97.

In spite of rapid demobilization, the United States generally kept its powder dry. It was apparent to most political and military leaders that one of the reasons why World War II had started was that the United States had opted out of becoming a world power at the end of World War I. The United States had refused to join the League of Nations and had retreated behind its historical strategic barriers, two large moats called the Atlantic and Pacific oceans. In 1945, however, it was apparent that those moats could be crossed easily by manned strategic bombers. Only the United States had them at the end of the war. In spite of major military reductions, the US maintained a *perceived* long-range manned strategic bombing capability. (A perceived capability is often just as good as a real capability when it comes to deterrence.)

The only place the Americans felt they might have to drop an atomic bomb was on the Soviet Union. In spite of the fact that the USSR was one of the Allies, and in spite of the fact that the Soviets had fought hard and valiantly against the Germans, Americans didn't really trust Uncle Joe. The Soviets and especially their dictatorial leader, Stalin, began acting with their usual Russian paranoia almost at once.

The Soviets didn't have the atomic bomb, and Joseph Stalin didn't like that. He also didn't like the way Harry Truman behaved. The feeling appeared to be mutual. In spite of the fact that Truman was the new kid in the Allied triumvirate, we know in retrospect that he was no one's fool. Neither was General of the Army Dwight David Eisenhower, who had almost as much political clout as military control over what happened in Europe in 1945.

It can't be said that the United States wasn't really comfortable being in the position of exclusive owner of the world's ultimate terror weapon, the atomic bomb. The bomb disgusted and dismayed military men in both the United States and Great Britain. As General Sir John Hackett wrote in his book *The Profession of Arms,* "The concept of total war between sovereign national states was now matched with a technique of total destruction. . . . As a result, if by war we still mean total war, as Clausewitz did, war can no longer be what Clausewitz called it—the continuation of policy by other means."

The obvious step was to attempt to bring atomic energy under control. Here again, in spite of what had happened as a result of the Treaty of Versailles or perhaps with some inkling of the failure of that agreement to control military technology, the obvious first step was to bring atomic energy in all its forms under the aegis of the newly formed United Nations for which such grand hopes ran rampant in those times.

But, in spite of American offers to internationalize nuclear power and atomic weaponry through the United Nations, the Soviets consistently said *nyet.*

The handwriting was on the wall. The Soviet Union intended to play by its own rules for its own benefit until it could assure itself, first, that it couldn't be invaded by the Allies as it had been at the end of World War I; second, that it could reach military parity with the United States; and, lastly, that it had become such a superior military power that it could continue to pursue the Marxist-Leninist policy of peace. Under Soviet doctrine, "peace" is that condition that will exist when all the enemies of socialism have been defeated.

The USSR's first priority was to rebuild its shattered country and industrial base. The Soviets sacked Germany and eastern Europe with a vengeance. On May 3, 1946, Gen. Lucius Clay, deputy American commander in Germany, halted delivery of reparations from the western zones of Germany to the Soviet Union and refused to resume them until the Soviets began to operate their zone of occupation according to the agreements hammered out at Yalta and Potsdam.

The USSR had further refused outright an American proposal for a 25-year alliance against the possible rise of German militarism.

The Soviets were well along on the first step of their plan to destroy the German industrial base. The next phase would be to bring the eastern European nations into the Soviet empire by forcing puppet communist governments upon them; this gave the Soviets some of the prime industrial real estate in the world populated by people such as the Czechs, who were highly industrialized.

Then they had to get the atomic bomb, and that meant opposing all attempts at international control of atomic energy.

On June 14, 1946, in the United Nations, the USSR vetoed the American plan put forth by Bernard Baruch for the international control of atomic energy. The Baruch Plan would have stopped the manufacture of all nuclear weapons, caused the destruction of all existing stocks, and set up an international inspection system. The Soviets demanded that the United States destroy its own stockpiles before the system of inspection was put into operation. They also demanded that their veto be retained in the UN's international atomic control agency.

The Soviets knew what the Americans knew: The ultimate weapon, the ICBM, was now possible. It would be created by marrying the ballistic missile with the atomic bomb. True, the ballistic missile was represented then only by the small V-2, with its range of 250 kilometers. And the atomic bombs of the time weighed more than 10,000 pounds, which was more than the V-2 could carry. But with some concentrated engineering, visionary experts on both sides of the Atlantic Ocean knew the ICBM was possible. Although the manned long-range strategic bomber was the only available delivery system then, recent wartime experience showed that bombers could be intercepted and destroyed by manned interceptor aircraft. The possibility of antiaircraft guided missiles made air defense even more effective in the short term—within ten years. However, because the technology for defending against a ballistic missile simply didn't exist at all and probably wouldn't for decades to come, the nation with exclusive possession of the ICBM was in a position to say, "Okay, boys, I've got the drop on you! Throw down your guns! Now you're going to do what I tell you to do!"

The Americans were pretty smug about it all, however. They had the long-range bomber that could carry the atomic bomb. The Soviet Union had neither, even though the USSR had made a carbon copy of the B-29s that had fallen into their hands when Superfortresses had made emergency landings in and near Vladivostok before the Soviets had entered the war against Japan. The Soviet copy, the Tupolev Tu-4, wasn't ready, however, until nearly 1950. Neither was the Soviet atomic bomb.

As a result of no immediate perceived need for an ICBM, the long-range ballistic missile program in the United States between the critical years of 1945 and 1950 languished.

Once the Peenemünde team had taught the personnel of U.S. Army Ordnance and the GE Hermes Project engineers how to assemble and launch the V-2 rockets at White Sands, the world's finest and most experienced ballistic missile engineers were put to work designing not ballistic missiles that they knew something about but air-breathing ramjets, supersonic versions of the V-1. These were, in effect, unmanned and expendable strategic bombers.

What funds existed as a result of wartime military construction budgets, money that really couldn't be put back into the Treasury, were spent building white elephants such as a 500,000-pound static test stand anchored in the granite of the Organ Mountains south of the White Sands cantonment area in New Mexico. It was used for two firings of modified V-2 rocket motors until 1953, when I was one of the engineers who helped convert it into a test stand for the 75,000-pound Redstone missile motor. But we're getting ahead of ourselves . . .

The thinking was short-range and tactical. The V-2 had shown that the ballistic missile was indeed a good long-range artillery piece if its many shortcomings could be worked out by continued engineering development. The V-2, after all, had revealed itself as a weapon that had been put into production and deployed quite prematurely. Some of the follow-on *aggregat* missiles planned by the

Peenemünde team deserved further study and development . . . but not the fantastic A.9/A.10 which was beyond reasonable belief at the time.

The Jet Propulsion Laboratory, part of the California Institute of Technology, was given the mission of designing a battlefield ballistic missile called Corporal that would carry a 1,000-pound warhead to a range of 90 miles. It was propelled by a 20,000-pound rocket motor using aniline and red fuming nitric acid, hypergolic propellants, that were fed into the combustion chamber by pressure instead of a turbopump. Out of the early Corporal development—the first Corporal wasn't fired at White Sands until 1951—came a series of upper atmosphere research rockets called the WAC-Corporal and the Aerobee. Piddling stuff compared to what could have been done by picking up where the Germans had left off at Peenemünde.

But except for the visionaries in the military services, Americans went to sleep, lulled by the assurances of the brilliant scientists who had come into prominence by developing the atomic bomb, thus permitting the United States to end World War II with the delivery of two of those weapons.

In December 1945, Dr. Vannevar Bush told a congressional committee, "There has been a great deal said about a 3,000 mile high-angle rocket. . . . I say, technically, I don't think anyone in the world knows how to do such a thing, and I feel confident that it will not be done for a very long period of time to come. . . . I think we can leave that out of our thinking. . . ."

As late as June 19, 1948, Lt. Gen. Leslie R. Groves, former head of the American atomic bomb program during World War II, wrote in *The Saturday Evening Post:*

> *It . . . will take Russia at least until 1955 to produce successful atomic bombs in quantity. I say this because Russia simply does not have enough precision industry, technical skill or scientific numerical strength to come even close to duplicating the magnificent achievement of the American industrialists, skilled*

*labor, engineers and scientists who made the Manhattan project
a success.*

Less than a year after Groves wrote this, the USSR successfully
detonated an atomic bomb and began producing them in quantity.

The Soviet Union was also doing things with the ballistic missile
that were unsuspected by the United States.

# V-2 at White Sands

Under the aegis of the Hermes Project, the 100 V-2 rockets stripped from the Mittelwerke by Toftoy and Hochmuth were shipped to Fort Bliss, Texas, and then to the new Army Ordnance Corps' White Sands Proving Ground about 40 miles north of there in the barren Tularosa Basin.

If there ever was a nearly perfect place to fly the V-2, it was White Sands. Located in the Tularosa Basin north of El Paso, Texas, between the San Andres Mountains on the west and the Sacramento Mountains on the east, it forms a 90-mile basin about 40 miles wide that is nearly flat at an elevation of 4,000 feet above sea level. It is crossed only by a single two-lane road, U.S. Highway 70, that runs from Las Cruces, New Mexico, in the Rio Grande valley on the west through Organ Pass northeasterly to Alamogordo, New Mexico. It is nearly isolated from the world except for El Paso on the south, Las Cruces on the west, and Alamogordo on the east. The climate is high Chihuahuan desert with weather for most of the year that can be best described as "severe clear." Humidity is practically nonexistent, and temperatures range from slightly below freezing in the winter to about 110 degrees F in the summertime. (One evening while driving home from the Proving Ground to Las Cruces, I measured the temperature at 107 degrees F and the humidity at 3 percent.) Less than 10 inches of rain waters the arid landscape, which is covered by hummocks about 6 feet high covered with clumps of hardy succulent grasses—the "boondocks" of White

Sands. Across the middle of the range is White Sands National Monument, a stretch of white gypsum sand. Up in the northwest corner of the range was a strange area covered with bubbly green glasslike rock, Trinity Site, where the first atomic explosion took place in July 1945.

The U.S. Army Ordnance Corps originally set up White Sands Proving Ground as an annex of its Aberdeen Proving Ground in Maryland, and many of the first engineers came from Aberdeen, where they'd been involved in artillery and explosives development. The first buildings weren't; they were tents. Eventually, World War II-style barracks were constructed, along with hangars for the assembly of V-2 rockets. Ten miles to the east of the cantonment area the Army built the world's safest above-ground building, a solid reinforced concrete blockhouse with walls 10 feet thick and a pyramidal roof 27 feet thick. It was designed to withstand the high-order explosion of a loaded V-2 100 feet away—which was eventually needed—or a V-2 rocket falling directly on it from an altitude of 100 miles—which never happened. In about 1950 they built an annex on the south side of it that wasn't quite as massive, and that is where I was during several launches, well aware of my lesser status as a young and therefore expendable engineer.

The flat basin was dotted with instrument stations—Askania cinetheodolites captured from Germany and then improved and modified by Americans, ballistic cameras, modified SCR-584 radars, a super-accurate Doppler radio positioning system known as DOVAP, telemetry receiving stations, and a new development called the tracking telescope which could take a photo of a V-2 at an altitude of 100 miles. Tying this all together was the job of the U.S. Army Signal Corps, which strung over 100,000 miles of open wires and set up some of the first microwave data links in the United States. For ten years, between 1946 and 1956, White Sands was *the* place to flight-test high-altitude and medium-range rockets because of the outstanding instrumentation and the good weather.

Since the U.S. Navy also wanted to test some missiles in an environment where they could be tracked during their flight with optical instruments—a luxury not always available at the Navy's

Point Mugu facility, and the China Lake facility was too small for some of the more powerful Navy missiles—the Desert Navy made its presence known at White Sands by building a blockhouse that duplicated that of the Army as well as the U.S.S. *Desert Ship*, an officially christened but completely landlocked duplicate of future guided missile cruisers. In addition, the Navy built an excellent officer's club that was nicer than the Army's made-over ranch house, plus a welcome and much-used swimming pool.

Forty miles to the northeast the U.S. Army Air Force reactivated the Alamogordo Air Base, renaming it Holloman Air Force Base, and establishing its White Sands presence there. The Air Force had its own launching area for high-altitude rockets, provided an important link in the radar chain, used the White Sands instrumentation to obtain data on air-to-air missiles, and provided a home for aircraft used on the range such as QB-17 drones, against which the Army and the Navy launched their Nike and Talos SAMs.

But until 1956 there was no thought or possibility of launching ballistic missiles with ranges greater than 100 miles at White Sands. The range wasn't large enough. Even at that, extensive flight safety procedures had to be established to prevent rockets from flying in a path that would cause them to impact off the range.

With the help of the Peenemünde rocket team brought to Fort Bliss under Operation Paper Clip, GE and the Army began firing V-2s not only to learn how to do it but also to utilize the V-2's then-prodigious payload capacity of 1,640 pounds to loft scientific measuring instruments to altitudes of 100 miles or so.

GE launched the captured V-2s under the Hermes Project. During the years 1946 to 1951, a total of 67 V-2s were launched by GE. Considering that the Germans had been producing V-2s at a rate of more than 900 per month in 1945 and launching more than four rockets a day at Blizna, this was indeed a very low priority and very low intensity program. Most of the time between shots was devoted to data reduction. The Germans had very little information about what happened to the V-2 after burnout. The famous astronomer Dr. Clyde W. Tombaugh came to White Sands in 1946 and is responsible for mating the high-power optical telescope to a motion-picture camera, the whole affair being mounted on a trainable gun mount so that the operator, watching the missile through a high-power aiming telescope of his own, could follow the missile during its entire flight. Photos of V-2s at an altitude of more than 20 miles showed that just before burnout there were strong wobblings caused by unsymmetrical thrust of the rocket motor running out of propellants. This is one factor that caused the high dispersion of the rounds fired against London and Antwerp.

Much of the V-2 matériel that arrived at White Sands was unusable because of wear and tear, shipping damage, corrosion, or age. Shortages of critical components plagued the program to the end. Douglas Aircraft had to make many V-2 tail sections; it was generally known by the launching crew that the American-made components weren't as good as the original German ones, and a lot of V-2s with Douglas tail sections shed their fins early in their flights. All the electrical wiring harnesses had to be replaced; the Germans had used solid wire that was prone to breakage because of vibration, and the GE harnesses were indeed one of the few parts that were better than the German counterparts. Honeywell and Sperry made American copies of the German gyros. Shortages didn't extend to all parts; in 1954 I got hold of about 100 motor-driven timing switches that provided us with some badly needed parts for other projects. I must have stashed nearly 50 of these in a cable duct in one of the rocket assembly buildings; I don't know what happened to them, but they are valuable museum pieces today. (I do have a few V-2 parts in my possession today. I went through some garbage cans full of unused V-2 parts when GE closed out the V-2 program in 1951, and I spent some time in the junkyard where recovered V-2 wreckage was stacked.)

By 1947 the Germans had left White Sands, and all V-2 firings after that time were carried out by American crews.

The V-2s turned out to be workhorses and could be modified if you knew what you were doing . . . and Americans learned. Seventy-one percent of all White Sands V-2s were above design weight, some carrying as much as 1,800 pounds of additional payload. The thick-skinned German warhead section was quickly replaced by an American-made version of much lighter construction capable of housing scientific instruments. To accommodate special payloads, nearly 52 percent of the White Sands V-2s had configuration modifications in the form of noses of different shapes.

Seven V-2 rockets were modified to carry Blossom payloads consisting of living organisms and seeds. Several monkeys flown in Blossom V-2s didn't survive their flights because of parachute or other failures.

A V-2 was launched from the deck of the U.S. Navy's aircraft carrier U.S.S. _Midway_ as Operation Sandy on September 6, 1947. This proved it could be done, although the V-2 turned at an angle of 45° after liftoff and climbed to an altitude of 12,000 feet before tumbling into the ocean. The GE Hermes launch team carried out Operation Sandy, and for many years thereafter Leo D. "Pappy" White, the Hermes project engineer, proudly displayed on his White Sands office wall the Operation Sandy diploma that certified he was capable of digging a 3-foot-deep foxhole in a steel deck in 15 seconds flat.

Robert P. Haviland of the GE Hermes team came up with the idea of replacing the V-2 payload with the little WAC-Corporal sounding rocket and launching the combination as a two-stage rocket christened Project Bumper. Strictly a product of American rocket engineering, this was the first two-staged rocket launched in the United States and was the immediate predecessor to the ICBM. Six of the eight Bumpers were launched at White Sands. Bumper 5, launched February 24, 1949, reached 244 miles, the highest altitude then achieved by a rocket vehicle. Bumper 8 was the first rocket launched at Cape Canaveral (July 24, 1950) and was used to test potential ICBM components.

The V-2 was also used to support other Hermes programs, as we'll see later.

The most famous of all V-2 shots is still not listed among the official White Sands shots. It was fired on the evening of May 29, 1947, carrying a special guidance system devised by Dr. Ernst Steinhoff, one of the Peenemünde engineers who was in America. As with Steinhoff's A.4 that had its wires crossed and landed in Sweden, this

V-2 behaved the same way and headed south instead of north. Steinhoff used the edge of the blockhouse roof as a reference as he watched it ascend. He knew it was going south, but he decided to let it go rather than take the chance that it would impact with a propellant load and cause great damage. It arced over El Paso and landed in a cemetery on the outskirts of Ciudad Juarez, Mexico. This nearly caused an international incident. But by the time the U.S. Army showed up a few hours later, enterprising Mexicans were selling any old piece of scrap metal they could find and claiming it was V-2 debris. This incident resulted in a stand-down of all flight testing at White Sands until Maj. Herbert Karsch and Nathan Wagner developed range safety procedures to prevent such a thing from happening again.

Four White Sands V-2 shots stand out in my mind.

V-2 Number 55 was a high-altitude shot with a sun-tracking spectroscope in its nose. It was launched at dawn on June 14, 1951. I was sitting on the hood of a truck 1,000 yards to the west. During thrust buildup, the V-2 skittered on the launch pad and shorted out the connections for the range safety explosives. I recall four explosions—the nose explosives, the alcohol-LOX tanks, the tail explosives, and the peroxide tank. I ended up on the ground on top of a cactus. In the blockhouse, 100 feet from the holocaust, project engineer Leo D. White was in his usual place between the firing panel and the bulletproof window. He had fired more V-2s than anyone in the United States. When he saw the nose explosives blow, he ducked instinctively. Everyone in the blockhouse figured if Pappy ducked, they'd better do the same. Then Pappy popped back up in time to see the alcohol-LOX tanks blow, so he ducked again . . . and so did everyone else. Two additional times this happened, and we can laugh at it today. It was also the day Pappy's mongrel dog wasn't in the blockhouse during a firing, and the GE engineers made sure the mutt was on hand thereafter.

V-2 TF-1 (Training Flight One) was fired on August 22, 1951, by the men of the Army's 1st Guided Missile Battalion. It was a hot rod that was fired for altitude. From a position 3 miles south of the launch pad, I watched it go straight up and out of sight to an altitude of 135 miles.

V-2 TF-4 was launched at night in June 1952. My wife and I watched with Dr. Clyde W. Tombaugh from a position 1,000 yards west of the launcher. The whole world lit up, and I didn't see anything like it again until I watched Apollo 17 launched at night to the moon from the Cape in December 1972. The sky was perfectly clear, and Tombaugh was able to track the rocket to an altitude of more than 100 miles through his binoculars, watching only the red-hot glow from the carbon vanes that had been in the engine exhaust.

V-2 TF-5 was the last V-2 launched in the United States. It was a party. In company with Dr. Tombaugh and science-fiction authors Robert Heinlein and Jack Williamson, we watched from 1,000 yards to the east of the launcher. This V-2 had been in trouble from the start. The 1st Guided Missile Battalion had loaded the alcohol and peroxide. The project officer then called for the LOX tanker to come into the launch area. "What LOX trailer?" Someone had forgotten to order LOX. It was on hand the following morning, but the rocket had stood for 24 hours with the hydrogen peroxide in it. That had corroded some of the ancient piping now seven years old. TF-5 took off beautifully. At 28 seconds, it was scheduled to pass the speed of sound. This causes all sorts of buffeting and vibrations in the rocket. These shook loose the peroxide piping. There was a huge explosion in the tail section. The last V-2 tumbled to the ground with a huge impact explosion. The end of an era.

"I could have had a V-2!" In 1956 White Sands tried to find a home for a V-2 that had never been fired. It was perched on its Meilerwagen transporter. The Army couldn't get a museum or university to take it. They asked me if I wanted it. All I had to do was sign for it. But I didn't have a place to park it. It ended up vertically with its tail full of concrete in the White Sands Missile Garden where it can be seen today.

For seven years German V-2s had been flown in the United States. We hadn't built any of them. No one wanted the last one. We squandered a legacy. It almost cost us our nation and our freedom.

# Hermes and NATIV

During the critical five years between 1945 and 1950 some American ballistic missile research was carried on other than launching captured German V-2s. But it was done at a very low level of effort with very limited funds. In many ways it was without definite goals as well. Americans seemed to be casting about in hopes of finding better ways to deliver the atomic bomb if they had to do it again. It was a period of "try everything and maybe something will work better."

As a result, the United States frittered away its lead in strategic weapons at a time when it was becoming more and more evident that we would need them if the Soviets continued to behave as they had since the end of World War II. But according to the experts and in agreement with the prevailing folk wisdom of the time, we had lots of time. Just as the British were almost totally unprepared when World War II started—and would have been had it not been for visionaries in the Air Ministry, Vickers Supermarine, and Hawkers—because they believed they would have ten years' warning before another brawl began to brew in Europe, so Americans felt there would be plenty of time because they could hold off the Russians with war surplus equipment. And plenty of that was everywhere because the United States had out-produced everyone else during World War II.

As for the technical abilities of the Russians, Americans considered them to be stupid, unschooled, bomb-throwing peasants who were so technically inept that they couldn't even get tractors to work right. Never mind that American and British military experts pointed out that the Soviet T-34 was the best tank of World War II, and even the Germans said so. Never mind that the Soviet "Sturmovik" attack plane was far better than the German Ju-87 Stuka and that the United States had nothing like it for tank-busting. Never mind that the Soviet MiG-3s and La-7s would fly and fight when the German Heinkels and Messerschmitts couldn't even be started because of the cold weather. Never mind that the Soviet "Katyusha" barrage rockets had terrorized the Wehrmacht. Most Americans believed the Russians were ignorant tank riders carrying primitive PPSh-41 submachine guns, and Patton could have whipped them if only we'd turned him loose. That was the gist of the thinking of the time. Americans were perplexed that the Russians didn't seem to be civilized, much less housebroken.

However, military men such as General Toftoy of U.S. Army Ordnance and General "Hap" Arnold had seen and understood what the Germans had done and how very close they'd come to winning World War II utilizing new technology if only Hitler had had real vision.

The Army had the Hermes Project. Only part of its scope was to launch captured German V-2s. That was the Hermes learning process that eventually would lead to a better American ballistic missile than the V-2. The Army's basic mistake was believing that Americans were the experts at mass production and couldn't learn anything by putting the V-2 into production in the United States. In the first place, as von Braun told Toftoy, Hammil, and Porter, the V-2/A.4 wasn't intended for production. The goal of the Hermes Project therefore was to learn how to design, build, and operate better ballistic missiles than the V-2, ending up with an ICBM at some indeterminate point in the future.

A strong feeling of nationalism ran through the American rocket engineers who at that time came through White Sands regularly. Americans, they believed, were as good, if not better, than the Germans, and they'd prove it. They did in the long run in some areas. But the Germans under von Braun were a far better team;

they'd had more practice and were farther along on what Americans called the learning curve. It was also obvious that the American rocket engineers were prone to the NIH (Not Invented Here) Factor. I was among them at the time and can now see it in retrospect.

The Hermes Project was ambitious for its time and its funding level.

First, GE had to develop a suitable rocket motor. This they began to do when the Rochester Ordnance District of the U.S. Army Ordnance Corps built a rocket engine test stand at the Malta Test Station near Balliston Spa, New York. GE engineers started out with a modest rocket motor operating at a chamber pressure about that of the German A.4 motor, 300 pounds per square inch (psi). It used alcohol and liquid oxygen and was fed with an advanced turbopump of GE design. GE had extensive experience in steam turbines and aircraft turbosuperchargers, and they put this to work for their rocket motor. If Americans are generally believed to think big in what they do, they certainly didn't think big when it came to rocket motors. For years, nearly all rocket motor manufacturers save one thought almost exclusively about motors with about 20,000 pounds of thrust. Thus, the initial GE motor developed 13,500 pounds of thrust. This was ready in the spring of 1949. During the next several years, this basic motor was continually up-rated and improved by jacking up the chamber pressure to 510 psi and the thrust level to 22,600 pounds by continual improvements in the turbopump design, something which GE was good at. A set of gimbals was designed into the motor, allowing it to be swiveled to provide directional control of the rocket vehicle, just as the carbon vanes had done for the A.4.

Eventually this rocket motor was developed into the X405 rocket engine of 27,000 pounds of thrust that powered the first stage of the Vanguard satellite launch vehicle in 1958.

The first Hermes design—the Hermes A-1—was started in 1946 as an antiaircraft missile patterned after the German Wasserfall because the design had already been tested in the Peenemünde wind tunnels and therefore was a good point of departure. However, in 1947 the Hermes A-1 became a test vehicle for the new GE radio-command inertial guidance system because the Douglas/Bell Labs

Nike had shown itself to be an effective SAM. It was also used to develop GE's telemetry system. Five of these Wasserfall clones were flight-tested at White Sands between May 19, 1950, and April 25, 1951.

The Hermes A-1E1 and A-1E2 were planned as interim tactical ballistic missiles, but only a single A-1E1 was assembled and tested. None flew. The requirements kept changing. This drove some of the GE engineers to distraction.

The Hermes A-2 was a wingless A-1, making it a little A.4 clone since the Wasserfall was a small winged A.4 configuration. A redirection in *that* part of the program showed that it would be a better ballistic missile if solid propellants were used, and it was converted into the RV-A-10, the largest solid-propellant missile built at that time with a diameter of 31 inches and a thrust of 32,000 pounds. The motor was made by Thiokol under contract, and three were launched from the Cape in March 1953, proving that a large solid-propellant motor was useful in a ballistic missile and paving the way for the later solid-propellant Minuteman ICBM.

The Hermes B was a ramjet development program tasked with developing the simple ramjet motor for an intercontinental cruise missile. GE designed and static tested the RV-A-6 ramjet capable of operating at Mach 4. On November 18, 1948, this ramjet was flown on the nose of V-2 rocket 44 at White Sands. It was also known as the Hermes II or "Hermes Roman Two," at White Sands, and it was probably the strangest of all the various V-2 configurations flown at White Sands. The Hermes B program was terminated in 1950 because, as we'll see later, the Air Force Navaho intercontinental ramjet-powered cruise missile became the one that was blessed by the Pentagon.

Hermes C was a study program, never got off the ground at all, and was later transferred to Redstone Arsenal, where the von Braun team did indeed do something with it under another name. Hermes C was supposed to be a 2,000-mile long-range missile with a supersonic glider as a payload. It would have had a takeoff thrust of 600,000 pounds and a liftoff weight of 250,000 pounds. It was an American version of the Peenemünde A.9/A.10.

The last Hermes missiles were the A-3AE2 and A-3B. These were designed to an Army specification calling for a tactically useful ballistic missile capable of carrying a 1,000-pound warhead to a range of 150 miles. A total of 7 A-3E2 and 6 A-3B Hermes missiles were flown at White Sands. They used the GE motor powered by alcohol and LOX, which immediately meant logistics problems in the field. But GE never had the chance to develop any support equipment. All but one of these Hermes A-3 ballistic missiles were successful.

When the Hermes Project was finally terminated in June 1953, the work that GE had done led directly to other ballistic missiles. However, from that time on GE was no longer at the forefront of ballistic missile development or rocket motor technology. Whether or not this was a conscious decision on the part of GE management not to pursue ballistic missile technology beyond this point remains to be told in a GE corporate history book. It wasn't or wouldn't be the first time GE led in high technology only to back away for unannounced corporate reasons. They did the same thing with computers twenty years later.

On the Air Force side of the house, things were equally active and equally confused at the same time. No one could envision a rocket large enough to carry the huge atomic bombs of the time. Besides, *a ballistic missile didn't have wings and didn't carry a pilot!* At the end of World War II, Gen. Henry H. "Hap" Arnold asked Dr. Theodore von Kármán to head up a committee that would look into the future and tell the Air Force what it would be flying in and fighting with in ten years, twenty years, and fifty years. This report, classified SECRET until 1960, was titled "Toward New Horizons" and was instrumental in determining Air Force research and development for at least 15 years.

Von Kármán had been an observer at Operation BACKFIRE. His report recommended that the Air Force conduct a continuing series of studies and technology demonstrations toward the goal of deploying an ICBM at some future time when the technology would permit it. Thus, with the support of this classified report to fall back on and in spite of the ascendancy of the bomber generals, the future missile generals began to work quietly behind the scenes.

The Air Force let two contracts for ballistic missiles. One will be discussed in detail later. The second was let to North American Aviation, builders of the P-51 Mustang, the B-25 Mitchell, and the T-6 Texan. North American was to conduct a feasibility study of guided missiles.

The result was the NATIV test vehicle. It was 18 inches in diameter, 14 feet 6 inches long, weighed 1,237 pounds, and was powered by a solid-propellant motor. NATIV was successfully launched to an altitude of 50,000 feet from the 144-foot Aerobee tower at Holloman Air Force Base on the White Sands range. This success led to a follow-on contract for the study of an intercontinental weapon system called Navaho.

The Navaho Project started out as a ballistic missile, the Navaho I, with a range of 500 miles. It would require a liquid-propellant rocket motor producing 75,000 pounds of thrust. North American started developing this, building static test stands in the Santa Susanna Mountains on the north side of the San Fernando Valley and an engine plant in Canoga Park.

The point of departure for the Navaho I engine was the A.4 motor. North American engineers got hold of some A.4 motors from the Army, analyzed them thoroughly, and began a program to build a better, simpler, more powerful, and more reliable motor.

In March 1950 North American successfully static tested its first 75,000-pound liquid-propellant rocket motor. It was a far simpler design than the A.4 motor. It used alcohol and liquid oxygen. It had a single-shaft turbopump powered by the decomposition of 90 percent hydrogen peroxide to produce high-pressure steam. It was the most powerful liquid-propellant rocket motor ever designed and built in the United States. It was basically an American-built V-2 motor.

North American Aviation therefore had gotten itself a lock on the technology needed to build big American liquid-propellant rocket motors.

Almost immediately, the Air Force canceled the Navaho I project.

# "We Won't Be Fighting Poland!"

The complete history of the development of the ICBM in the Soviet Union can't be told here and hasn't been told anywhere. It is not likely that the Soviets will talk very much about it in the future in spite of glasnost and perestroika because it involves the development of weapons. The Soviets do not like to talk about such things. At some point more details may come to light as the Soviets reveal more of their early work with rockets for space flight. The history of the development of their ballistic missiles will have to continue to be pieced together from these bits and pieces.

That's exactly what's had to be done for the story of the history of Soviet ICBM development that follows. Like anything else having to do with trying to figure out the Soviet Union from a vantage point in a western country, one must rely on whatever one can get one's hands on. People who don't follow Soviet science and technology are continually amazed at how much the Soviets talk about these things in the open literature. Soviet documents such as scientific papers are available in both Russian and English. So are books published in English by the Soviets. Soviet leaders, scientists, engineers, and other spokespeople have made public statements that are on record. Some of these statements may have been intended only for propaganda value, and all of them are intended to put the Soviets in the best possible light. In dealing with any Soviet documents, books, or statements, one must be doubly careful because the Soviets often use a sort of doublespeak in which they put their own spin on the meanings of English words. Sometimes it's possible to learn things from what they *don't* say. In all cases, it's like putting together a complex jigsaw puzzle where the pattern of many pieces together is often more important than the shape of an individual piece or the color and design that's on it.

Much of the history of Soviet ballistic missile development was obtained by the intelligence activities of western nations. Therefore it's still classified by the U.S. government. Because of the requirement to time-downgrade classified material, it's been possible to obtain some of this information through the Freedom of Information Act. But you have to know exactly what you're looking for, and this in itself is often a tall order.

Unclassified U.S. government publications are also helpful, especially those from the Congressional Research Service of the Library of Congress. However, these haven't been up to their previous level of quality or accuracy established by the late Charles S. Sheldon in the 1960s and early 1970s.

Over the years the publications of the British Interplanetary Society (BIS) have become excellent resources for Soviet space information from which data on the Soviet ICBM programs can be pieced together. The BIS seems to be one of the channels that the Soviet Union has developed over the years for the dissemination of both information and disinformation.

The most active resource is an unofficial, unorganized network of Soviet space watchers that has grown up in the western nations. On at least a weekly basis I am in touch with this network through various individuals. None of these people is to my knowledge a professional intelligence operator or analyst; the network is composed of private individuals who are interested in the enigma of the Soviet rocket programs. I became an early member of this network in about 1955 after writing a few unclassified magazine articles about Soviet rocketry in the days when no one believed the Soviets had any rockets. Long before it was officially admitted by the U.S. government or known by the news media, this network knew that the Soviets had an ICBM and that they would launch a satellite with that ICBM sometime in the fall of 1957. We even knew something about its size and weight, although we missed by estimating too low! And we missed the launch date of Sputnik I by a couple of weeks. We thought it would go on September 17, 1957, the 100th birthday of the Soviet space pioneer Konstantin Eduardovich Tsiolkovski. We also underestimated the size and power of the Soviet ICBM.

Therefore this history of Soviet ICBM development must be considered as the author's assessment based on all the inputs mentioned above plus the author's learned ability to "think Soviet." This capability to "think Soviet" means understanding a bit about how the Russians think because of the structure of their language which reflects their thinking patterns (or vice-versa) and how they are forced to develop weapons because of the shortcomings, limitations, advantages, and peculiarities of their system of doing things. It's also become necessary to know something about the history of science and technology in both czarist and bolshevik Russia. One of the most important attributes of a Soviet aerospace watcher is the ability to realize that science and technology know no national boundaries, that efforts to prevent "technology transfer" can't and don't work, and that the Soviet Union had and still has some very good engineers and technologists. But they think and act differently than we do in the western countries.

In this story, we've met some Soviet rocket engineers already. They showed up for the British Operation BACKFIRE launchings at Cuxhaven. Not much was known or said by the Soviets about their rocket engineers over the years. Usually, we found out about them only when their obituaries were published by a grateful Soviet government.

The Soviets who were present at BACKFIRE played major roles in Soviet ballistic missile development over the next ten years.

Going back earlier than 1945, it is helpful to know that the Soviets had an active liquid-propellant rocket research program before World War II (or the "Great Patriotic War" to a Soviet person). Immediately after the October Revolution, Lenin ordered Professor Nikolai Egorovich Zhukovski (1847–1921) to set up an aeronautic research center under the name of *Tsentralnyi Aero-Gidrodinami-*

*cheskii Institut* (Ts.A.G.I.), the Soviet counterpart to the National Advisory Committee on Aeronautics (NACA) in the United States and what was to become the Zhukovski Academy of Aeronautics in Moscow. In 1930, Ts.A.G.I. established a working group to carry out basic research in rocket flight. In 1931 this became the Group for the Study of Reactive Motion (G.I.R.D.) in Leningrad. It finally became the State Rocket Scientific Research Institute.

In 1933, the liquid-propellant rocket GIRD-09 was launched near Moscow. It was 2,457 millimeters long, 160 millimeters in diameter, and weighed 20 kilograms. It reached an altitude of 4,500 meters. The people involved were Valentin P. Glushko, Sergei Pavlovich Korolev, Mikhail K. Tikhonravov, Yuri A. Pobedonostsev, and others who were to become the leaders of the Soviet ballistic missile development programs.

Up until 1937, Soviet rocketry was almost on a par with that in Germany, which in turn was far ahead of that anywhere in the rest of the world, including the United States. The resources and efforts that had to be concentrated on winning the Great Patriotic War (we'll use the Soviet designation for this as we will for other things when discussing Soviet ballistic missile history) meant that their liquid-propellant rocket engineers had to concentrate on immediate war needs.

Political ramifications also interfered.

In 1937, Stalin initiated a massive purge of the Soviet intelligentsia that included military, scientific, and technical people. It almost cost the Soviet Union the war four years later. The G.I.R.D. rocketeers had the blessing and were working with the full approval of Soviet armaments minister Mikhail N. Tukhachevskiy who saw in rockets what Becker in Germany had seen. Tukhachevskiy and his staff were arrested by the secret police on June 10, 1937, and put to death. The purge continued to reach downward through all levels of Soviet life, and the G.I.R.D. rocketeers were therefore suspect. They were rounded up by the secret police and shipped to the GULags. This is where the official Soviet biographies of the men who were to lead postwar Soviet rocketry suddenly become very

vague and incomplete. Most of these men were saved by the inter-
vention of the Soviet aircraft design bureau chief, Andrei Tupolev,
who got the secret police to send the rocket engineers back to special
prisons for scientists and engineers, *sharashkas,* where they could be
put to work on aeronautical projects.

Thus, in 1945 most of the Soviet engineering and technical visi-
tors to Operation BACKFIRE were in effect political prisoners
under the control of Gen. Grigori A. Tokaty from the Zhukovski
Academy of Aeronautics, who had been appointed Chief Rocket
Scientist of the Soviet Government in Germany.

Shortly after returning from Operation BACKFIRE, Tokaty reported to Stalin on the disposition of German rocket resources.
Stalin was furious. "This is absolutely intolerable!" Stalin said, according to Tokaty, who later defected to the West. "We defeated
Nazi armies; we occupied Berlin and Peenemünde; but the Americans got the rocket engineers. What could be more revolting and
inexcusable? How and why was this allowed to happen?"

Tokaty was assigned to find out. On March 14, 1947, he reported back to brief the Politburo. G. M. Malenkov made it quite
clear at that point that the V-2s alone did not conform to the
long-range plans of the Soviet Union. "We cannot rely on such a
primitive weapon. Besides, should there be another war, we will
not be fighting Poland! Our strategic needs are determined by the
fact that our potential enemy is to be found thousands of miles
away."

The following day, March 15, 1947, in a follow-up meeting,
Tokaty, who was present, reports that Stalin stated, "Do you realize the tremendous strategic importance of machines of this sort?
They could be an effective straitjacket for that noisy shopkeeper
Harry Truman. We must go ahead with it, comrades. The problem of the creation of transatlantic rockets is of extreme importance to us."

On the "suggestion" of Stalin, the Council of Ministers on that
date approved the formation of the *Pravitel'stvennaya Kommissiya
po Raketam Delnego Deistviya* (PKRDD), the Special State Com-

mission for the Study of the Problems of Long Range Rockets.

The Soviet ICBM program had begun. At that point the Soviets and the Americans were running almost neck and neck in the race to get the ICBM. But with the full support of Stalin and thus the entire Soviet government, it is not surprising which of the two contenders pulled ahead of the other.

# Pobedas and 8-Zh-38's

The Soviet Union is not helpful when it comes to designations of its ballistic missiles. In the west, the various Soviet ballistic missiles are known primarily by their NATO code names which begin with the letter S such as Sapwood and by alphanumeric designators such as SS-4. In the USSR, they are apparently known by two different designations—an R designation such as R-7 and an industrial production designation such as 8-K-63. To make matters more confusing—which is just what the paranoid Soviet Politburo, KGB, and Defense Ministry want—it doesn't appear to western observers or analysts that the numbers match the sequence of the NATO designations.

If it seems confusing, I'll try to do the best possible job of keeping the various ballistic missiles sorted out, because the Soviets have designed a lot of them. Perhaps they have built prototypes of them. Perhaps some of them are actually in the field. However, it is known that some of their ballistic missiles pulled through Red Square as part of military parades are dummies—"dimensional replicas," Soviet spokesmen have called them when these dummies were pointed out to them by western observers and newsmen.

The Soviet Union was likewise very secretive about the people who designed and developed its ballistic missiles. In many cases we didn't know who they were until they died and their obituaries were published in the USSR. Some were given state funerals. The reason for such secrecy that was given by the Soviets was typical: They did not want the identities of their rocket men known in order to protect them from assassination by the CIA, MI6, and other intelligence agencies. And the KGB wanted to prevent other intelligence organizations from attempting to get the Soviet rocket engineers to defect to the West.

As it turned out, several did defect. But since we don't know if they were _permitted_ to defect in order to spread disinformation, some of their stories have to be analyzed carefully. Often the reports of defectors didn't match what really happened or what the official Soviet histories later "revealed."

In most cases Soviet history must be kept in a loose-leaf binder. It is rewritten often. In some cases it is rewritten simply because the Soviets are slowly changing their language and forcing many words and terms into disuse. Many modern Russians cannot read the inscriptions on czarist buildings in Leningrad. The old words no longer exist or their meanings have been changed so that the inscriptions are nonsense today. It's a situation where George Orwell's "NewSpeak" has become reality.

But it is becoming possible to piece together more and more information about the early days of the Soviet ballistic missile program from the works of Tokaty, Grottrüp, Suvarov, and others.

The Soviets got no V-2 rockets from Germany. Practically every workable one had been taken from the Mittelwerke and shipped to White Sands by the Americans. The others had been taken by the British.

In 1945 the Soviet situation in ballistic missile research and development can best be summarized by what Tokaty wrote about that period in his book _Stalin Means War_ in 1951:

> _We have no leading V-2 experts in our zone; we have no complete projects or materials of the V-2; we have captured no fully operational V-2s which could be launched right away. But we have lots of bits and pieces of information and projects which may be very useful to us. We have the free or compelled co-operation of hundreds of German workers, technicians, and second-rate scientists, whose experience could be of value to us._

*In the circumstances, I think the best thing to do is to organize
all these into a group, in Peenemünde, to give it a set task, and
to find out what it can do for us here in Germany.*

Thus, the Soviets would have to make their own V-2s. And they
set about doing this by establishing the *Institut Rabe—Raketenbau
und Entwicklung* (Rocket Manufacture and Development) with
headquarters in Berlin. The first priority was to re-create a full set
of production drawings.

Tokaty assigned Sergei P. Korolev to head the effort at the Mittelwerke, re-creating the production drawings and procedures. Valentin P. Glushko was ordered to reestablish the V-2 rocket motor
acceptance testing facility at Lehesten, which the U.S. Army had
left practically intact. Both men were political prisoners at the time,
under sentence of life imprisonment from the time of the 1937
Stalin purges. How could such men work for a regime that had held
them as political prisoners? Very willingly if they had the choice to
follow orders or be sent back to the GULags.

The Soviets rounded up as many of the Mittelwerke engineers and
technicians as they could find and began scouring their occupation
zone for German rocket people.

They found Helmut Grottrüp who had been the assistant to Dr.
Ernst Steinhoff in the Guidance, Control, and Telemetry Labora-
tory at Peenemünde. Grottrüp had decided to stay in Germany with
his wife, Irmgard, because he didn't like the contract terms of
Operation Paper Clip that the Americans were offering to the
Peenemünde rocket team. So he and his wife returned to their home
in Bleicherode in the Russian zone. He was quickly contacted by the
Soviets from Mittelwerke. Early in 1946 Grottrüp was in charge of
Zentralwerke, a pilot production line that had been set up at the old
V-2 repair depot near Klein Bodungen. Zentralwerke Nordhausen,
Werk II, assembled V-2 motors. At Sommerdia, east of Leipzig, in
the former Rheinmetall Borsig plant, a large design office was set up.
A factory for manufacturing V-2 electrical equipment was set up in
Sonderhausen south of the Mittelwerke. The Gema plant in Berlin
continued production of missile control systems.

By September 1946 the V-2 drawings had been redone, the pilot production line had turned out 30 flightworthy V-2s, and those V-2s were static-tested at Lehesten by Glushko, first under the tutelage of the Germans, then without them. Those V-2s were never flown; they were used for ground testing.

By the summer of 1946 Korolev was working on an improved V-2. He stretched the V-2 tankage by 3 meters and increased the motor thrust from 25 tons to 32 tons by adding a second turbopump assembly in series to increase the injection pressure and thus the propellant flow rate and combustion pressure. Korolev's improved V-2, known to British intelligence as the K1, had an estimated range twice that of the V-2. Furthermore, its accuracy would have been better because Korolev called for the separation of the warhead from the missile body after burnout, something that would eliminate any errors introduced by the wobbling of the missile body as it plunged back into the atmosphere.

The K1 production drawings were in Russian. When it went into production later in the USSR, it was the R-2, also known as the Pobeda. We know what it looks like because Korolev did the same thing with ballistic missiles that the Americans did: used some of them as space launch vehicles. The R-2 became the Soviet V-2A suborbital launch vehicle in the years to come.

At this point the Soviets were clearly independent of the Germans in ballistic missile development. It took them just about a year to do it.

Then all the ballistic missile facilities, equipment, and other material in Germany was packed up and sent to the USSR. The Soviets wanted to get it out of Germany as a counterintelligence move, and they had far more room in which to flight-test ballistic missiles in the Soviet heartland. Most of the equipment relating to the missile itself was sent to Zavod 88 (Factory 88) at Zhegalovo, part of Kaliningrad northeast of Moscow. Most of the rocket motor equipment was sent to Zavod 456 in Khimki just northwest of Moscow.

When the production lines got rolling in Zhegalovo, the Soviet V-2 copy was known as the R-1 or 8-Zh-38.

At 4:00 A.M. on the morning of October 22, 1946, Grottrüp, along with some 6,000 Germans involved with the Institut Rabe, were suddenly rousted out of their homes, put on 92 trains waiting for them all over the Russian zone, and sent to Moscow where they arrived on October 28, 1946, to be greeted by General Professor Pobedonostsev. One group under Grottrüp was settled in northeastern Moscow near Kaliningrad and the Zhegalovo Zavod 88, where the Soviets had established *Nauchnii isledovatelskii institut Nii-88* (Scientific Research Institute 88). Others were sent to the island of Gorodomyla in Lake Seliger, about 250 kilometers northwest of Moscow. Not all of the thousands of Germans transported to the USSR were used for rocket research. They were attached to various design bureaus and factories in the Soviet aviation industry, where Soviet engineers picked their brains. By 1950 most of these non-rocket engineers and technicians had been sent home, all of them totally unaware of what they might have been working on.

At Nii-88, the Germans were asked to design the R-10 ballistic missile on which they'd done some preliminary work in Germany as the G1. It was 14.2 meters long, 1.62 meters in diameter, weighed 18,600 kilograms at launch, was powered by an alcohol-LOX motor producing 32 tons of thrust, and would carry a payload more than 900 kilometers. It was guided by a "beam-rider" guidance system with a Doppler-type radio cutoff system, and its accuracy would have been approximately 1 mil or 1 meter for each kilometer of range. Essentially it was a little V-2 with one exception: It was the first ballistic missile to use an ablatively cooled nose cone to protect the payload against the heat of reentry into the atmosphere. The ablative material would burn, char, and sluff off without transmitting the heat to the interior. This ablative material was the same as that used on the first Soviet ICBM ten years later: laminated plywood. In 1947, when the R-10 was designed, it was the most advanced ballistic missile in the world.

The R-10 *might* have been the direct prototype of the Soviet SS-2 Shyster ballistic missile. On the other hand, its dimensions and performance characteristics nearly match those of the Soviet R-5 rocket. Someday we may know, when the Soviets decide to tell us.

The work at Nii-88 came to an abrupt halt on August 26, 1947, when Grottrüp and several other Germans—gyroscope expert Dr. Kurt Magnus, guidance and control expert Dr. Johannes Hoch, radar expert Karl Munnich, and propulsion engineers Alfred Klippel and Otto Meier—were ordered to board a train at once. Grottrüp wasn't even allowed to call his wife. Almost a week later the train pulled onto a siding near the village of Kapustin Yar about 120 kilometers east of Stalingrad on the Volga River. They were at the railhead of the first Soviet ballistic rocket range. Several thousand Red Army engineers were already there, along with another train bearing Soviet military officers. The Germans were there to assist in the launching of the first R-1s or 8-Zh-38s, Soviet-built copies of the V-2.

Kapustin Yar in 1947 was almost as primitive as White Sands at the time. It was a tent city. Curiously, the tents were lend-lease U.S. Army tents. More camels than trucks or cars wandered over the barren plain east of the river. Eastward stretched the steppes of Khazakstan. In place were Askania cinetheodolites captured from Peenemünde to record the flight trajectory. German telemetry receiver stations were sited along the rocket's proposed ground track.

The first 8-Zh-38 of twenty that were fired at Kapustin Yar in the fall of 1947 was ready on October 30.

The countdown proceeded to minus five seconds when the weight of the loaded rocket caused one leg of the launcher to collapse, tilting the rocket sideways. The count was stopped, and dozens of fearless Soviet technicians rushed out, jacked it back up to vertical, and propped it up with timbers and girders.

Then it was launched and flew.

It was a nearly perfect flight, landing near the target 284 kilometers to the east.

Gen. Dmitriy Fedorovich Ustinov, then Minister of Defense Armaments and later to become Soviet Minister of Defense in 1976, grabbed Sergei P. Korolev in a bear hug. Korolev then did the same with Grottrüp.

The ballistic missile program of the Soviet Union was off the ground.

# The Matter of the Payload

As a weapon, the long-range ballistic missile was considered by many to be a very expensive and complicated way to deliver a ton of high explosives on a target more than 100 kilometers away. This was beyond the range of any cannon-type artillery device.

However, the active and vocal proponents of strategic air power repeatedly pointed out that the long-range bomber, perfected by the United States during World War II, was quite effective in that role.

In retrospect, long-range strategic bombing didn't turn out to be the ultimate weapon envisioned by its proponents. To understand this and to gain perspective on the ICBM as a weapons system, it's helpful to quickly review the whole concept of strategic bombing, which is the linchpin of the concept of general war.

On the night of August 25, 1914, a German zeppelin dirigible appeared in the night skies over Antwerp, Belgium, and dropped a few bombs. Little damage was done. The British Royal Flying Corps retaliated in November 1914 by flying three AVRO biplanes 250 miles across German territory to bomb the zeppelin sheds at Friedrichshafen. Little damage was done. The Germans then used zeppelins to raid Dover and Erith in southeastern England but lost several of the huge, hydrogen-filled airships to interceptor aircraft. So they shifted to night bombing and went after the London docks on the night of May 31, 1915. But losses were still prohibitive because of the cost of dirigibles.

As a result, the Germans developed the first strategic bomber, the

Gotha G-IV. On June 13, 1917, fourteen of these Gothas dropped 118 bombs on London and killed 160 people. The current antiaircraft and fighter interceptor defenses were ineffective, and all Gothas returned to their base on the continent.

It seemed to the British that London lay at the mercy of the Imperial German Air Service. Prime Minister Lloyd George called in an imperial statesman to survey the situation and make recommendations.

This first strategic bombing study concluded that this new form of warfare would prove so powerful that all other forms of military and naval action would become "secondary and subordinate." It further concluded that the only defense was an overwhelming counterattack. (We shall encounter the modern counterpart of this doctrine later.)

The man who wrote this also wrote the preamble to the Charter of the United Nations 28 years later. He was Gen. Sir Jan Smuts of South Africa.

Smuts' concepts were taken up by the British Chief of Air Staff, Sir Hugh Trenchard, after World War I. He created the Trenchard Doctrine, which proclaimed that the moral effect of strategic bombing is far more effective than the physical effect on military targets. Trenchard stated that the way to victory in future wars was to develop a heavy bombing offensive against the enemy's civilian population. The Trenchard Doctrine also claimed that there is no defense against such an offensive and that interceptor fighters are merely a sop to civilians and politicians.

As a result, there arose the belief that the enemy would start the next war at a time of its own choice in a theater it selected, and with overwhelming military superiority. Bombers would strike a "knockout blow" with such suddenness and intensity that it would cause grotesque destruction, death, and suffering. The next war would therefore be over in minutes with no survivors and no winners because those attacked would strike back with equal intensity.

What really happened, of course, was something else. The bomber turned out to be vulnerable without escort fighter cover. The Luftwaffe discovered this during the Battle of Britain. The U.S.

Army Air Forces discovered this when it attempted to carry out daylight precision bombing of Germany in 1943. Strategic bombing worked in the final days of the Pacific war against Japan only because submarines had cut off vital fuel supplies for Japanese interceptor aircraft and because Gen. Curtis LeMay had resorted to indiscriminate night firebombing of cities to burn the industrial heart out of Japan. Bombers dropping conventional explosives or firebombs turned out to be very expensive and not at all that effective.

A multimillion-dollar long-range bomber with an expensive human crew delivering a few tons of conventional high explosives could make perhaps half a dozen sorties over a heavily defended target before being shot down. When escort fighter cover was available or the enemy air defenses had been destroyed, perhaps a few more sorties could be made. This was proved in Europe, over Japan, in Korea, and over North Vietnam.

The long-range ballistic missile seemed to be the answer, but its proponents were never able to overcome the objection that a ballistic missile costing far less than a bomber was a cost-effective way to deliver high explosives. (It should be pointed out at this juncture that no one has ever fought, much less won, a cost-effective war.)

The situation changed when it was realized that the long-range ballistic missile could be used to carry a nuclear warhead. The German high command knew this during World War II, but German nuclear research had not produced an atomic bomb by 1945. If the war had gone on another two years, the Germans might have gotten such a bomb.

But even if they had, the state of the art in ballistic missiles and atomic weapons in 1945 was such that no missile could have carried the weight and size of an atomic bomb. The Little Boy and Fat Man atomic bombs weighed about 5 tons and were a dozen feet long and about 10 feet in diameter. The B-29 Superfortress was the only 1945 aircraft that could carry an atomic bomb, and it had to be highly modified to do it. The Convair B-36 could carry a 72,000-pound bomb load but only four "gravity nuclear weapons" because of the size of those devices.

The matter of ballistic missile accuracy was also a factor. If you were going to expend an expensive and scarce atomic bomb—in 1949, the United States had a stockpile of only 200 atomic bombs— you wanted some insurance that it was going to hit close enough to a very important target to destroy it. The guidance system of the V-2 was too inaccurate for intercontinental ranges; a dispersion of 3 mils at a range of 10,000 kilometers means a miss distance of 10 kilometers or more than 6 miles which, for a 20-kiloton bomb of the Nagasaki type, is a miss.

In addition, no one yet knew how to get this huge, expensive atomic payload back through the atmosphere at speeds of Mach 10 or more without having it burn up or get so hot that it wouldn't explode properly when it got there. (Getting the early atomic weapons to explode properly was a delicate art and a very difficult proposition.)

Finally, the reliability of the V-2 was terrible. More than 25 percent of them used operationally against London and Antwerp failed. This is a far higher failure rate than can be accepted by even an artillery officer in charge of a battery of 155-millimeter guns, much less a naval gunnery officer in charge of the 16-inch guns of a battleship. It didn't seem a good idea to the artillery and gunnery experts to put an atomic warhead aboard a ballistic missile that could fail in one out of four launches and thus create a real hazard to the launch crews and the immediate neighborhood. Even if the atomic warhead didn't explode, the chances were good that the warhead materials would be widely scattered and that the high explosives used for implosion squeeze might go off in unexpected ways.

Engineers can always build something bigger and more powerful once it has been shown that it can be done in the first place. Improving the accuracy and reliability of ballistic missiles are also engineering tasks. And engineers in both the United States and the Soviet Union knew it could be done in the late 1940s.

There was little or no incentive in the United States to expend the money to do more than merely study long-range ballistic missiles in the 1945–1950 period. The United States had staked its military doctrine on the long-range bomber, and it had the B-29, the improved B-50, and the huge B-36. Furthermore, it had a monopoly on atomic weapons.

The best estimates made by experts in the United States said that the Soviets couldn't possibly have an atomic capability before 1951.

The experts neglected to consider the effects of espionage on this timetable.

With the assistance of agents and sympathizers in Great Britain and the United States, and possibly with the help of some equipment obtained through channels from the west, the Soviet Union had set about to break the atomic monopoly.

On September 23, 1948, President Harry S. Truman called a press conference in the White House. The statement in the press release was brief. "We have evidence that within recent weeks an atomic explosion occurred in the U.S.S.R."

In the west, we have no information that has been declassified about where the shot known as Joe I took place in the Soviet Union or who were the Soviet scientists and engineers involved.

The most immediate consequence of Joe I was the approval for Dr. Edward Teller to proceed with the development of Super, the code word for a thermonuclear weapon. It took four years to design and build the 65-ton Shot Mike fired in the Ivy series at Eniwetok Atoll on October 31, 1952. The Fat Man detonated over Nagasaki had produced an explosive force equivalent to about 22,000 tons of TNT. Shot Mike produced a 10.4 megaton explosion.

The United States felt better now. It would take the Soviets years to come up with a weapon as complex as Shot Mike.

But the Soviets approached the problem differently. Shot Mike had used liquid tritium. Most of the 65 tons of equipment needed to make it work was dedicated to the refrigeration plant needed to liquefy the tritium. Dr. Andrei Dmitrivich Sakharov designed the first Soviet thermonuclear weapon. It used "dry" lithium hydride. It was detonated on August 12, 1953, less than a year after Shot Mike.

The United States didn't explode a dry thermonuclear device until the 15-megaton Castle shot in the spring of 1954.

A 10-megaton thermonuclear warhead doesn't have to be delivered with the pinpoint accuracy of a 20-kiloton atomic warhead. You can "miss" by many kilometers and still "kill" a "soft" target such as a city, an air base, or a military installation. A near miss with 10 megatons can also wreak havoc with the aircraft carriers and other surface ships of the naval task forces the U.S. Navy possessed. The Soviets understood this.

And if a few ballistic missiles blow up or fail, the Soviets were ready to take this into consideration in building up a ballistic missile force. All they had to do was to keep the production lines running and build more ballistic missiles than they really needed. They felt the same way about killing a few peasants by having failed missiles and warheads drop on them. The Soviet Union took 16 million casualties in the Great Patriotic War and had killed more than 35 million of its own citizens during the purges and collectivizations of the 1920s and 1930s.

As for building a bigger ballistic missile to deliver a large and heavy thermonuclear warhead, the Soviets merely shrugged and started to work. They'd always been enamored of very large airplanes and other engineering projects, so they weren't intimidated by large machines.

Stalin had decreed that the Soviet Union would have a transatlantic rocket, and now he had just the right warhead to go with it.

# The MX-774 and Its Progeny

If the thermonuclear warhead was ready by 1953, the intercontinental ballistic missile, its carrier vehicle, was not. Neither the
United States nor the Soviet Union had a ballistic missile large
enough and powerful enough even to begin to mate the two devices
into the ICBM system.

While Korolev, Glushko, and others in the Soviet Union were
hard at work doing something that the American looting of the
Mittelwerke had forced upon them—the reestablishment of the V-2
production lines first at Mittelwerke and later at Zhegalavo—American developments continued in a sporadic manner, funded even
more sporadically by a Congress that didn't yet understand exactly
what the Soviets were up to.

Americans were becoming more and more uneasy about their
former Soviet allies. With the refusal of the Soviet Union and its
eastern European satellites to participate in the Marshall Plan, and
in light of the Berlin blockade beginning in June 1948, it was
becoming apparent that the United States would have the Soviet
Union as an nonwar opponent for an indeterminate time. But little
was done in the ballistic missile area because the United States had
captured all the V-2s and the German rocket scientists, hadn't it?
And weren't the Russians ignorant and inept peasants who had to
steal all their technology from elsewhere if they couldn't buy it from
willing U.S. companies or get it from American war surplus once we
were through with it?

The launch of the Convair MX-774 (RTV-A-2) from White Sands Proving
Ground's Army Launch Area on July 13, 1949.

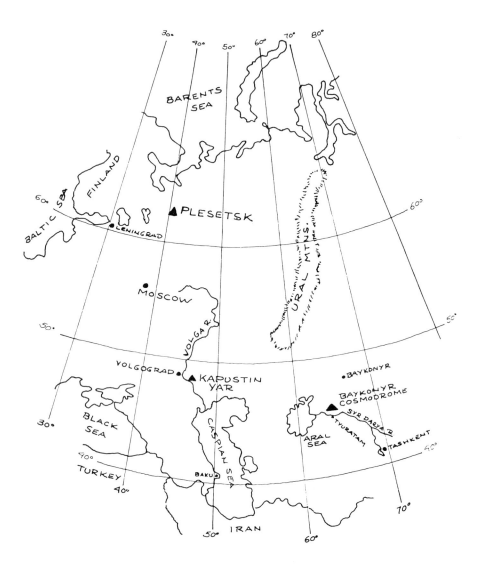

The general location of the three Soviet rocket flight test facilities.

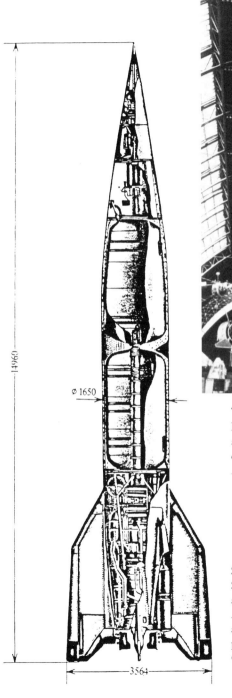

The research rocket version of the Soviet R-1 with payload compartments on the side and a research nose. The missile is displayed in the Kosmos Pavilion in Moscow.

Soviet cutaway drawing of the R-1, the Soviet-built German A.4 rocket, as it appears in the book *Sergei Pavlovich Korolev*, by Yuriy Vasilyevich Biryukov and Nikolai Aleksandrovich Vasraravov, published in Russian in Moscow, October 7, 1978.

The first photo of the first Soviet ballistic missiles revealed to the world during the parade in Red Square, Moscow, on November 7, 1957. These are R-3s (NATO SS-3 Shysters).

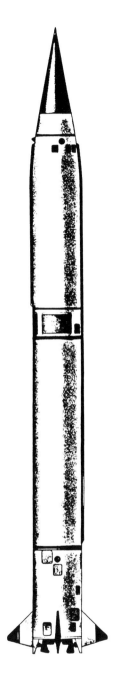

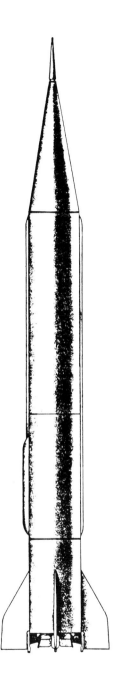

Soviet drawing of the R-3 (NATO SS-3 Shyster) that appears in *Sergei Pavlovich Korolev*.

Soviet drawing of the SS-2C Scud tactical ballistic missile that also was used for upper air research. This is taken from *Sergei Pavlovich Korolev*.

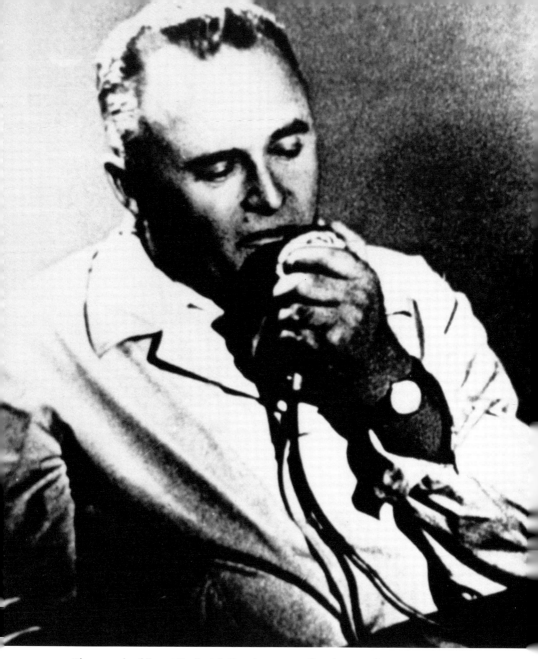

Photograph of Sergei Pavlovich Korolev reportedly taken on the evening of October 4, 1957, in the blockhouse at the Baykonyr Cosmodrome as he gave the clearance to launch the R-7 ICBM carrying the world's first artificial earth satellite, Sputnik 1.

This aerial photograph of the Soviet R-7 launch pad at the Baykonyr Cosmodrome, Tyuratam, was taken in the summer of 1957 by an American U-2 spy plane.

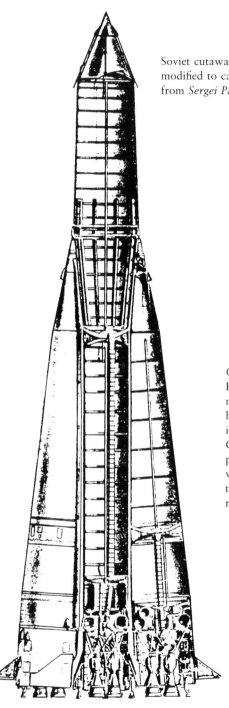

Soviet cutaway drawing of the R-7 ICBM with its nose modified to carry the Sputnik 1 satellite. This is taken from *Sergei Pavlovich Korolev*.

*Opposite:* This photograph of the Soviet R-7 ICBM with the elongated conical nose cone is now strongly suspected to be one of the five R-7 ICBMs launched in mid-1957 from the Baykonyr Cosmodrome. The conical nose was a plywood-sheathed ablative reentry body, which contained the large Soviet thermonuclear warhead of the time, rated at about 15 megatons yield.

View of the thirty-two rocket chambers of the Soviet R-7 ICBM revealed to the world for the first time at the Paris Le Bourget Air Show in 1967. The version shown in Paris was fitted out as the R-7 that had launched Maj. Yuri Gagarin on his single orbital flight in Vostok 1 on April 12, 1961.

The four-chamber Soviet RD-107 rocket engine designed by Valentin Glushko and used to power one of the four strap-on boosters of the R-7. A similar engine with four verniers instead of two, the RD-108, powered the central core of the vehicle. A single turbopump fed propellants to all four chambers and verniers.

Single frame from a Soviet 35-millimeter motion picture purporting to show the launch of Sputnik 1 from Tyuratam's Baykonyr Cosmodrome. However, a study of the photo indicates that this had to be the launch of the R-7 that placed Sputnik 2 in orbit on November 3, 1957, carrying the dog Laika. The Soviet Soyuz vehicle for the joint Soviet-American flight was launched from this same facility in 1975, but the Soviet engineers had added an ejector duct by 1960 to prevent the ignition flames from coming back up around the R-7 as shown here.

The Soviet SS-10 Scrag ICBM being paraded in Red Square on November 7, 1968. There is no evidence that this missile ever reached operational ICBM status and may, in fact, be one of the Soviets' "dimensional simulations"—i.e., dummies.

Dr. Theodore von Kármán, the Hungarian-born fluid dynamics scientist who contributed to rocket and jet propulsion, was one of the founders of the Cal Tech Jet Propulsion Laboratory (JPL), a founder of the Aerojet Corporation, and one of the early advocates for an American ICBM program.

Dr. Charles Stark Draper, founder of the Draper Laboratories at MIT and the developer of the first all-inertial guidance system as well as most of the gyroscopic flight instruments used in today's aircraft for instrument flight.

The elements of a simple all-inertial gyro-stabilized guidance system pioneered by Dr. Charles Stark Draper for aircraft, then for ICBMs. Today inertial navigation systems are widely used in transoceanic jetliners.

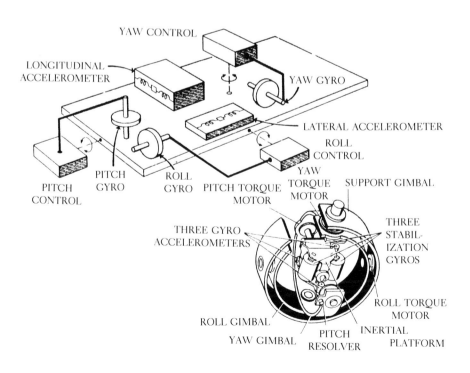

Sketch from an early Convair Atlas
report showing the elements of
"half-staging," or dropping four of
the five rocket thrust chambers of
one of the early Atlas ICBM designs
in order to reduce weight and extend
range.

The launch of Thor IRBM Missile
Number 120 from Cape Canaveral
on February 28, 1958, carrying the
GE Mark 2 heat sink reentry nose
cone and reentry body.

The Rocketdyne MB-1 rocket engine used to propel the first Douglas Thor IRBMs. This engine generated 135,000 pounds of thrust. Compare its simplicity with the V-2 engine of less than half the thrust shown earlier. Photo taken by the author at the First World Congress of Flight, Las Vegas, Nevada, April 1959.

The launch of one of the production Jupiter IRBMs from Cape Canaveral. Designed by the Army Ballistic Missile Agency at Huntsville, Alabama, the Jupiter was built by Chrysler Corporation and became an Air Force program alongside Thor. Jupiters were deployed in Turkey until the early 1960s.

The Army's Hermes Project limped along, hampered by constant redirection of efforts and no clear short-range goal but with influential supporters in the Army Ordnance Corps. However, the talents of the "Paper Clip" Germans from Peenemünde under von Braun were largely wasted by putting them to work designing ramjet-powered cruise missiles. The Jet Propulsion Laboratory was working on the Corporal tactical ballistic missile with a range of 90 miles but hadn't flown even a prototype by 1950.

The U.S. Navy was primarily interested in developing an effective missile defense against kamikaze attacks but managed to find a little money to put into the development of the Martin Viking high-altitude research rocket, a poor American replacement for the V-2 which, by 1950, had resulted in the launch of only 4 Viking rockets.

The U.S. Army Air Force became the U.S. Air Force (USAF) as a result of the National Security Act of 1947, which merged the two cabinet organizations, the War Department and the Navy Department, into a single Department of Defense and created a separate Department of the Air Force. The USAF had an interest in ballistic missiles just as the other two services did. However, the USAF was and is a group of pilots. Sometimes the predominant group was the fighter pilots, but the major group in charge of the new USAF consisted of bomber pilots.

One of the most farsighted of all World War II Allied military leaders was General of the Armies Henry H. "Hap" Arnold, who saw the forthcoming need for the ICBM at the war's end. Even though Arnold got a very fine, far-looking report from Dr. Theodore von Kármán on the technology needs of future Air Force machines and vehicles, he wasn't supported by the rest of the suddenly important civilian scientists and academicians who seemed content with "logical" and "evolutionary" development of existing weapons. Few of these scientists believed that a need for an ICBM would develop within the foreseeable future. Most of them reflected the opinions of Dr. Vannevar Bush whose public statement about the long-range ballistic missile was quoted earlier.

The Air Force intended to move ahead in ballistic missiles and had let a contract to North American Aviation for the development of the NATIV and the propulsion systems for the Navaho I, as noted earlier. But to introduce some redundancy into the system in case of the failure of the NATIV and Navaho technologies, the Air Force initiated a very hush-hush study and development plan for a long-range ballistic missile—an "evolutionary extension" of the strategic bomber. On April 22, 1946, a contract for $1,400,000 was given to Consolidated-Vultee (now General Dynamics), the builders of the B-24 Liberator, the B-32 Dominator, and the in-development B-36. The company was to study the development of an ICBM under the MX-774 contract.

Karel J. "Charlie" Bossart, a Belgian-born aeronautical engineer and chief of the structures group at the Downey, California, plant was the leader of this effort. He was in many ways an American von Braun in his leadership abilities, technical expertise, and missionary zeal. His associates on the MX-774 were assistant project engineer Lloyd W. Standley; design engineer Charles S. Ames; aerodynamicists William H. Patterson, Frank J. Dore, and Willis B. Mitchell; thermodynamicist Dr. Howard F. Dunholter; and electronics engineer James W. Crooks. This was the first genuine American long-range ballistic missile team that wasn't under the tutelage of the German Peenemünde group. They were basically aircraft people, not rocket enthusiasts. They became rocket enthusiasts because of what they had to do and what they accomplished. Their contribution to American rocket technology has been little noted, and it's time their names were linked with aerospace history leading to the ICBM.

In June 1946 the Air Force Materiel Command at Wright Air Force Base upped the MX-774 budget to $1,893,000. Those were the days when a million dollars bought a *lot* of engineering effort.

The initial statement of work from the Air Force to Bossart and his team told them to conduct study and research leading toward the design of a missile capable of carrying a 5,000-pound warhead to a range of 5,000 miles and impacting within 5,000 feet of the intended target. They were to determine whether a glide vehicle—sort of a hypersonic cruise missile like the A.9/A.10—a subsonic cruise missile, or a true ballistic missile would be most suitable for the task.

Early in the study, a subsonic cruise missile version was canceled by the Air Force.

The next casualty was a vertical takeoff rocket vehicle with a gliding supersonic warhead.

The pure rocket ballistic missile design looked like the best bet. But given the structural and materials technologies of the time, Bossart's team recommended the use of liquid oxygen and liquid hydrogen as the only propellants having the energy to propel that heavy payload to the required range.

By June 1946, with the additional funds from the Air Force, Bossart and his group began detailed design work on the first purely American ballistic missile. Their first step was to build a series of three experimental test vehicles.

Except when they are relying on a great deal of research and development data, engineers prefer to start from a known point and proceed. In the case of long-range supersonic ballistic missiles, only one example existed as a point of departure: the V-2. But Charlie Bossart didn't want to build an American V-2. He and his team wanted to incorporate some badly needed improvements. In the first place, Bossart's team wanted to save weight by using integral tanks—a design where the walls of the tanks were also the skin of the missile just as an airplane's wing tanks are essentially sealed-off portions of the inside of the wing structure. Bossart also wanted to use a rocket motor that would swivel on a gimbal to provide directional control rather than using the carbon vanes of the V-2. He also wanted to use a separable nose warhead section to improve postboost flight characteristics and lower the dispersion.

The resulting missile, called the RTV-A-2, or "Hi-Roc" (although it was to be known to history by its contract number, MX-774), used the basic configuration of the V-2 rocket. This shape had been extensively tested in the German wind tunnels, and engineers knew it would be stable from subsonic to high supersonic speeds. Thus, the RTV-A-2 was a baby V-2 in appearance. It was a little over 30 feet long with a body diameter of 30 inches and four tail fins spanning 82.24 inches shaped like those of the V-2.

An existing American rocket motor was used to power the RTV-

A-2. It was the Reaction Motors, Inc. (now a moribund division of Morton-Thiokol) RMI 1500-C-4. Another version of this four-chamber rocket motor was to propel the famous Bell X-1 experimental aircraft that Chuck Yeager first flew through Mach 1. It had originally been developed by RMI to power an improved, large version of the U.S. Navy's Lark antiaircraft missile. The RTV-A-2 version used a single turbopump driven by steam from the decomposition of hydrogen peroxide to deliver liquid oxygen and alcohol to the four chambers and produce a thrust of 8,000 pounds.

Consolidated-Vultee had started to cut metal and "bend tin" on the RTV-A-2 vehicles when the budget ax fell. The MX-774 contract was canceled on July 1, 1947, by the Air Force as a result of a budget crunch.

The design and assembly work was far along, and Bossart and his team were planning to launch within a year. Even though the Air Force had withdrawn its support, Consolidated-Vultee decided to complete the three missiles and flight-test them with company funds.

The first RTV-A-2 was launched from the Army launch area at White Sands Proving Ground in New Mexico on July 13, 1948. It suffered a premature engine cutoff at 12.6 seconds, rose to an altitude of only 6,200 feet, and impacted at 48.2 seconds, 415 feet from the launch pad.

The next RTV-A-2 performed better when launched at White Sands on September 27, 1948. Although its radio command guidance system worked well, it exhibited 10-degree oscillations in roll which reduced its performance because of increased drag. The engine cut off at 48 seconds at an altitude of 54,000 feet when the vehicle had attained a velocity of 2,350 feet per second. It reached an altitude of 24 miles and didn't impact; it exploded on the downward leg of its flight at an altitude of 20,000 feet and at a supersonic speed of 1,900 feet per second.

Round number three turned in the best flight of all. When launched from White Sands on December 2, 1948, its RMI engine burned for 51.6 seconds, boosting the RTV-A-2 to a velocity of 2,653 feet per second. The missile then coasted up to an altitude of

30 miles. The nose separation explosives fouled the recovery parachute, which opened at an altitude of 121,000 feet on the way down, at a speed of 1,500 feet per second. The parachute therefore tore loose from the vehicle, allowing it to impact on the desert floor.

Then what? No Air Force money was available to continue the work. The Bossart group had achieved a number of technical firsts in ballistic missiles well in advance of the Army with its Paper Clip rocketeers from Peenemünde. Consolidated-Vultee had about as much, if not more, experience in ballistic missiles as GE with its Hermes Project or the Glenn L. Martin Company with its Navy Viking rocket. Hermes, Viking, and Hi-Roc had all used and proved the swiveling or gimbaled rocket motor concept, the integral or monococque propellant tank concept, and the separable payload/warhead section. The Army was still shooting V-2s. The Navy was launching about one Viking per year. At this point, the Air Force was no longer launching ballistic missiles.

Consolidated-Vultee had become General Dynamics (GD) and continued to support its ballistic missile development team with company funds from 1948 through 1951. Bossart and the GD team, building on their experience, continued to study and design ballistic missiles on paper. Their ideas began to take interesting new twists and turns, and some new concepts came forth from this company R&D effort.

In November 1948 GD proposed two designs of a 1,000-mile ballistic missile to the Air Force. For the first time, a "stage-and-a-half," or 1½-stage, design was put forth.

The first design used a cluster of five rocket motors—the RMI 20,000-pound LOX-alcohol motor developed for the Navy's Viking rocket—to produce 100,000 pounds of thrust at lift-off. Partway into the flight when a large amount of the propellant was burned out of the 63-foot missile's tanks, the four outer rocket motors would be shut down and jettisoned with the fin-carrying tail section to get rid of their weight, since the fins were no longer needed in the thin upper air and the additional motor thrust was no longer needed with the lighter missile.

The second version was a three-engine missile 49.5 feet long with

60,000 pounds of thrust and a lighter payload. Three RMI Viking motors were to be used. The outer two motors and the tail housing with its stabilizing fins were to be jettisoned when the high thrust needed at takeoff was no longer required to accelerate the missile later in flight.

A workable new concept of a unique long-range ballistic missile was taking shape here. Nothing had been built by GD except the "baby V-2" (the RTV-A-2), but the ideas that came about as a result of this were being refined. A unique American-generated ballistic missile was under gestation.

The 1½-stage concept, a form of "parallel staging" as distinct from "series staging," was new and important for several reasons. One of them was the fact that starting a liquid-propellant rocket motor was and still is a black art. Everyone who becomes involved in liquid-propellant rockets has his share of "hard starts" resulting in "catastrophic disassembly" of the vehicle. Parallel staging permitted all the rocket motors to be started on the ground before launch— an important factor in the early days, when little was known about "air starts" for series-staged rockets. At the time, the only multi-staged rocket flown was the Hermes Project combination of the V-2 and the WAC-Corporal, the Bumper.

Starting all motors on the ground was a safer thing to do at the time. Better to have the missile blow on the pad with blockhouses and such all around than burst in the air and create a scrap-metal rainstorm.

Bossart and the GD group weren't the only ones who figured out that parallel staging might be the way to go.

# The Korean War Stimulus

On June 25, 1950, ten divisions of the North Korean army invaded South Korea. The North Koreans were armed with Soviet-made rifles, tanks, aircraft, and other military equipment.

The cold war had suddenly become hot. The intentions of the Soviet-led communist bloc of nations were no longer a matter of debate to most Americans. Still weary of fighting and slowly recovering from World War II, the United States supported the United Nations' police action to defend South Korea and drive the North Koreans back above the 38th parallel, the border between the two Koreas which had been drawn arbitrarily under an occupation agreement between the United States and the Soviet Union in September 1945. The USSR had proceeded to set up a communist government in North Korea and in January 1948 had refused to allow the UN commission into North Korea to supervise free elections that were to be held by UN mandate throughout Korea.

America sighed with frustration, sent the military reservists into Korea, called up other World War II servicemen, reinstated conscription, and came to the reluctant conclusion that the country was going to have to build up and maintain a strong military posture vis-à-vis the Soviet Union that would last for an unknown number of years or decades.

The funding and the political will were suddenly present to permit ballistic missile R&D to accelerate.

The U.S. Army tried to make the best of it, particularly in the area of guided missiles and ballistic missiles. The preceding five years had been full of political infighting among the three armed services, especially in the area of missiles. The talk after World War II was about future conflicts that would be push-button wars. Like the German Wehrmacht prior to and during World War II, the U.S. Army believed that long-range ballistic missiles were a logical extension of artillery. The U.S. Air Force contended that guided missiles, even ballistic missiles, were unmanned aircraft and should come under its jurisdiction. The U.S. Navy pointed to the 16-inch guns on its battleships and to the naval aircraft on its carriers and combined the arguments of the other two services. The first delineation of this conundrum was made by the War Department in September 1944 by assigning all wingless ballistic missiles to the Army Ordnance Corps and all winged pilotless aircraft missile types to the Army Air Forces.

In 1946 the Air Force claimed that Army Ordnance was infringing on its turf because the army missiles under development— primarily antiaircraft missiles, or what are now called SAMs (Surface to Air Missiles)—were supersonic pilotless aircrafts. So in 1946 the War Department gave the Army Air Forces the responsibility for all guided missile development. When the Department of Defense was formed and the USAF gained separate service status, it gave back those missiles which met the needs of the Army Ground Forces.

But the question of jurisdiction still lingered on like an unwanted weekend houseguest. Decision after decision was made within the Defense Department on the basis of the reports and studies of numerous boards and commissions. Finally, in 1948, the Chairman of the Joint Chiefs of Staff, Gen. Omar N. Bradley, set forth the policy that "guided missiles would be employed by each armed service in a manner and to the extent required to accomplish its assigned missions." If the Joint Chiefs hadn't dodged the issue at that time and had established some dividing line based on the range of missiles, the Army might have been limited to developing and using ballistic missiles with a maximum range of 100 miles because it was generally considered, although not officially voiced, that missiles of greater range were an extension of aircraft rather than an extension of artillery.

Thus, the chaos of American ballistic missile development continued to the detriment of the country. In the Soviet Union no such dichotomy was allowed to develop; all Soviet ballistic missiles remained under the control of the Soviet army until later in the 1950s. With the creative energies of the American military people devoted to such infighting, American technologists couldn't move steadily ahead without having their ballistic missile projects redirected or canceled on the basis of the latest new policy statement.

This came to a halt in 1950. Secretary of Defense Louis A. Johnson suddenly had the Korean War in his lap. The early months of fighting clearly showed that the North Koreans were armed with Soviet weapons, displaying the fact that the USSR had developed a whole new arsenal of weapons far more modern and effective than the World War II vintage weapons of the American forces. The need for renewed military R&D became evident. Johnson saw what was happening with missiles. He asked K. T. Keller to take over as Director of Guided Missiles, acting on the recommendations of the Johnson-established Special Interdepartmental Guided Missiles Board.

Keller put the JPL Corporal project on a crash program track as an interim battlefield ballistic missile system. He sorted out the SAM mess but allowed the Navy to keep its shipboard SAMs because of the special environment of shipboard use. He canceled most of the Hermes Project except the Hermes A-3, which was to run out its development as an experimental ballistic missile in order to harvest the data and expertise of the program.

He reassigned the responsibility for the Hermes C-1 long-range ballistic missile to the new U.S. Army Ordnance Missile Command established by General Toftoy at the Redstone Arsenal in Huntsville, Alabama. In the fall of 1950 Huntsville got some new residents from Fort Bliss, Texas: the Peenemünde Paper Clip rocket scientists under von Braun.

The German rocket scientists were initially greeted with suspicion and distrust because of their Old World ways and because the "redneck Southerners" didn't like the idea that the Germans whom they'd just fought in World War II were moving in as neighbors. But most of the Germans got their library cards before applying for their driver's licenses. In fact, the Huntsville library grew to be one of the best in the South. The integration of the Germans into the life of Huntsville turned out to be a major social experiment—successful in the long run. A sleepy little southern city of 85,000 people in 1950, Huntsville gained a symphony orchestra, an astronomical observatory, a major space and missile museum, and a whole new flavor over the following decades. The Germans joined local churches and civic groups, introduced German pastries into church bazaars, and raised the level of science education in the local schools. On April 15, 1955, forty German scientists with their wives and children gathered for an impressive ceremony in the Huntsville High School auditorium, where they became naturalized citizens of the United States.

The Hermes C-1 missile that had been assigned to Redstone Arsenal was originally intended to be a rocket-boosted glide missile. The German rocket team, working with their American counterparts, quickly converted this into a ballistic missile with a 500-mile range. This was first called Ursa, then the Major, and finally was given the name of the arsenal where it was designed and developed: Redstone.

Von Braun and his rocket team wanted the Redstone to be available quickly, so they settled on a ballistic missile that was basically a larger, improved A.4 quite comparable to what Korolev and Glusko had already done in the USSR in developing the Shyster ballistic missile out of the V-2 and R-2 Pobeda—although we didn't know it at the time.

The Redstone was a major step forward in American ballistic missilry. It was 70 inches in diameter and 69 feet long. It weighed 61,000 pounds at lift-off. Because of changes in Army requirements and Pentagon policies limiting Army ballistic missiles to ranges of 250 miles or less, in its final form it could throw a 5,000-pound nuclear payload to a range of 200 miles. It used the 75,000-pound-thrust liquid-propellant rocket engine developed by the Rocketdyne Division of North American Aviation from the A.4 engine for the canceled USAF Navaho I missile. It was guided by a simple, reliable, and accurate gyro-stabilized and accelerometer-commanded inertial guidance system and was steered by both carbon vanes in the rocket exhaust jet and air vanes on the four fins, just like the A.4. It was built of aluminum with integral propellant tankage. It had a separable warhead nose. It was a true American version of the German V-2.

On August 20, 1955, the first Redstone was launched at the USAF Long Range Proving Ground at Cape Canaveral, Florida. It had guidance problems and went only 8,000 yards downrange. However, because the state of the art of radio telemetry had progressed since the days of Peenemünde, the data transmitted back to the ground from the errant missile allowed the problems to be identified and corrected. The Redstone R&D flight test program ended in 1958. During that time 37 test vehicles were launched. Twenty of these were manufactured by Chrysler Corporation, the prime contractor for the production of the Redstone.

The Redstone engine underwent development and acceptance test firings on the "white elephant" 500,000-pound static test stand at White Sands that we modifed for it. That is where many of us postwar "third-generation" rocket men got to know von Braun and the German rocketeers. It is also where many American rocket engineers were introduced to big, high-thrust, long-burning rocket motors. These tests were under the supervision of Charles M. Mansur and Lowell N. Randall, two members of Dr. Robert H. Goddard's crew from the prewar days at Roswell, New Mexico. If it did nothing else, the Redstone merged the German and American rocket people as the Hermes Project had never done. The Redstone had American and Peenemünde rocketeers working side by side rather than the latter teaching the former and then leaving the scene. (I had the dubious distinction, as the controls engineer on the stand, of drenching von Braun and several others one day when I accidentally tripped the emergency water deluge system while conducting pretest checkouts.)

And the Redstone engine under static test at White Sands turned many people into true believers. To watch and hear and feel 75,000 pounds of thrust for 120 seconds was awesome.

We never blew a Redstone engine at White Sands. We did develop a number of new starting techniques in a series of tests during which it was quite possible to have had a hard start.

The Army wasn't alone in getting its ballistic missile projects jump-started again by the Korean War.

In January 1951 the USAF Air Research and Development Command had the funds to crank up the Air Force ballistic missile program again.

North American Aviation was to redirect the Navaho Project to achieve a very large ramjet-propelled Mach-3 cruise missile with a range of 5,000 miles. Navaho II (Navaho G-26-G-38) was to be boosted vertically into the air and to the supersonic speeds required for ramjet operation by a rocket booster developing 240,000 pounds of thrust. This was the largest rocket booster yet projected in the United States. North American Aviation's Rocketdyne Division began the development of a totally new rocket engine of higher thrust and lighter weight. By 1953, the choice had narrowed to a cluster of two rocket combustion chambers side by side using a single turbopump driven by the two propellants—LOX and alcohol— burned in a separate gas generator to run the turbine. Instead of using heavy double-walled construction, each 120,000-pound rocket chamber was made up of a bundle of thin-walled tubes through which alcohol was circulated. This tubular-wall thrust chamber design subsequently was adopted by all large liquid-propellant engines and is still used today. The Navaho II engine was undergoing static tests by 1952. The first Navaho booster and its piggyback winged ramjet-powered supersonic missile was launched for the first time from Cape Canaveral in September 1953. The United States finally had a rocket engine with more than 50 tons thrust.

In January 1951 the USAF Air Research & Development Command also restarted the Consolidated-Vultee long-range ballistic missile project with a new contract, MX-1593. It was a great day for

Charlie Bossart and his team who had worked on MX-774, and for General Dynamics, which had supported their low-intensity studies with company funds. The objective: Deliver a strategic (i.e., nuclear) warhead to a range of 5,500 miles.

Thus was born a project that was quickly to get the code name Atlas.

# The Peenemunde
# Pfiel and the R-7

Rocket engineers in the Soviet Union were also pressing hard to develop a long-range ballistic missile, especially Stalin's transatlantic rocket. By 1950 Korolev and Glushko had the R-1 (8-Zh-38) and the improved R-2 Pobeda in production. Both missiles were being introduced into the first two rocket divisions of the Soviet army. These rocket troops also provided Korolev with additional technicians for launching the R-1 and R-2 research versions as high-altitude sounding rockets from Kapustin Yar. The arrangement allowed the rocket troops to gain operational experience with the R-1 and R-2, the engineers to learn the nasty little problems and bugs that had to be eliminated, and the scientists to utilize the payload space for both biological experiments leading to manned space flight and for measuring the characteristics of the upper atmosphere through which long-range ballistic missiles would have to pass in their trajectories.

One should not get the impression that the Soviet effort was monolithic, dogged, directed toward a single goal, and totally integrated. It was not. We know little about the internecine power struggles within the USSR because the Soviets do not air their dirty laundry in public; they do not have to do so in a closed society such as theirs.

We do know that Sergei P. Korolev was still a political prisoner during the late Stalin years even though he was basically in charge of the R-1 and R-2 programs. One of Korolev's close associates was Mikhail Yangel. Valentin P. Glushko, also a political prisoner because of his association with Stalin's enemies purged in 1937, was the primary Soviet rocket engine designer and had established a major rocket motor design and test center at Zagorsk about 58 kilometers northeast of Moscow. Aleksei M. Isayev was chief of another rocket engine design bureau.

Not all the Soviet rocket designers got along well. We know that Korolev's greatest adversary was a competing engineer named Chelomei or Chelomey, who had managed to remain trusted by Stalin, had not been sent to the GULags, ran a competing design bureau, and did not get along well with Korolev.

Gen. Grigori A. Tokaty, who in 1947 was a professor at the Zhukovsi Aeronautical Institute in Moscow, had led a group in the design of a three-staged liquid-propellant long-range rocket called TT-1. Apparently internal politics within the growing Soviet missile establishment stopped the TT-1 in the design phases. As late as 1961, Tokaty, who had by then defected to the west, was still strangely reticent about discussing both the technical and political details. However, he did write in an article published in the March 1963 issue of *Spaceflight* magazine by the British Interplanetary Society:

> Had the group been allowed to continue its work without interference from the outside, the USSR might well have succeeded in putting a Sputnik round the earth sometime in 1950–1952. But for reasons that had nothing to do with the project itself or with our professional qualifications, we found ourselves in a difficult position. Towards the end of 1947, our work was paralyzed. Some of us were compelled to seek refuge in the West, and others were arrested; the rest had to wait.

Helmut Grottrüp and the other German engineers and technicians were doing some useful work at Nii-88 and Gorodomlya. They had been asked to work on the R-10 as well as a multistaged rocket, the R-12, which would carry a one-ton warhead to a range of 2,500 kilometers. However, on April 4, 1949, Ustinov visited Gorodomlya and proposed that the Germans begin the design of the R-12 that would carry a 3-ton warhead at a range of 3,000 kilometers. The result was a cone-shaped missile about 24 meters long with a base diameter of 3 meters. With an empty weight of 7,000 kilograms and using liquid oxygen and alcohol as propellants, its gross weight was 71,000 kilograms. It used a gimballed rocket motor with a thrust of 100 tons. Control was totally by the gimballed engine, and no fins were used on the vehicle. The structure was monococque, or self-supporting, with integral tanks made from stainless steel. The 3-ton warhead used laminated plywood as an ablative material to keep the payload cool during reentry.

I saw drawings of the R-12 in the classified section of the technical library at White Sands Proving Ground in 1954. It was classified SECRET at the time. It was an elegant design.

I didn't think too much about it until October 1976, when another German rocket engineer, Rolf Engel, visited my home in Phoenix, Arizona. Engel saw my model of the Soviet R-7, which was fitted out as the Vostok manned space launch vehicle. He smiled and pointed to one of the four conical boosters of the vehicle.

"Do you know where that came from? And why Korolev used that configuration?" Engel asked me rhetorically. "That is a vehicle called the _Peenemünde Pfiel_, or 'Arrow.' It was one of the design studies that von Braun and his team came up with in late 1944 or early 1945." Engel then sat down and made a rough dimensioned sketch of the Pfiel.

"It was also called the R-12 by the Soviets," I told him. I'm still searching for that scrap of paper, which I _know_ I saved. The dimensions sketched by Rolf Engel were within 10 percent of the booster dimensions on the R-7.

Korolev found a use for the R-12 in 1954.

The R-15, an unmanned rocket-boosted supersonic glider vehicle, was the last project the Soviets asked the Germans at Nii-88 and Gorodomlya to work on. Gröttrup was the last of the Germans to be repatriated to East Germany on June 21, 1952. The Soviets had wrung them dry. No justification existed to keep them in the USSR because young Soviet designers and engineers had learned everything they could from them.

Joseph Stalin died on March 5, 1953, to be succeeded by Georgi

M. Malenkov as premier and Nikita S. Khrushchev as First Secretary of the Communist party. Very quickly, Korolev, Glushko, and other scientists and engineers who had been held as working political prisoners were rehabilitated. We know Korolev was offered membership in the Communist party. Regardless of his feelings at the time, he accepted because he probably realized that it would increase his political influence and allow him to get on with his work on large rockets. Korolev had known the Soviet "Father of Cosmonautics," Konstantin Edouardovich Tsiolkovski, and, like von Braun, knew that the only way to get big rockets built for space exploration was to allow the military to pay for them as long-range ballistic missiles.

Khrushchev met Korolev, Glushko, and the other Soviet rocket engineers only after he came to power. Stalin had kept rocket development secret from nearly everyone, and the new "collective leadership" was in awe when they found out about it.

Khrushchev wrote in his memoirs:

> Korolev came to the Politburo meeting to report on his work. I don't want to exaggerate, but I'd say we gawked at what he showed us as if we were sheep seeing a new gate for the first time. When he showed us one of his rockets, we thought it looked like nothing but a huge cigar-shaped tube, and we didn't believe it would fly. Korolev took us on a tour of the launching pad [probably Kapustin Yar] and tried to explain to us how a rocket worked. We were like peasants in a marketplace. We walked around the rocket, touching it, tapping it to see if it was sturdy enough—we did everything but lick it to see how it tasted. . . . We had absolute confidence in Comrade Korolev. When he expounded his ideas, you could see passion burning in his eyes, and his reports were always models of clarity. He had unlimited energy and determination, and he was a brilliant organizer.

As the new Soviet leadership slowly took over and began the initial de-Stalinization process, one area that did not receive redirection was the Soviet long-range ballistic missile program. What was apparent to Stalin and the Politburo in 1946 was still a fact of life in 1953:

The Soviet Union's major adversary was the United States.

With the detonation of the first Soviet "dry" thermonuclear weapon on August 12, 1953, and the apparent progress of Soviet rocket engineers, the State Commission for the Study of the Problems of Long-range Rockets, the Soviet Academy of Science, or a combination of several groups reported to Malenkov and Khrushchev—or perhaps Khrushchev alone, because he was certainly hard at work almost at once consolidating all power in his own hands—that the elements were in hand at last to finalize the design of the first transatlantic rocket only six years after Stalin and the Politburo had established the goal.

Korolev's design bureau was given approval for the construction and testing of the R-7 design.

We now know what the R-7 looks like. The Soviets did what the United States later did: use its ICBMs as space launch vehicles. But it took until 1967 for the Soviets to display the R-7 in its Vostok manned launch vehicle configuration at the Paris Air Show at Le Bourget. It seemed strange and alien to western rocketeers at the time. However, as the pieces were put together over the next two decades, Korolev's R-7 turned out to be an elegant engineering approach to a difficult problem. He used what he had available.

Liquid oxygen and hydrocarbon (like gasoline or jet fuel) turned out to be the favorite Soviet propellant combination, just as it had in the United States. Gasoline or jet fuel is not only more widely available in quantities of hundreds of thousands of liters or gallons, but its characteristics can be altered in the petrochemical refinement process to produce the desired viscosity, volatility, flash point, ignition temperature, and heat content. The R-7 was designed for those propellants.

It had to be large enough to throw the 3-ton Soviet dry thermonuclear warhead to a range of at least 8,000 kilometers in order to reach the continental United States.

The easiest and quickest way to deploy it would be on railway sidings along the broad-gauge Soviet railway system. Good roads don't exist in most of the USSR, but it has an extensive railway system over which most freight and people move. The R-7 could be large because the Soviet loading gauge—the required clearances through tunnels, over bridges, and past railside structures—is much more generous than that in Europe. (The Soviets had deliberately built their railways "nonstandard" so that invaders such as the Germans would not be able to run their own locomotives or railway wagons on Soviet railways.)

So the R-7 could be designed for horizontal assembly and checkout just as the Soviets had learned how to work with rockets such as the V-2.

To loft the Soviet thermonuclear warhead, a big rocket would be required, one that had very high total impulse—total thrust multiplied by the rocket burning time. Korolev's R-7 was a parallel-stage vehicle—a central core vehicle surrounded by four strap-on vehicles. The huge rocket would thus take off with all rocket engines burning, and the four boosters would exhaust their propellants and fall away about two minutes into the flight. The lighter central core would then continue to thrust the payload to the proper velocity.

Glushko had developed a rocket engine producing 100 tons of thrust (220,000 pounds). He had done this by taking a well-developed improved version of the German 25-ton V-2 motor that had been used in the R-2 and R-3, clustering four of the chambers, and supplying propellant to all four chambers with a single turbopump driven by a gas generator that used LOX and gasoline. The engineering logic of doing this is straightforward: It is easier to design and build a good, small liquid-propellant rocket chamber and a very big turbopump to supply a cluster of these small chambers. Big rocket motors are prone to combustion instability. Glushko also had improved the efficiency of the V-2 motor by increasing the combustion or chamber pressure from 20 atmospheres to 60 atmospheres.

To provide steering, Glushko and Korolev depended on small swiveling vernier rocket motors mounted on both the boosters and the core. Two verniers were mounted with the engine package in each booster; this was the RD-107 rocket motor. Four verniers were used with the core rocket engine, the RD-108.

Why did Korolev use conically tapered boosters? Structurally, they could be made lighter than boosters that were cylindrical with conical noses. And Korolev already had the design and perhaps even the jigs and tooling of the R-12 clone of the Peenemünde Pfiel, assuming that the R-12 was built at all (which I suspect it was).

The result was a monster. Standing at least 30 meters tall with its conical nose cone and with its base at least 10 meters across over the boosters, it weighed about 325 tons at takeoff. In its parallel-stage configuration, with four main chambers in the core and four chambers in each of four boosters, plus four verniers in the core and two in each booster, Korolev had to achieve a cluster ignition of 32 rocket chambers at once! Von Braun had proposed the clustered ignition of 51 250-ton motors in his 1952 orbital spaceship in *Collier's* magazine, and most American rocketeers at the time scoffed at the idea; the best Rocketdyne had done at that time was three 60-ton motors at once in a cluster for Navaho III. Korolev solved the ignition problem very neatly: The propellant lines between the tanks and the injector heads were loaded with a hypergolic or spontaneously igniting "starting slug"—i.e., the LOX was replaced with red fuming nitric acid to which a little potassium permanganate had been added.

The R-7 *Semyorka* ("Old Number Seven" in Russian) couldn't be launched from Kapustin Yar. It was super-secret, and the launches would certainly be seen by the Volga River traffic. So Korolev had a new long-range testing facility built near Tyuratam just north of the Oxus River on the steppes of Kazakhstan east of the Aral Sea. Korolev had a lot of support because the party secretary of Kazakhstan at that time was a rocket enthusiast by the name of Leonid Brezhnev.

American intelligence organizations were aware that the R-7 was being developed. They actually knew a lot about it. By 1955, negotiations were well under way to establish a long-range radar tracking station in Turkey to watch Soviet missile development. But that wasn't good enough. As we shall see, the Soviet ICBM was an ongoing program by 1955, and it was vital to know what the status of Soviet ICBM testing was. So the CIA contracted with Lockheed Aircraft Company for the design and construction of a very high altitude, very long range spy plane. To give it an innocuous cover, it was assigned a designation as a utility plane: U-2. Almost before the concrete was dry for the R-7's launch complex at Tyuratam, U-2s were overflying the site far above the maximum altitude of any Soviet interceptor or SAM.

In April 1957 the first R-7 was on the pad at the raw new base at Tyuratam.

The first launch attempt was a failure. The R-7 blew up shortly after ignition.

Five more R-7s went on the pad and suffered failures of one sort or another in the months of May, June, and July of 1957.

But on August 3, 1957, the first successful R-7 got off the pad, followed a few weeks later by a second successful flight that shot the huge, heavy conical nose cone with its laminated plywood ablative heat shield for the full 8,000 kilometers into the Pacific Ocean. It landed not far from the GULags of the Kolyma gold mines on the Kamchatka peninsula where Korolev had been worked almost to death during the winter of 1938–1939.

# *Teapot*

An enormous amount of information about the Soviet ICBM program was available to the intelligence community of the United States during the period 1950–1957. This is apparent from the fact that I saw a classified drawing of the R-12 in 1955. Along with my colleagues at White Sands Proving Ground, I also knew that the Soviets were working on an ICBM variously known as the TT-1 or T-5, only one of which was actually a real project as we know now.

The U.S. leadership had to have known about Soviet progress in ballistic missiles. Otherwise, the General Dynamics work on the MX-774 and the North American Navaho II program would have remained in limbo with all ballistic missile work being concentrated on the development and deployment of tactical ballistic missiles such as the Corporal and the Hermes C-1/Redstone with their limited 90- and 200-mile ranges respectively.

The real jolt, of course, came with the discovery that the Soviets had exploded a dry thermonuclear bomb less than a year after the United States had fired the 65-ton "wet" Shot Mike. The first U.S. dry thermonuclear bomb wasn't fired until the Castle shot of 15 megatons in the spring of 1954 at Eniwetok Atoll in the Pacific.

It comes as a real shock to most people to realize that the Soviets beat the United States to the thermonuclear warhead. No one can properly consider the American thermonuclear test, Shot Mike, as a warhead or even a weapon; at best it was a complex, bulky, building-sized, 65-ton proof-of-principle test gadget. It showed the

United States that a thermonuclear reaction could be triggered but that it would have to be made smaller, simpler, and lighter to be considered as a weapon. It took a year and a half to get it. On the other hand, the Soviets went directly to the dry thermonuclear weapon. Unlike the situation with the atomic bomb where the USSR reacted to what the United States had done, it was the United States that reacted to the Soviet achievement with the dry thermonuclear bomb. In view of how the Soviet Union was behaving at the time and in light of its Marxist-Leninist doctrine and accompanying military doctrines, the Soviet thermonuclear bomb, whether deliverable by long-range bomber or ballistic missile, wasn't just a perceived threat; it would be a real one within a few years.

By 1950 the U.S. Air Force hadn't rejuvenated the MX-774 contract but had let a whole new contract, MX-1593, to General Dynamics to study and design an ICBM.

While we know now how the Soviets solved some of the problems of an ICBM, Charlie Bossart at GD and the Air Force officers at the Air Research and Development Command knew they faced an array of extremely difficult engineering and technical problems.

A ballistic missile capable of lofting even a nuclear warhead would be very large, requiring a high-thrust rocket engine. A big rocket engine could probably be built, and the 220,000-pound Navaho II rocket engine was under development by the Rocketdyne Division of North American.

But two problems appeared to be almost insoluble: (a) how to attain an accuracy—called "circular error probable" or CEP—of less than a mile at a range of 5,500 miles; and (b) how to keep the warhead from burning up as it plunged back into the earth's atmosphere at near-meteoric speeds.

Engineers are lazy or they wouldn't be engineers in the first place. Basically, engineers look for a better way to do something, usually an easier way. So they tend to search for the easy way out because that's part of their training. In addition, the easy way out is just that: Easy—meaning that they don't have to work so hard and have more time for coffee breaks, fishing, or their families. When faced with extremely difficult problems, they tend to moan and complain about how difficult and expensive and complex the solutions will be. I can say this and am prepared to fend off criticism from engineers because I am one and I've done a lot of engineering in my time. The complaints of engineers faced with difficult technical problems are like the complaints of soldiers about how bad the chow is or how much better the enemy's weapons are. It doesn't mean that they won't knuckle down, get to work, and do their jobs. In the case of engineers, they usually find more than one solution to a problem.

The first step toward the solution of the manifold and complex problems of building a successful ICBM, of course, was to get some idea of the size and shape of the ballistic missile, the long-range cannon shell. This would help the engineers determine the sizes, shapes, performance requirements, and allowable weights of other subsystems.

By June 1951 Charlie Bossart and his crew had come up with two proposed test vehicles using the existing Navaho I rocket engine with 75,000 pounds of thrust and a 1½-stage cluster of four RMI 20,000-pound Viking motors. Basically the same, one vehicle would have a gliding warhead and the other a ballistic warhead.

Typical of the reentry thinking of the time, the nose on each test vehicle was a needle-sharp cone whose objective was to keep the supersonic aerodynamic drag force very low and thus keep the heating rate low as well. High-temperature materials such as tungsten were specified for the nose cone. It didn't occur to them then— because they had no hypersonic wind tunnel data on reentry vehicles yet—that the narrow tip would get quite hot very quickly and burn away to a blunt shape with high drag.

Various proposals for full-size Atlas ICBMs were presented by GD in July 1951. Those vehicles were predicated on delivering a very large and very heavy wet thermonuclear warhead to a range of 5,500 miles. Lengths varied from 70 to 180 feet with diameters from 7 to 14 feet. Thrust requirements ranged from 190,000 to more than 600,000 pounds.

GD and Rocketdyne studied various liquid-propellant combinations, too—hydrogen-oxygen, hydrogen-fluorine, hydrazine-fluorine, ammonia-fluorine, ammonia-oxygen, gasoline-oxygen, alcohol-oxygen, gasoline-nitric acid, and hydrocarbon-oxygen. The goal was to achieve the highest possible efficiency balanced against operational requirements and resulting missile size. Some combinations were rejected at the start; for example, fluorine and ammonia have corrosive and toxic characteristics which would make them not only dangerous and deadly but also nearly impossible to handle under operational conditions. The final choice was a hydrocarbonlike jet fuel called RP-1 (Rocket Propellant Number One) and liquid oxygen (LOX).

In October 1953 Bossart came up with a proposed configuration for the Atlas that was huge (for the time). It was a ballistic missile 12 feet in diameter and 108 feet long. Using the 1½-parallel-stage technique, it would have been propelled by a cluster of rocket engines generating 656,900 pounds of thrust at takeoff. This thrust level was to be provided by a cluster of five up-rated Navaho II rocket engines, four of which would be jettisoned at staging. Further design work refined this monster to a proposal put forth a few months later that would have been 90 feet long and 12 feet in diameter with a takeoff thrust of 650,000 pounds.

I recall seeing drawings of these various Atlas design proposals and photographs of the wooden mockup that were in the classified section of the White Sands technical library. We tried to keep up with these developments because there was always the possibility that we would have to beef-up the big test stand at White Sands to handle the engine testing. We were also looking at the flight safety problems involved if we were to flight-test these Atlas missiles at White Sands (which was never officially considered because the USAF Long Range Proving Ground at Cape Canaveral was always the prime site for ICBM flight testing).

The successful test of a dry thermonuclear warhead in the spring of 1954 meant that an Atlas of smaller size could be built.

But this took some doing. And intelligence reports from the Soviet Union provided the motivation.

In October 1953 the U.S. government knew about the Soviet dry thermonuclear bomb. They also got word of Korolev's proposed R-7 ICBM. Trevor Gardner, then Special Assistant for Research and

Development in the Department of the Air Force in the Pentagon, organized a group of high-level scientists to form the Strategic Missiles Evaluation Committee, code name Teapot. Backing Gardner on this were Secretary of the Air Force Harold E. Talbott and Air Force Chief of Staff General Nathan F. Twining. Gardner persuaded Princeton physicist and digital computer expert Dr. John von Neumann to head up Teapot.

Other members of Teapot included Professors Clark B. Millikan, Charles C. Lauritsen, and Louis G. Dunn of Cal Tech; Dr. Hendrik W. Bode of Bell Labs; Dr. Allan E. Puckett of Hughes Aircraft Co.; Dr. George W. Kistiakowski, former Manhattan project explosives expert and then at Harvard University; Professor J. B. Weisner of MIT; Mr. Lawrence A. Hyland of Bendix Aviation Corporation; and Dr. Simon Ramo and Dr. Dean Wooldridge of Ramo-Wooldridge Corporation.

The Teapot objective: Evaluate—quickly—in light of Soviet developments and all available information about American ballistic missile and thermonuclear warhead development the feasibility and practicality of developing an intercontinental ballistic missile as a weapons system. The Air Force wanted to overcome the hurdle placed in the way of the ICBM in 1945 and 1946 when many high-level American scientists had pooh-poohed it.

In February 1954, Dr. John von Neumann presented the report of the Teapot committee. It is obvious from the Teapot report that the committee members concluded that the United States had waited almost too long again before doing something and had probably wasted valuable time in the 1945–1950 time period. Teapot concluded that an effective ICBM could be developed and deployed early enough to counter the pending Soviet ICBM threat *if*—and they were big ifs—exceptional talents, adequate funds, and new management techniques suited to the urgency of the situation were authorized. The United States couldn't keep stumbling ahead in ballistic missile technology and development as it had been doing since the end of World War II. We had lost five years, and it was going to take a lot of hard work and extra money to make up for those lost years.

Furthermore, Teapot recommended that the huge five-engined Atlas proposal be redesigned as a smaller ballistic missile to take advantage of the smaller dry thermonuclear warhead.

The Atlas development schedule would have to be accelerated as well. No more leisurely build-and-test, then move on to the next problem or the design of the next subsystem. It would all have to be done almost simultaneously if the United States was to have an operational ICBM by the end of the decade, in time to head off either nuclear blackmail or a potential preemptive ICBM strike by the Soviet Union. The USSR had surprised us with its MiG-15s over Korea; these had shown that the USSR was no longer a peasant nation unable to handle the modern technology of jet propulsion.

To do all this, the Teapot committee's report went on, the Air Force would have to set up a new type of development management group that had to be supported with proper funding and priorities, given the ability to shortcut many contracting and procurement regulations, and provided with the authority to redirect, expand, and accelerate the ICBM program.

Only by doing *all* these things, not just some of them, could the United States get a long-range ballistic missile, an ICBM, that was militarily useful and strategically effective within a reasonable span of time, i.e., before the Soviets deployed the R-7 in sufficient strength to pose a real threat to the free world.

Time had run out, the Teapot report revealed. It told the Air Force and the Department of Defense and Pres. Dwight D. Eisenhower what needed to be done.

How to do it was something else.

# *Hooking Up the Push Buttons*

Having the Teapot report in hand cleared the way for the U.S. Air Force, the Department of Defense, and the Eisenhower administration to do something about the ICBM with the support of the scientific and academic community.

This is less of a critical factor today than it was in February 1954. Ten years earlier, World War II had been in full swing. It had become common knowledge—if incorrect—that the United States had won that war because scientists had developed radar, rockets, and especially the atomic bomb. The scientists who had been involved were, by that time, back in their academic environment, and they hadn't objected to the false impression that they'd created all those things. This perception had permitted them to seek and get large grants and extensive funding for their postwar research programs. While the scientists had indeed played a role in these developments, the news media neglected the fact that these were *engineering* projects. The scientists involved did indeed provide a lot of the basic knowledge that formed the foundation for the engineering development, and in many cases, scientists had to accept the role of program managers because they understood something of the technologies behind the projects. But the influence of the scientists on subsequent technical progress, especially in the field of ballistic missiles, had gotten far out of proportion to their actual involvement in or their awareness of the technologies involved.

To some extent, this strange involvement of theoretical scientists in the practical application of technology still exists.

With the Teapot report in hand, Trevor Gardner had to get something done, and he now had the clout to accomplish this.

With the help and concurrence of Air Force Chief of Staff Gen. Nathan F. Twining and Lt. Gen. Donald Putt, Deputy Chief of Staff for Research and Development, Gardner pushed through approval for a special management agency within the Air Force with the specific responsibility and authority to develop an ICBM in accordance with the Teapot findings and recommendations. It was called the Western Development Division (WDD) of the Air Research and Development Command. It was supported by a Special Aircraft Project Office of the Air Materiel Command. WDD was to be responsible for R&D and would direct the latter's procurement and production activities.

The choice for the WDD "vice president in charge of getting things done" was a man Gardner and Putt had known and watched for years. He was a career Air Force officer, a German-born naturalized citizen, a graduate of Texas A&M, a bomber pilot in the 19th Bomb Group in the South Pacific during World War II, and an officer who had been a strong advocate for the ICBM during the lean years of 1945–1950.

His name was Bernard Adolph Schriever.

The orders given to General Schriever told him, in essence, to get an operational ICBM in place at the earliest possible date. It had to be the best possible weapon built with the smallest possible budget. Basically, Schriever was told that good enough was the enemy of the best in this situation, that a workable system that was ready as quickly as possible was preferable to a perfect one that could be available a few years later. The United States didn't have the extra time; that had been frittered away earlier. Many people believed that it was the most important job in the country. It would have the highest priority in the nation. Schriever was to make the concept of push-button warfare a reality. As Sen. Brien MacMahon remarked, "All we have now is the push-buttons." Schriever had to hook the push-buttons up to something that would work if the buttons were pushed—yet everyone fervently hoped that the push-buttons would never have to be pushed.

As General Putt later observed, "Schriever is a natural. He was born for the job." As a colonel, Schriever had shown no reluctance to stand up and be counted when principle was at stake, even when his convictions required him to stand up against four-star generals. He wasn't given to snap judgments. Once he'd reached a decision, he was willing to stand behind it. He was patient when the opposition was persistent, willing to outwait them or slowly to convince them with logic and data. Schriever was therefore known as a man with complete integrity and sound judgment, neither a rebel nor a nonconformist. Furthermore, he could stimulate action and get things done. And he had a rare understanding of the intricacies and internal politics of the aerospace industry.

Backed by the clout of Gardner, Twining, Putt, and von Neumann, Schriever set about building his staff, his team, to carry out what seemed to be an impossible job. He selected his people carefully on the basis of what he later revealed were his criteria:

> The one overriding qualification in my opinion is a man's loyalty. If he has a deficiency in his loyalty, I don't care how smart he is or what he can do, I won't have him around. This doesn't mean I want a lot of "yes" men; because I try to give all my key staff people adequate opportunity to state their case in any major issue. But if you don't have loyalty in an organization, you don't have anything. And I like people who are smart, who have the attribute of wisdom as well as intelligence— particularly in key spots. Also, I want to see initiative. I like aggressive people.

We don't know the Soviet engineers who worked with Korolev and Glushko, so their names are probably lost to history. But we do know those men picked by Schriever to be on his initial team, and their names are: Col. Harold T. Morris, Col. Harold W. Norton, Col. William A. Sheppard, Col. Charles H. Terhune, Jr., Lt. Col. Benjamin P. Blassingame, Lt. Col. Beryl L. Boatman, Lt. Col. Philip

C. Calhoun, Lt. Col. Roy L. Ferguson, Lt. Col. Otto J. Glasser, Lt. Col. Edward N. Hall, Lt. Col. Joseph D. Heck, Jr., Lt. Col. John B. Hudson, Lt. Col. Norman J. Keefer, and Lt. Col. Edwin A. Swanke.

In July 1954 this group set up shop in Inglewood, California.

New technology usually requires new forms of social organization to make it work. In the case of the ICBM and WDD, this new form of social organization was the "systems engineering corporation." Such a firm doesn't manufacture anything. It acts like a catalyst in a chemical reaction; i.e., it makes the reaction happen more quickly but does not appear to take part in the reaction itself, emerging afterward as it was at the start. Schriever knew that military officers, brilliant as they might be, looked at the world from a particular viewpoint and with a special emphasis that were not necessarily either compatible with or even understood by industrial managers and engineers. From another viewpoint, the industrial managers and engineers could do things that military men could not. Industrial people, for example, don't worry about being killed in an operation, and military men don't have to worry about meeting a payroll or making a profit. To get an operational ICBM before the end of the 1950 decade—which Schriever as well as Gardner and others knew was the most probable date of "initial operational capability" or IOC for the Soviet ICBM—WDD would be like a juggler keeping dozens of balls, Indian clubs, batons, frangible china plates, and fire wands in the air at once. One juggler couldn't do it. He'd need help from experts. Thus was born the systems engineering corporation.

The first one was Ramo-Wooldridge Corporation, formed by two members of the Teapot committee, Dr. Simon Ramo and Dr. Dean Wooldridge. In essence, Ramo-Wooldridge was a consultant corporation. Ramo graduated from Cal Tech, spent his early career with General Electric, became operating vice president of Hughes Aircraft Company, and got together with Wooldridge in 1953 at the time of Teapot. Wooldridge was primarily the financial and administrative expert of the team. As Ramo-Wooldridge Corporation, the company wasn't the classical "prime contractor" that had been used on aircraft development projects in the past. Ramo-Wooldridge produced no hardware. It was made up of the civilian managers equivalent to the usual staff of civilian engineers and specialists that supported the military project directors, but with one significant difference: The engineering and production management people gathered together by Ramo and Wooldridge were employees of a private contractor to the WDD; they didn't have to worry about civil service procedures, salary grade levels, and the rest of the bureaucracy that had grown up even then around government service in order to assure that the government was indeed getting its money's worth out of the civilians who worked directly for it. Ramo-Wooldridge could go out and advertise for the best, hire the best, pay for the best, give them the best tools for the job, and eliminate the constraints under which civil service employees had to operate. There wasn't time to follow the rules set up for the leisurely pace of peacetime development.

Nor was time available to do the ICBM job using the usual procedures of a military R&D program. Too many things had to be done, too much research had to be conducted, too many things had to be developed, and none of them could wait on any of the others. A new approach to the management of technology had to be used.

One of the reasons that Schriever had been chosen to head WDD was a special staff study written in 1950 entitled, *Combat Ready Aircraft,* by then-Colonel B. A. Schriever. This study set forth the concept of a management technique dubbed "concurrency." In a sense it's a way to accommodate the chicken before the egg is hatched.

Concurrency means not only developing a series of subsystems simultaneously but also making decisions well in advance of the receipt of test data that are basic to the decisions themselves.

It means making the best educated guess, perhaps backing it up with two or more redundant approaches to the solution in case one fails to live up to expectations, then proceeding with the planning and construction of industrial facilities for test and production, military programs for the construction of operational bases and support elements, and even training of personnel before the initial testing of the weapon itself.

It's a grand gamble whose elements have to be very closely watched and directed lest one get out of hand.

Concurrency as developed and practiced by Schriever and WDD depended and still depends on three conditions.

First, authority and responsibility have to be consolidated in one agency with unity of command. Otherwise, the management side of the house cannot react quickly enough.

Second, to support and maintain high management confidence in the validity of the technical decisions, great technical competence is essential, especially when the management decisions involve the commitment and expenditure of vast sums of money to technical directions that are not easily reversed, especially when made well in advance of tests that prove their validity.

Finally, funding and program decisions outside the authority of the program director have to be both timely and firm. Special management channels have to be set up to expedite the decision processes leading to funding and program decisions and commitments.

The controlling factors in most program decisions are usually performance and availability, so sound financial management with stringent cost controls became an essential part of the program.

All of this had to produce flexible ICBM designs with "stretch" and adaptability built into them that could be started into production before the first test flights were made. Could an all-inertial guidance system be used, or should the missile be designed for radio guidance? What kind of thermal projection system would be necessary for the warhead, and how would this affect the design of the missile, its drag during powered flight through the atmosphere, and its ultimate weight? Could it be fired out of a hole in the ground, or would the unknown environment of a silo launch be too much for the structure and the subsystems to withstand? Would an above-ground launch system be better, and, if so, how could it be protected against an enemy preemptive first strike by R-7 thermonuclear missiles? Could the missile survive a first strike, given the guessed-at CEP of the Soviet missile and thus be launched post-strike, or would it have to have the sort of reaction that would allow it to be launched before the R-7 landed? A sporty game.

It was made even sportier by the complex interacting factors that could not be controlled by the program management team. For example, warhead technology was proceeding rapidly. Constant changes were made in the assessment of thermonuclear blast effects which in turn affected both missile basing and guidance system accuracy.

Finally, back in Washington, an existing deterrent military force of long-range bombers had to be kept in being while this new weapons system was being developed. And it had to be done in such a way that it didn't bankrupt the nation in the process.

This "program package" concept was new and untried when WDD first set up business in 1954. Along with concurrency, it had been tried in the past with varying degrees of success but never attempted with all elements in operation at once. Now Schriever and his WDD team had to make it work. Too much depended on the successful outcome.

# Aiming a 5,000-Mile Artillery Shell

Many people think that the biggest problem in developing an ICBM was getting bigger rocket engines and making bigger missiles. Those were only two of many, and they were probably the easiest to solve.

Making a bigger rocket is like making a bigger airplane. It's an engineering job. It's a matter of telling the structural and aero-dynamics engineers how big the missile is to be and what it should weigh. The rest is a matter of working with tables of materials, doing lots of sketching, and fiddling with finicky figures for months on end until the best compromise between size, weight, strength, and cost is achieved. Basically, save for a few little tricks, a big liquid-propellant rocket is nothing more than a huge flying sewer pipe that can carry up to nine times its own weight in propellants.

Bigger rocket engines are another matter. Even today the design and development of large liquid-propellant rocket engines are almost black arts. An engineer may start with some basic equations. But very quickly the whole approach becomes almost one of "applied black magic." A liquid-propellant rocket engine simply cannot be scaled up according to an established set of rules or formulas. This is because a rocket engine is a complex system involving the interaction of heat flows, hydrodynamics, combustion kinetics, and a host of other esoteric subjects.

One of the most difficult problems involved with rocket engine design is combustion instability. In a way, a liquid rocket engine combustion chamber is somewhat like an organ pipe open at one end. Like an organ pipe, it has a resonant frequency set up by pulses of pressure racing back and forth within it. The frequency of these pulses changes with changes in pressure, density, temperature, and all the other factors that influence fluid dynamics. No one really understands it all yet. Even a little 3,000-pound-thrust liquid rocket motor can exhibit combustion instability; it literally screams when it's operating. The dynamic pressure pulses inside the combustion chamber can tear it apart. When engines get larger, they can become very prone to combustion instability; then they don't scream, they blow up.

The secret seems to lie in the proper design of the injector system, that part of the combustion chamber where the two liquid propellants are injected into the chamber at a pressure higher than the combustion pressure. Recall that Dr. Walter Thiel solved the injector problem in the A.4 rocket motor by clustering 18 of the proven injectors from a small motor. When it came to running the rocket engines for the Navaho II project and, later, the Atlas, Rocketdyne engineers were working with rocket motors that were about the same size as the A.4 engine but weighed less, operated at almost twice the combustion pressure, and generated more than three times the thrust.

It isn't only the painfully high noise level that makes rocket engine test engineers seek refuge behind ten feet of reinforced concrete during static tests.

One of the major problems of developing and deploying an effective ICBM was to give it a suitable guidance system. If a gun isn't aimed properly or an ICBM, a long-range modern "gun," isn't guided correctly during its powered flight, it won't hit the intended target. Accuracy and dispersion are two allied factors that an artillery officer worries about when developing a gun or, these days, a guided missile.

The accuracy and dispersion requirements that Dornberger set forth for the A.4 rocket had to be improved greatly to produce an effective ICBM. With a 10-megaton warhead, it's permissible to miss the target by a couple of miles at a range of 5,500 miles.

However, if you want to really make sure you've hit the target and taken out the Brand X ICBM silo, it's necessary to get the CEP or miss distance down to a matter of a hundred yards or less.

This may not seem to be a difficult job. After all, a truck driver can start out in Los Angeles and go through the Holland Tunnel into Manhattan with an accuracy measured in inches. That's why truck lines use human truck drivers. To duplicate that feat with a robot . . . Well, no robot has yet been built that will do it. But an ICBM guidance system comes close.

The A.4 rocket used a combination of gyros and accelerometers to tell the missile where it was at any given instant in its flight. A reasonably simple analog computer can compare the actual position in space with the desired position, send a correcting signal to the autopilot, and have the missile steer itself back onto its intended flight path.

Gyros sense up and down, right and left, and back and forth. They provide a "stable platform" that tells the missile "which way is up." As a long-range ballistic missile proceeds in its flight, it's true that "up" changes because the earth is spheroidal in shape. But this factor can be taken into account by the missile's on-board computer if it has a reference to the starting point.

Accelerometers measure acceleration or change in velocity. A guidance system uses three accelerometers. They measure the change of velocity (acceleration) along the three main axes of a ballistic missile—pitch (nose up/down), yaw (nose right/left), and velocity (nose forward/backward).

The outputs of the three accelerometers are sent electrically to a reasonably simple computer. This computer performs a number of mathematical operations. By integrating the outputs of the accelerometers as a function of time since launch and knowing where the starting point was from the stable gyro platform, the computer tells the guidance system where the missile is.

The computer also tells the guidance system where the missile *should* be at that instant in its flight. If the ICBM has deviatated from its intended course or trajectory, an error signal is generated. This error signal tells the guidance system to make a correction. This is done by swiveling the rocket motors, for example, to steer the ICBM back onto its path. When the error signal is zero, the ICBM is where it is supposed to be when it is supposed to be there.

It wasn't as easy as that in 1954.

Two men were perhaps the experts in inertial guidance systems.

One was Dr. Ernst Steinhoff, who had been in charge of the A.4's guidance system. In 1954, Steinhoff was with the von Braun team at the Army's Redstone Arsenal in Huntsville, Alabama, working on the Redstone missile's inertial guidance system.

The other was Dr. Charles Stark Draper, a professor at the Massachusetts Institute of Technology, who was the American expert on gyros. Draper was in charge of the Instrumentation Laboratory at M.I.T. He had known Elmer Sperry, Jr., the inventor of the modern gyroscopic stable platform, and had worked with Sperry to invent, build, and test gyro flight instruments for airplanes. In 1939, Sperry Gyroscope had provided financial support for Draper to make a gyroscopic turn indicator for airplanes. During World War II, Draper developed gyro-stablilized gunsights for aircraft. When the war was over, he concentrated on developing inertial guidance systems for aircraft. And in 1953, Draper was the brains behind the first full inertially-guided transcontinental flight from Massachusetts to California.

The big problem with inertial guidance systems for ICBMs was the gyro. It has to be a precision instrument. Any imbalance or slop in the bearings will create drift. The gyro will slowly lose its inertial alignment and begin to wander. For a short-range battlefield tactical ballistic missile, fairly sloppy gyros can be tolerated because an error of a fraction of a degree won't result in a large CEP at a range of 100 miles. But at a range of 5,500 miles, the gyros have to be almost perfect and drift-free. On top of all that, gyros tend to do strange things and become very inaccurate in the polar regions.

Now it can be done, of course, even with mechanical gyros. The invention of the laser ring gyro produced a gyro with practically zero drift over a long period of time because it has no mechanically moving parts at all, just photons of light. The transoceanic jet airlines of today have better gyros and inertial guidance systems than Steinhoff or Draper even dared to dream possible back in 1954.

Having a precision inertial guidance system is only part of the solution to getting an ICBM to its assigned target.

The solution also has to account for other factors.

The aerodynamic drag produced by an ICBM ascending through the atmosphere to near space and then back through that atmosphere also must be taken into account. In 1954 atmospheric scientists had a reasonably good idea of the density and temperature of the atmosphere up to about 50 miles. These data had been gathered from vertically launched sounding rockets over the preceding ten years or so. But these rockets had been launched from places like White Sands and Cape Canaveral and Kapustin Yar. What were the characteristics of the atmosphere over the North Pole? A good guess can be made, but is a guess good enough when dealing with guidance systems that must be accurate to within a fraction of 1 percent?

Another factor is something called Coriolis Force, which isn't a force at all. It's a perceived force created by the fact that the earth is spheroidal and rotating on its north-south axis. A launch site at the equator has a far greater eastward velocity due to rotation than one at a latitude of, say, 40 degrees north latitude. After the ICBM has been launched and is traveling, say, northward over the Pole, it still has an eastward component to its velocity because of the greater eastward velocity of the ground from which it was launched. Over the North Pole, the ground has zero eastward motion because of the rotation of the earth. Thus, as a ballistic missile changes latitude in its flight, the earth underneath it turns at a different rate, and the missile is seen from the ground as having an eastward or westward component to its flight path that really isn't there insofar as the missile is concerned. Without Coriolis Force taken into account, the guidance computer will think the missile is east of its intended path as it travels northward and west when it is traveling southward. Since guidance is limited to powered flight, in this case the computer would correct and make the ICBM warhead land east of its intended target. To know how to correct for Coriolis Force, the designer of an ICBM's inertial guidance system must know the exact shape of the earth so that the precise numbers for the Coriolis Force can be calculated and taken into account.

In 1954 no one knew the exact shape of the earth.

Therefore, if you wanted to shoot from, say, New York to Moscow, no one knew exactly how far New York City was from Moscow. The error could be a matter of several miles. No one knew. There were two reasons for this.

The first was simple when you think about it. "First-order" surveys accurate to within inches had been made all over North America, and an accurate geodetic grid had been established. Surveyors with surveying transits and measuring tapes had actually measured the distance between Miami and Nome. They had stretched measuring tapes all over the continent. They knew with reasonable precision—within a matter of feet even in the worst cases—precisely where locations were with respect to each other. Another first-order grid had been established in Europe and other places. But the actual distance between Newfoundland and Ireland had never been measured because no one had stretched a measuring tape across the Atlantic Ocean between Newfoundland and Ireland. The same held true for the Pacific Ocean. The Soviets weren't about to let the Americans tie into the Siberian grid across the Bering Straits, and the Americans weren't overly anxious for the Soviets to be able to tie into the North American grid, either, for obvious reasons: Tying the grid together would improve the accuracy of ICBMs. It wasn't until both the United States and the USSR got satellites—launched by ICBMs—that first-order surveying accuracy was obtained on a worldwide basis.

The second reason is that the planet earth isn't a sphere but a lumpy piece of rock. We didn't know where all the lumps were, and we didn't know the exact shape of the earth. If the planet were truly spherical—which it isn't because of its daily spin and nonuniform composition—the solution would have been easy. One of the important findings of the first satellites—Sputnik I and Vanguard—was the revelation of the true shape of the earth. It's sort of pear-shaped. And it's got lumps in it. These lumps of heavier, denser material affect the local gravitation force. For example, the presence of a large nearby granite mountain will cause a plumb bob to be deflected a minute fraction of a degree toward it; this upsets the determination of true vertical which, compounded over thousands of such measurements required to set up a geodetic grid, results in inaccuracies in maps and charts. Not much, but enough to make a difference between a hit and a near miss at intercontinental ranges. The lumps of stronger gravitational force also cause slight alterations in the flight path of an ICBM. Again, we didn't have this information until we were able to place satellites into orbit with ICBMs later in the decade.

These problems were solved by the persistent urgency of WDD and its people, who didn't keep regular office hours. The next time you fly a 747 on the polar route between Los Angeles and Europe, you can bet the aircraft is being steered by an inertial navigation system that had an ICBM guidance system as its ancestor.

In keeping with the principles of concurrency and redundancy, WDD selected the AC Spark Plug Division of General Motors and the Arma Division of American Bosch Arma to develop an inertial guidance system with the help of Stark Draper's MIT lab.

And just in case the inertial guidance system didn't work out as planned, WDD hedged its bets by getting both General Electric and Honeywell to work on radio-command guidance systems. Since all the guidance possible for an ICBM must be carried out during its first few minutes of powered flight, the missile could be tracked by precision radar that would determine its position and velocity. Radio commands could then be sent from the ground to the missile to tell the guidance system how to make the necessary corrections to the flight path.

Some of the problems facing inertial guidance systems weren't fully solved until ICBMs became available to launch satellites. And some of the problems of radio-command systems ran into trouble with differences in air temperature bending radar signals, for example.

Thus, in the 1950s the state of the art in guidance systems posed serious problems if you wanted to put a pickle in a pickle barrel 5,500 miles away. But if you could be content with just getting close, interim solutions would work. And since the mission of WDD was to get a workable ICBM quickly, the good was the enemy of the best. The problems were soluble if you worked hard enough and didn't insist on absolute perfection. "We don't want it perfect; we want it Tuesday!" was the initial philosophy of WDD.

And WDD was willing to hedge its bets by placing parallel and redundant contracts.

# Getting the Warhead Down

The flight path of a ballistic missile is just like that of an artillery shell. An initial period of acceleration brings the warhead to the necessary speed and sends it in the proper direction to hit the target. In a gun, this happens inside the gun barrel in a fraction of the time of the flight of the shell's warhead. A rocket-propelled artillery shell such as an ICBM can achieve much higher velocities and thus much greater range because it carries its own propellant along and makes its own imaginary gun barrel by using a guidance system. Thus, because of the shorter range, the velocities of a gun-launched projectile are usually much lower than those attainable with a long-range ballistic missile. In a ballistic missile, the accelerations are much lower, which means the warhead doesn't need to be as robust as that for a gun-launched warhead. And the powered portion of a ballistic missile's trajectory also covers a greater distance.

After reaching the proper velocity—speed and direction—a warhead launched either by a gun or a ballistic missile then coasts the rest of the distance to the target. In the case of a cannon shell, most of the flight takes place in the earth's atmosphere, where air drag slows the warhead during its entire flight; it doesn't get very hot because its speed may be only twice the speed of sound or Mach 2. But a ballistic missile warhead is nearly in space—30 miles up or more—when the propulsion phase of the flight is over, and it coasts to its target hundreds or thousands of miles away in almost empty space 60 to 100 miles up. There is some air at those altitudes, although not very much. It's a better vacuum than can be created in most surface laboratories. But when the ballistic missile warhead comes back into the lower portion of the atmosphere at speeds ranging from Mach 5 to Mach 20, it encounters very high drag forces because of its speed. It also gets a lot hotter because of air friction and because it compresses the air ahead of it.

Everyone in the ICBM program was well aware of the fact that temperatures of thousands of degrees would be encountered by long-range ballistic missile warheads as they slammed back into the atmosphere. Some indication of this had already been seen by von Braun and his team with the A.4 at Peenemünde and Blizna, but the temperatures encountered by the warhead of a 200-mile missile moving at Mach 2 weren't enough to really matter.

Not so when an ICBM warhead reenters at Mach 20 or more.

The warhead not only can get hot enough to melt, but it can melt away in an asymmetric manner, causing aerodynamic drag to be different on one side than the other. This unbalance of drag forces can pull the warhead to one side, slow it down too much, or cause it to overshoot the intended target. The CEP grows very large unless the reentry conditions can be known in advance, controlled by the way the warhead's outer structure burns away or melts, and accounted for in advance by the guidance system while the missile is still in powered flight.

The Soviets had taken the quick and easy way out. They opted to use a very large 15-megaton dry thermonuclear warhead. To protect it from reentry heating, they sheathed it in a lot of laminated plywood which would char and thus ablate or burn off. Since they had little information on how spotty ablation might change the shape and thus alter the final trajectory of the warhead coming through the atmosphere, decreasing its accuracy, they were willing to live with a high CEP because of the large radius of destruction of the big warhead. Soviet leaders from Stalin through Khrushchev realized the political, diplomatic, and propaganda values of having an ICBM first, no matter how clumsy, inaccurate, and crude it might be.

General Schriever and the WDD wanted the Air Force ICBM

to hit military targets with some degree of precision. If an ICBM was going to be used against a target more than 5,000 miles away, the Air Force wanted the warhead to land as close to the target as possible, preferably as close as a gravity bomb delivered by a B-52 manned bomber. An ICBM might get through to targets that couldn't be reached by B-52s because of air defenses. If the CEP of an ICBM warhead could be reduced, fewer missiles and thus fewer warheads would be required to ensure that an important target was indeed hit. With a large CEP, a military command always frets and worries about a number of questions: Did I really disable the target? Do I have to shoot another ICBM at it to make sure? Do I have to send a reconnaissance airplane over—or use a recon satellite in later times when they became available—to take a look? An artillery officer wants at least a reliable miss distance—i.e., lower CEP—if he can't get extremely high accuracy. In short, whether a commander is running an artillery battery or a bombing squadron, he wants to be able to hit the target with as much accuracy as possible.

This was basically the philosophy behind the American doctrine of precision daylight strategic bombing that was developed before World War II. Except for the final days of the strategic bombing of Japan, when there were no specific military targets for precision bombing because the Japanese had dispersed their industry, American strategic bombing doctrine had always stressed precision. The legacy of this doctrine formed the foundation, knowingly or otherwise, for the USAF requirement for a low CEP.

So control of the warhead reentry conditions was important to Schriever and WDD. It was a two-pronged problem: surviving reentry and knowing where the warhead would hit.

Early ICBM proposals put forth by Charlie Bossart at GD for the MX-774 and the early MX-1593 ballistic missile design studies showed warheads that were very slender cones. However, other approaches were coming out of the Ames Research Center of the National Advisory Committee on Aeronautics (NACA), the predecessor of NASA.

Immediately after World War II a valuable legacy of German

high-speed aerodynamic research fell into the hands of the Allies. A great deal of data on supersonic flight became available. Ames began building supersonic and hypersonic wind tunnels and test facilities. By 1950 they had a 10-inch by 14-inch hypersonic facility ready. It was clear that problems would exist with reentry of ICBM warheads. The warhead could not be permitted to burn up due to aerodynamic heating, and that was a research area in which the Ames scientists had been deeply involved.

Harvey Julian Allen at Ames knew that the kinetic energy lost by a warhead as it reentered the atmosphere would be totally converted to heat energy. The heat would be generated in two places: inside and outside the shock wave. The heat generated inside the shock wave is transmitted readily to the warhead itself, while that ahead of or outside the shock wave is removed from the body and can't easily reach it through the intervening layers of air. He reasoned that the overall rate of heat generation and thus the temperature of the warhead would be lower if the largest portion of the reentry heat were generated ahead of the shock wave. That meant a radical departure from the sharp-nosed ICBM designs. Allen maintained that an ICBM nose warhead should be blunt in order to strengthen the shock wave, increase the pressure drag, and keep the heat away from the surface of the warhead. A blunt nose would also keep the shock wave standing out well ahead of the nose.

Allen and a colleague, Dr. Alfred J. Eggers, who was in charge of the hypersonic test facility, analyzed the consequences of this hypothesis and jointly published the first report as a classified document in 1951. But the idea wasn't picked up by Bossart and others. It just sat on the back burner and simmered for a few years.

Eggers designed and built an interesting new device called an atmospheric entry simulator (AES) in which a gun fired a test model into a hypersonic test tunnel, thus achieving the sort of speed an ICBM warhead would attain. Ames became the center for government reentry research, and Eggers further refined the Allen-Eggers blunt-body concept. The Ames researchers began to get some data on the stability of blunt reentry bodies as well as their supersonic drag characteristics. The engineers now had the tools that would allow them to predict where the warhead would land.

The first nose cone shapes considered for Atlas warheads were very blunt "heat sink" types using the Allen-Eggers blunt-body concepts combined with a heavy copper heat sink, a material that would absorb the reentry heating just long enough to allow the warhead to descend to the altitude where it would be triggered.

Others became interested in solutions to the reentry problem. Dr. Arthur Kantrowitz at Cornell University's School of Aeronautical Engineering had been working under contracts with the Office of Naval Research on high-temperature gases and became aware of the reentry problem. He developed a shock tube test facility that would allow him to test entry body models in supersonic high-temperature gas flows. One of the contractors selected by WDD to develop the Atlas reentry body that would enclose the warhead was Avco Corporation, and Kantrowitz began to run models of the Avco blunt nose cone designs in his shock tube at Cornell. He made such great progress that Avco Corporation established the Avco Everett Research Laboratory in 1956 for him, whereupon he left Cornell to devote full time to the reentry work. Kantrowitz's results convinced Avco that the ablative approach was the way to go, and Avco Research and Development Division produced Avconite, an ablative composite material that was used on the RVX 1-5 nose cone design.

General Electric also had a contract for the reentry body and it settled also on the ablative approach. Dr. Leo Steg developed a glass-fiber ablative material that was used on the Mark 3 nose cone.

Meanwhile, the engineers at the Army's Redstone Arsenal also were at work on ablative nose cones, but they took a direct approach to testing the shapes and materials: They merely placed nose cone test models in the hot supersonic exhausts of rocket engines.

Both the Air Force and the Army utilized a series of test rockets to loft nose cone models high into space and then slam them back into the atmosphere under rocket power to achieve reentry velocities under real conditions. The development of radio telemetry greatly enhanced this type of testing in the real environment because information on temperatures and accelerations could be transmitted to the ground.

Lockheed Aircraft developed for WDD a reentry test vehicle known as the X-17, a multistaged solid-propellant rocket whose first two stages accelerated its payload to an altitude of about 100 miles. There the payload, consisting of another solid-propellant rocket plus the instrumented nose cone model, fired back down into the atmosphere to bring the model to the proper speeds at the proper reentry altitudes.

The Army at Redstone Arsenal built a similar test vehicle, a Redstone tactical ballistic missile that had been stretched and upgraded to carry a cluster of solid-propellant rockets aloft with a nose cone model at the tip. In 1956 this Army vehicle, known as the Jupiter-C, launched a test nose cone to a range of 6,000 miles down the Long Range Proving Ground from Cape Canaveral. Twelve test flights were planned; only three were actually made before von Braun and his team got the data they needed. The remaining nine Jupiter-C rockets were carefully placed in storage.

Concurrency was paying off. It had been an enormous risk. But by 1957 nearly all the "insoluble" problems had not one but several solutions. It was only a matter of putting them all together in a ballistic missile that would work.

# Atlas Comes Alive

Gen. Bernard Schriever's concept of concurrency, which had to be used to quickly develop an American ICBM, was fraught with dangers. It was a very high risk situation.

To get an ICBM in the least amount of time meant that WDD had to start with what was known and available, then support applied research to get specific answers as yet unavailable. This meant developing an ICBM system design with great flexibility as well as utilizing multiple-path approaches to problem solving. The use of redundant approaches to known problems had been used, tested, and proved in the U.S. Army Corps of Engineers' Manhattan District, the project cover name for the development of the first atomic bomb in 1942–1945. (Contrary to popular belief, the "Manhattan Project" never existed; the real, proper name of the atomic bomb's development program was the Manhattan District. Since it was carried out under the aegis of the Corps of Engineers which had "districts" already in existence to build such things as flood control and harbor facilities, the use of the word "district" was a perfect cover.)

When General Schriever and his WDD people surveyed what was available in 1954, they found scraps and pieces of former programs but no organized, unified program. They'd have to put it all together themselves, and this meant developing a new management technique for military programs.

The American ICBM program was the most complex technological juggling act in history. Although the Manhattan District's work on the atomic bomb had been carried out under the pressures of wartime exigency, WDD had to operate in a unique atmosphere of nonwar that was the hallmark of the early years of the Cold War between the United States and the USSR. General Schriever and his team were military people; it was their job to defend the nation, and they knew about the serious threat created by a paranoid, militant, aggressive Soviet Union armed with an ICBM force capable of striking the American heartland with less than 30 minutes' warning time and no possible American defense against ballistic missiles. Schriever and the WDD had to pioneer *the management of technology,* initiating procedures and techniques that are often commonplace or even obsolete today. Clear lines of authority and responsibility were established. Closely integrated into the WDD management organization were people from the Air Materiel Command, the Strategic Air Command, and the Air Training Command; the first one had to procure the Atlas, the second had to operate it, and the third had to trian the people to use it. WDD officers, NCOs, and civilians worked sixteen hours a day seven days a week, even on such holidays as Christmas. Leaves or vacations were out of the question. The multiple-path approach also meant extensive travel to ensure proper communications and coordination. A small fleet of Air Force airplanes—usually obsolete North American B-25 Mitchells and other World War II aircraft; this was before the days of the corporate jet or the "VIP Liaison Transport"—were kept at nearby at Los Angeles International Airport. Nearly all the WDD officers were rated pilots, and they put in a lot of cross-country flying time during those years as they crisscrossed the nation for face-to-face meetings and conferences. The parking lots around the buildings housing WDD and its later organizations were rarely empty at midnight. Saturday differed little from weekdays except that California sport clothes were accepted in lieu of the uniform of the day. Schriever also introduced a management concept known as "Black Saturday," an all-day monthly meeting during which Schriever and his staff would probe every nook and cranny of the program, looking for problems or potential difficulties. No holds were barred. No punches were pulled during those intense, soul-searching, and often soul-searing sessions. Each program director would be "put on the rack." But he was usually rewarded with Schriever's accolade, "Okay, let's get on with it!"

But what the von Neumann Teapot Committee had found and the WDD people had confirmed was encouraging. In spite of the wasted five years from 1945 to 1950, enough progress had been made in several fields and enough tested hardware existed that the ICBM program could at least get started.

When it came to propulsion, North American's Rocketdyne Division had a series of liquid-propellant engines developed for the Air Force Navaho Project, the intercontinental supersonic ramjet-powered cruise missile. The most important engine was the 120,000-pound thrust chamber. To achieve the necessary thrust to accelerate the Navaho to supersonic speeds where its ramjets could operate, two of these chambers were clustered to provide 240,000 pounds of thrust.

The Navaho rocket engine was probably the most advanced in the world in 1953. It pioneered many rocket engine technologies that became widely used in the United States and abroad. Among these was the lightweight combustion chamber using a cluster of thin-walled tubes banded together. This method of constructing a rocket combustion chamber, a high-pressure gas generator with a specially shaped hole in one end, was much lighter than the solidly built welded double-wall combustion chamber developed in the United States by James H. Wyld of Reaction Motors, Inc., during World War II and by von Braun, Thiel, and the German team at Kummersdorf in the early 1930s. The Navaho engine also used an advanced turbopump propellant feed system whose turbine was driven by the output of a gas generator burning the same fuel and oxidizer as the engine itself. This "bootstrap" power cycle eliminated the need for a separate propellant system such as that used in the V-2 and Redstone missiles. The ability to control and increase the gas generator flow rate and combustion pressure meant more horsepower from the turbine. This meant that the propellant pumps driven by the turbine could pump more liquids at higher pressures into the combustion chamber. In turn, this allowed the engine to be run at higher combustion pressures and higher thrust levels.

The first Navaho booster with its piggyback ramjet-powered supersonic intercontinental cruise missile was launched from Cape Canaveral in September 1953.

With the bootstrap power cycle and the ability to run the Navaho combustion chambers at higher flow rates and pressures, each chamber could be uprated to 135,000 pounds of thrust without a great deal of redesign. A thrust level of 150,000 pounds per chamber was not out of the question in the minds of the Rocketdyne engineers. Given a little development work, the Atlas had a propulsion system.

The only feasible airframe design concept available was the five-engine General Dynamics Atlas proposal. This would have required a liftoff thrust of 650,000 pounds which meant using five uprated Navaho II chambers. This huge Atlas proposal would have been 108 feet long with a diameter of 12 feet. But seeing the strong likelihood of smaller, lighter thermonuclear warheads becoming available later in the 1950 decade, the von Neumann Teapot Committee had recommended putting this 1953 Atlas design concept on a diet to reduce its size and power requirements. However, this lightweight warhead didn't exist in 1953. Schriever, WDD, and the nation would have to bet on the Atomic Energy Commission being able to deliver it on schedule.

So much for the good news. The bad news was not as sanguine.

In 1953, available inertial and radio guidance systems were complicated, unreliable, and too inaccurate for use at ranges of 5,500 miles or more if an acceptable CEP was to be attained. The nation and its Air Force had never been supportive of area bombing such as the British had pursued under the Trenchard doctrine. When Gen. Curtis LeMay had to resort to area fire bombing of Japanese cities in the final year of World War II, America was on a wartime footing and operating under a wartime philosophy of winning what was considered a just and good war; later peacetime revelations of the results of fire bombing Dresden, Hamburg, Tokyo, Nagoya, and other cities, plus the nuking of Hiroshima and Nagasaki, were viewed with revulsion by both American civilians and military people alike. American long-range bombing doctrine had always stressed precision bombing of military targets. Thus, there was no question of just firing an ICBM at Moscow or Leningrad with a CEP of tens of miles; American ICBMs were to be targeted against military installations under the existing Strategic Air Command doctrines. The Atlas had to take out the Soviet ICBM launching capability as a first priority; the second priority, in the argot of the time, was to be able to put one through the window of the men's room of the Kremlin.

Provided that the warhead survived coming back through the earth's atmosphere at 25,000 feet per second. Make a reentry body big enough and heavy enough, and it would get through, of course, which is what the Soviets did. However, no proof existed in the free world of the ability to make a reentry body small enough and light enough for the capabilities of the down-sized Atlas.

A great deal of unplowed ground lay ahead of the American ICBM program in areas that had received little if any attention at that time. No one knew very much about vibration effects on the missile's structure and subsystems. Contrary to popular belief, a rocket engine doesn't operate with a smooth push; combustion goes on in a series of tiny explosions that pulse many times per second. The muted sound of the gas burner on a kitchen stove is an example of this. As combustion pressures increase and the flow rate of gas goes up, this sound can become a low whistle and finally a shriek. If the combustion frequency goes into resonance with the natural frequency of the missile airframe and its subsystems, it can shake a large rocket vehicle apart. Or it can set up fore-and-aft pulsing known as the pogo effect because it creates the same sensation as bouncing around on a pogo stick.

All these problems and more had to be tackled and solved simultaneously. Keeping this technological juggling act going was the major job of WDD and its civilian helpmate, the Ramo-Wooldridge Corporation.

Since no one knew much about igniting high-thrust liquid-propellant rocket engines at high altitudes in flight, the 1½-stage procedure was selected; all engines would be ignited on the ground while the missile was held down. When the proper thrust level was built up—liquid rocket engines require a second or so to smooth out and come up to their design thrust levels—the missile would be released. The booster portion of the propulsion section—two rocket chambers in the case of the Atlas—would be jettisoned 140 seconds into the flight, with the central or sustainer engine continuing to operate for 160 seconds more.

In accordance with the recommendations of the Teapot Committee, WDD instructed Charlie Bossart and his GD team to scale back the Atlas configuration using best estimates of the likely weight of the yet unbuilt and untested small thermonuclear warhead.

When Bossart looked at all the elements involved and redesigned the Atlas, it came out as a missile about 75 feet long with a diameter of 10 feet.

But to get its weight down, Bossart and his group couldn't build the Atlas the same way as all previous ballistic missiles. They couldn't use straightforward aviation structural technology and build the Atlas like a big airliner with semimonocoque aluminum skin riveted and welded to internal formers and stringers. Even if the propellant tanks were made integral with the skin and structure, the Atlas would have been too heavy for the available propulsion system. Bossart had to utilize an entirely new approach to a structure.

The result was a stainless-steel balloon.

The skin of the Atlas was as thin as a dime, varying in thickness from 0.020 inch to 0.040 inch, depending on the loads the skin had to support. The liquid oxygen and hydrocarbon fuel (RP-1) tanks _were_ the airframe, and a single insulated bulkhead separated the two tanks. The Atlas airframe had no internal structure such as formers and stringers to support the thin skin. The missile had to be kept under an internal pressure of 10 pounds per square inch—a little less than half that required by a radial tire. Otherwise, it would have collapsed under its own weight.

It's not hard to understand how this pressurized airframe worked. A toy rubber balloon doesn't seem to be very strong when it isn't inflated; when blown up, it becomes stiff and strong. A deflated tire is fairly flexible; put 24 pounds per square inch of air pressure in it, and it will support half a ton of load or more.

It sounds simple, but the problems associated with such a huge steel balloon were many. General Dynamics still doesn't talk very much about how it made a steel balloon ten feet in diameter and over sixty feet long. Special stainless steels had to be developed, and GD worked with steel companies to do this as well as to work the bugs out of ways to weld such thin steel sheets. The completed Atlas could be stored or shipped on its side as long as it was kept pressurized, but moving the huge balloon around was often delicate work.

In addition, when the Atlas balloon was loaded with 173,000 pounds of liquid oxygen at −297 degrees Fahrenheit, the upper tank suddenly got much colder than the rest of the airframe; shrinkage caused by temperature difference had to be accounted for. On top of that, no one had handled that much liquid oxygen that quickly before, and the Atlas project had to pioneer whole new ways to handle, pump, transfer, and store very large volumes of the supercold liquid.

When loaded into the Atlas tanks 10 feet in diameter, the liquid oxygen and RP-1 fuel didn't just sit there during flight; they sloshed back and forth and they exhibited the same sort of vortex you can see in bathwater when it twists down the drain.

Liquid oxygen does not like to come into contact with organic materials such as oil or even the residue from human sweat that's left on a surface after being touched by human hands. The Atlas project developed techniques for keeping LOX systems superclean and detecting the presence of contaminants down to a level not previously considered possible—175 microns in size and no more than 2 micrograms of contaminants per milliliter of volume.

The structural dynamics of a stainless-steel balloon loaded with sloshing liquids and with a heavy warhead at one end and a heavy rocket engine at the other were complex. The steering action of the rocket motors puts sideways forces into the balloon that tend to make it bend. Aerodynamic forces from subsonic to supersonic speeds will cause the airframe to bend back and forth like a sheaf of wheat in the wind. Take a long, skinny, inflated party balloon and place a coffee cup over each end and you'll get some idea of the complexity of the problem.

But the Air Force, GD, Rocketdyne, GE, Avco, Burroughs, and the other outfits involved in this crazy juggling act could see a glimmer of light out there a few years away. It could be done. Atlas could be built. But could it be built and tested and ready in time?

The full go-ahead for Atlas production was ordered in January 1955. The Air Force gave it the code name WS-107A-1. At the Convair Division of General Dynamics, Atlas was known simply as Model 7.

Was it a coincidence that both the United States and the USSR called their first ICBM Model 7?

The land launch of a Polaris A-1 SLBM from the Ship Motion Simulator at Cape Canaveral.

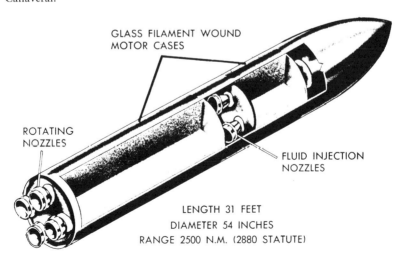

GLASS FILAMENT WOUND
MOTOR CASES

ROTATING
NOZZLES

FLUID INJECTION
NOZZLES

LENGTH 31 FEET
DIAMETER 54 INCHES
RANGE 2500 N.M. (2880 STATUTE)

Cutaway drawing of the two-stage Polaris A-3 SLBM.

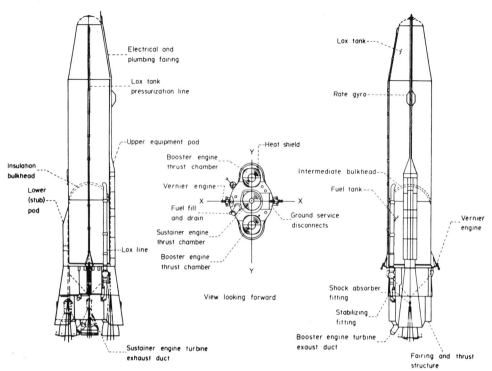

Layout drawing of the Convair SM-65 Atlas-D ICBM without its nose cone,
showing the location of the various components.

Looking up the working end of the Atlas three-engine MA-3 propulsion system,
showing the two 150,000-pound outer booster engines and the single
60,000-pound center sustainer engine, which keep on thrusting after the boosters
were jettisoned.

The first successful flight of Atlas 12-A from Cape Canaveral on December 17, 1957. The Atlas-A used only the two outboard booster engines for propulsion because the 60,000-pound center sustainer engine wasn't yet ready. The A-Series allowed verification of aerodynamics, airframe integrity, guidance system suitability, and ground support equipment.

3 ┌ 10
METERS ┤ FEET
0 ┴

1942
A.4

1948
MX-774

1948
3-ENGINE
ATLAS PROPOSAL

1948
5-ENGINE
ATLAS PROPOSAL

1951
ATLAS PROPOSALS
GLIDER (l) & BALLISTIC (r)

1953
5-ENGINE
ATLAS PROPOSAL

Series of six sequence photos showing the launch of an Atlas-A from Cape Canaveral.

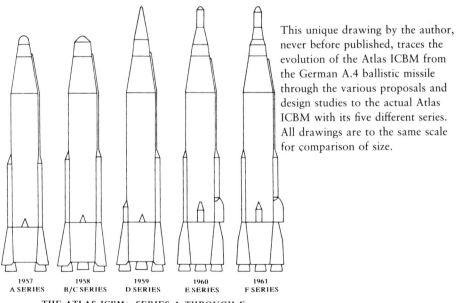

This unique drawing by the author, never before published, traces the evolution of the Atlas ICBM from the German A.4 ballistic missile through the various proposals and design studies to the actual Atlas ICBM with its five different series. All drawings are to the same scale for comparison of size.

| 1957 | 1958 | 1959 | 1960 | 1961 |
| A SERIES | B/C SERIES | D SERIES | E SERIES | F SERIES |

THE ATLAS ICBMs, SERIES A THROUGH F

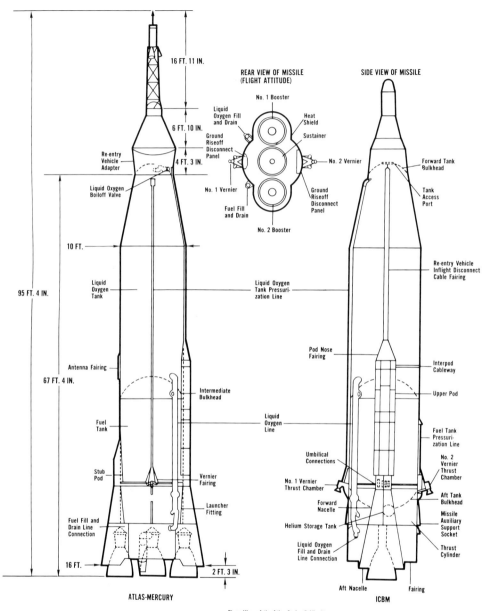

**REAR VIEW OF MISSILE
(FLIGHT ATTITUDE)**

No. 1 Booster

Liquid Oxygen Fill and Drain

Ground Riseoff Disconnect Panel

Heat Shield

Sustainer

No. 2 Vernier

No. 1 Vernier

Ground Riseoff Disconnect Panel

Fuel Fill and Drain

No. 2 Booster

**SIDE VIEW OF MISSILE**

Forward Tank Bulkhead

Tank Access Port

Re-entry Vehicle Inflight Disconnect Cable Fairing

Interpod Cableway

Upper Pod

Fuel Tank Pressurization Line

No. 2 Vernier Thrust Chamber

Aft Tank Bulkhead

Missile Auxiliary Support Socket

Thrust Cylinder

Aft Nacelle

Fairing

Pod Nose Fairing

Umbilical Connections

No. 1 Vernier Thrust Chamber

Forward Nacelle

Helium Storage Tank

Liquid Oxygen Fill and Drain Line Connection

Liquid Oxygen Tank Pressurization Line

Liquid Oxygen Line

**ICBM**

16 FT. 11 IN.

6 FT. 10 IN.

4 FT. 3 IN.

Re-entry Vehicle Adapter

Liquid Oxygen Boiloff Valve

10 FT.

Liquid Oxygen Tank

Antenna Fairing

67 FT. 4 IN.

95 FT. 4 IN.

Fuel Tank

Stub Pod

Fuel Fill and Drain Line Connection

16 FT.

Intermediate Bulkhead

Vernier Fairing

Launcher Fitting

2 FT. 3 IN.

**ATLAS-MERCURY**

Three-View of the Atlas Series D Missile

Drawing showing the general configuration of the Atlas-D ICBM with a reentry nose cone *(right)* and the Atlas-D configuration used to launch the NASA Project Mercury manned capsules into orbit in 1962 *(left)*.

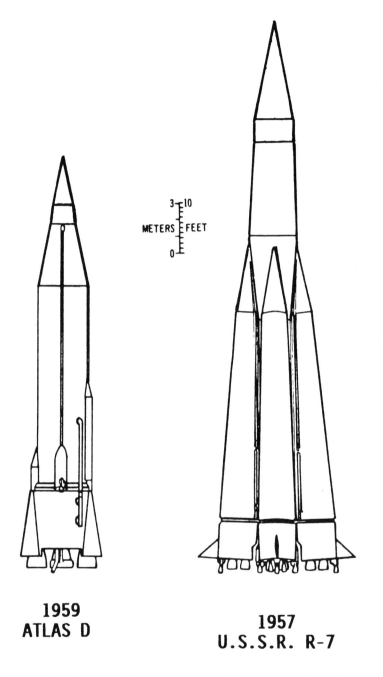

3 ⊢10
METERS ⊢FEET

0 ⊢

**1959
ATLAS D**

**1957
U.S.S.R. R-7**

Size comparison between the USAF Atlas D (Convair Model 7) and the USSR
R-7 ICBM.

The launch of an operational USAF/Martin Titan I ICBM from Cape Canaveral on October 7, 1960: The missile used LOX/RP-1 for both stages.

The first launch of the USAF/Martin Titan II ICBM from Cape Canaveral on March 16, 1962. The large GE ablative nose cone is seen. Note the nearly transparent exhaust flames from engines burning storable liquid propellants. This vehicle was identical to the 54 Titan II missiles installed in operational silos.

A sequence of four photos showing the hot launch of a Minuteman I from an underground silo. The smoke ring seen in the left photo is typical of a silo-launched Minuteman.

*Opposite:* The first launch of the USAF/Boeing Minuteman I ICBM from Cape Canaveral on February 1, 1961. All three stages used solid propellants.

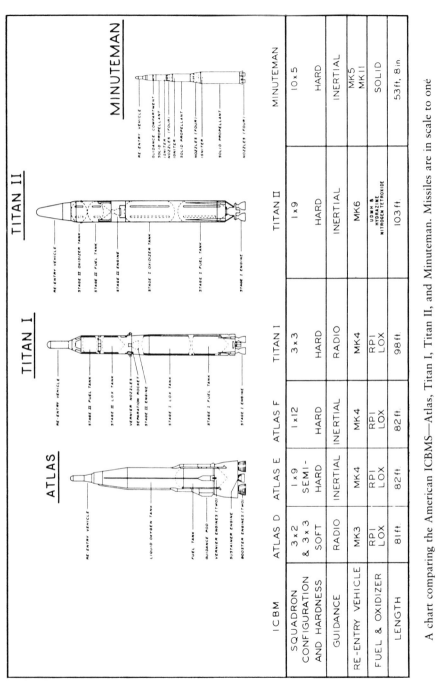

ATLAS

TITAN I

TITAN II

MINUTEMAN

| ICBM | ATLAS D | ATLAS E | ATLAS F | TITAN I | TITAN II | MINUTEMAN |
|---|---|---|---|---|---|---|
| SQUADRON CONFIGURATION | 3 x 2 & 3 x 3 | 1 x 9 | 1 x 12 | 3 x 3 | 1 x 9 | 10 x 5 |
| AND HARDNESS | SOFT | SEMI-HARD | HARD | HARD | HARD | HARD |
| GUIDANCE | RADIO | INERTIAL | INERTIAL | RADIO | INERTIAL | INERTIAL |
| RE-ENTRY VEHICLE | MK3 | MK4 | MK4 | MK4 | MK6 | MK5 MK11 |
| FUEL & OXIDIZER | RP1 LOX | RP1 LOX | RP1 LOX | RP1 LOX | UDMH & HYDRAZINE NITROGEN TETROXIDE | SOLID |
| LENGTH | 81 ft | 82 ft | 82 ft | 98 ft | 103 ft | 53 ft, 8 in |

A chart comparing the American ICBMS—Atlas, Titan I, Titan II, and Minuteman. Missiles are in scale to one another to provide comparison of size.

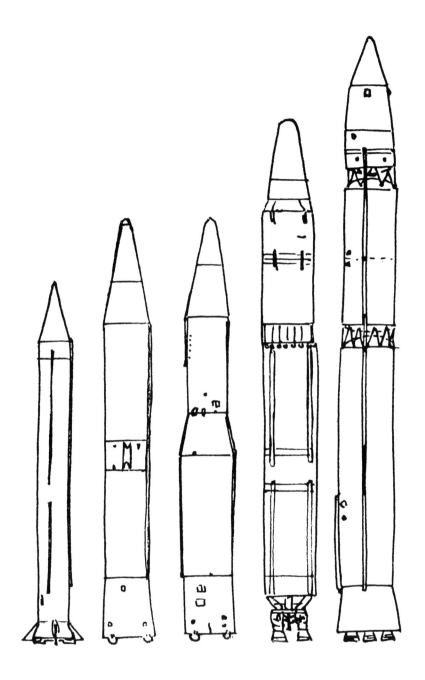

A drawing of ICBMs to the same scale for purposes of comparison made free hand by the dean of American students of the Soviet space program, the late Dr. Charles S. Sheldon of the Library of Congress. *Left to right:* SS-4 Sandal, SS-5 Skean, SS-8 Sasin, USAF/Martin Titan II, and SS-10 Scrag.

The Rolls Royce RZ.2 liquid-propellant rocket engine licensed from Rocketdyne and used in the British Blue Streak IRBM. The two rocket chambers, each capable of producing 137,000 pounds of thrust using LOX and RP-1, were modifications of the Rocketdyne engines that powered the Thor and Jupiter IRBMs. Each chamber had its own turbopump.

*Opposite:* The launch of the British Blue Streak IRBM from Woomera, Australia in the late 1950s. The program was canceled by the British government, and Blue Streak was unsuccessfully promoted as the first stage of an abortive European satellite launch vehicle, the Europa.

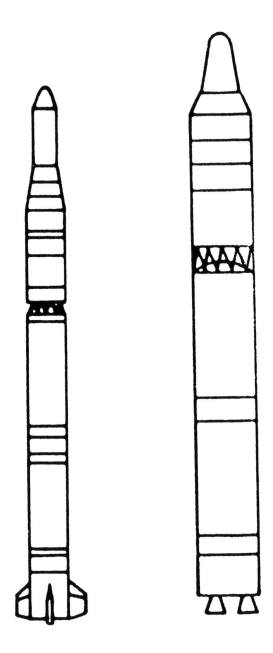

Drawings of the ICBMs built by the People's Republic of China as shown in a Chinese brochure promoting the use of their rockets as space launch vehicles. Show to the same relative scale are the DL-4 on the left and the DL-5 on the right. Both missiles have been named East Wind. Both use storable liquid propellants.

# Filling the Gaps

One of the problems involved in trying to tell a consistent story about the U.S.'s ICBM development is that the Air Force philosophy of concurrency meant that a lot of different things were going on simultaneously. The best that can be done is to take hold of a given thread and try to follow it through, keeping in mind that other threads exist alongside and that things happened there, too.

Gen. Bernard Schriever's concept of concurrency not only meant the very risky simultaneous development of entire systems instead of a step-by-step approach, it also meant a reduction of risk and insurance of success by parallel or redundant developments. This was a well-learned lesson from the successful Manhattan District in which engineers tried five different ways of extracting U-235 from U-238 in the hope that one would turn out to be workable; all of them turned out to work, thus allowing a choice of the most efficient and productive method. In the Western Development Division, Schriever and his team embraced the development of redundant systems.

For example, General Electric and Burroughs Corporation were put to work developing the radio-inertial guidance system. This was considered to be the best bet for early availability because a gyro inertial platform in the missile would be updated continuously by radio command from the ground, where accurate tracking of the missile in flight was possible. However, radio-inertial guidance meant that ICBMs could not be salvo-launched; the number launched was limited by the availability of ground tracking and command stations. Radio-inertial guidance might also be susceptible to interference (electronic warfare). Therefore, American Bosch Arma Corporation and the AC Spark Plug Division of GM, both working in conjunction with Dr. Draper's guidance laboratory at MIT, were contracted to develop a parallel, self-contained all-inertial guidance system. If the all-inertial system proved out, it could be incorporated into later models of the Atlas.

The same dual or redundant approach was used with the reentry body in which the warhead rode. As mentioned earlier, two solutions to the reentry heating problem were considered. The first was to use a quantity of metal such as copper to absorb the heat; if enough mass is used in such a heat sink approach, it stores the heat, allowing an insulated interior to remain relatively cool. The second was to get rid of the heat by allowing some of the external surface of the body to burn or ablate away, carrying the heat from the body by dissipation.

In 1954 WDD felt that more was known about the heat sink principle, so this became the basis for the first generation reentry bodies typified by the General Electric Mark 2. This was a blunt sphere-cone shape about 64 inches in diameter containing more than a thousand pounds of copper as a heat sink material. The Mark 2 weighed about 3,000 pounds and was scheduled for the first Atlas missiles.

The problem with the Mark 2 was that it lost a lot of speed high in the atmosphere and came in relatively slowly, which meant a longer period during which it could be detected and possibly intercepted by an anti-ballistic-missile missile. (Some advanced planning was being done even in 1954 to scope out the technical problems of actually intercepting an ICBM nose cone in flight; in the 1950s it was a difficult and expensive task, but thirty years later, under the Strategic Defense Initiative, it was neither difficult nor expensive.) An ablative reentry body also was under development under the redundancy philosophy. Dr. Arthur Kantrowitz at AVCO developed the Avcoite ablative material, while Dr. Leo Steg at GE's Missile and Space Vehicle Division developed and tested nearly a hundred materials. The GE RVX-2 ablative reentry body weighed about 2,200 pounds, making it lighter than the Mark 2. Again, both redundant development programs paid off.

Getting a reentry body successfully through the aerodynamic heating was only one of the problems that had to be solved. The Mark 2 had a higher acceleration, which meant a more robust warhead; this was ameliorated by the RVX-2 and the second generation Mark 3 body. Ensuring that both the heat sink material and the ablative material retained integrity during reentry was yet another because asymmetrical melting or burning that changed the external shape would have caused aerodynamic lift to deflect the nose cone from its intended target point. The warhead inside must be armed at some point in the flight when it won't fall back in friendly territory, then fused and set off so that the thermonuclear charge achieves the desired blast effect, whether this be in the air for air-burst shots or underground for demolishing enemy missile silos and command centers.

WDD wanted a backup for the Rocketdyne rocket engines, so it contracted with Aerojet General Corporation for a parallel engine development program.

The "basing" of an ICBM—i.e., how it would be deployed in the field—was also considered. Underground silos were obviously the best place to store ICBMs to protect them from the weather as well as from possible preemptive attacks. But no one knew whether a large missile could be launched out of a silo and withstand the hell-fire environment of the rocket engines igniting "in the hole" or whether it would have to be raised aboveground first. Therefore, redundancy dictated that the first facilities be "soft" aboveground launch sheds from which the Atlas could be raised to the vertical, loaded with propellants, and launched. Next could come the underground silo with a huge elevator capable of lifting the missile vertically out of the silo so it could be loaded and fired. Finally, once some data were in hand from testing, the "fire-in-the-hole" launch from a silo could be considered. It didn't look like the fragile Atlas would withstand an underground silo launch anyway.

In May 1955, with the Atlas configuration firm, it became apparent to General Schriever and the WDD team that for about 5 percent additional expenditure, it would be possible to build and deploy a second ICBM, again as a backup in case something went wrong with the Atlas. This second ICBM was the Titan, and a contract was let with the Glenn L. Martin Company to design and build it.

Titan was a different approach and used some of the advanced features "forbidden" to the Atlas because Titan could have a longer lead time and thus greater sophistication. Titan used a self-supporting semimonocoque airliner-type airframe with a chemically milled skin shaped by formers and stringers. It was also a true two-stage missile with an upper stage that would be started in flight when the lower stage had exhausted its propellants and was dropped. Because of the "package concept" of the concurrency philosophy, the rocket engines, guidance systems, and reentry bodies could be used on either the Atlas or the Titan. However, Titan never used anything but the two-chamber 350,000-pound-thrust Aerojet first-stage engines and an 80,000-pound upper-stage engine. And Titan was designed to be deployed vertically in a silo, lifted to the surface for loading, and then launched from the surface.

The Martin Company built a totally new factory in the foothills of the Front Range of the Rockies southwest of Denver. Several static test stands were also constructed in the hills, all of them capable of testing the entire two-stage Titan, the second stage being mounted alongside the first stage and fired in sequence. Many White Sands rocket engineers went up to Denver to work for Martin, myself included. Lowell N. Randall of Dr. Goddard's crew, formerly with the White Sands Propulsion Branch in charge of the Redstone engine testing there, took over as head man on the Titan test stands.

It became apparent by October 1955 that an intimate linkage existed between the Air Force military satellite program—reconnaissance and surveillance satellites, communications satellites, and weather satellites—and the only large rocket boosters being developed in the United States. WDD suddenly was assigned the entire satellite development of the Air Force. Then, in mid-December

1955, Schriever's successful little technology management "shop" in Inglewood, California, was charged by the Air Force with the total responsibility for an initial operational capability (IOC) of an ICBM at the earliest opportunity.

Again, Trevor Gardner came into the picture from the Department of the Air Force in the Pentagon. The Air Research and Development Command (ARDC) in Baltimore was looking for a replacement for the Martin B-61 Matador (also later called the TM-61), a 1940s-vintage subsonic tactical cruise missile under the aegis of the Tactical Air Command (TAC). ARDC was about to invite studies for a so-called TBM (tactical ballistic missile) with a range of 1,000 miles to replace the Matador. Gardner had a prophetic idea: A medium-range ballistic missile was just what the British needed as their intercontinental ballistic missile. Certainly Britain would be within range of the Soviet tactical missiles exemplified by the Shyster and the improved Sandal. So he set out to see if the British could build their own and if the United States could help them, and he set up an investigative committee under the Aircraft Industries Association (AIA). One of the committee members was Lt. Col. George R. Vanden Heuvel who was to direct the ARDC's TBM studies; another was Elmer Wheaton, chief missiles engineer at Douglas Aircraft Company, who had headed up the successful Nike SAM program.

Wheaton knew that one tool was absolutely necessary for the quick development of ballistic missile systems: an electronic computer. This was in the days when computers were big mainframes that used tens of thousands of vacuum tubes. In the fall of 1954, after searching all over England, Wheaton found only one suitable computer there. It belonged to a delicatessen chain and was used for keeping inventory. The company rented out time on it when it wasn't being used to keep track of kosher pickles.

Col. Vanden Heuvel summed up the committee's findings concerning Britain's ability to build its own ballistic missile: "They would be three years behind us with our help, five years behind without it."

The United Kingdom simply didn't have the resources.

But the British government expressed an interest in either buying an American medium-range ballistic missile or permitting the Americans to base those missiles in the British Isles.

Schriever found out about this when he invited Douglas Aircraft to bid on building the Titan. Douglas said it was concentrating on the thousand-mile TBM wanted by ARDC. Schriever met with Gen. Thomas S. Power, the ARDC commander, and asked that the TBM program be transferred to WDD, where it could enjoy the same high priority as the ICBM program. Vanden Heuvel, who was at the meeting, didn't like the idea because he thought it would deal a death blow to the TBM, which would be overshadowed by the ICBM. Schriever assured him it would not and offered to take the TBM only if Vanden Heuvel went with the package.

Why Schriever moved when he did was revealed a few weeks later. The National Security Council (NSC), acting on recent intelligence on Soviet planned deployment of their Shysters in eastern Europe, issued a request to the Air Force for the best approach to achieving a 1,500-mile Intermediate Range Ballistic Missile (IRBM). NSC requests are not made lightly. Schriever and WDD were ready and waiting. Said WDD's commander, "We in this business should be able to outguess people outside the business."

An outstanding Navy rocket expert on loan to WDD, Comdr. Robert Truax, was put in charge of the IRBM program by Schriever. Truax was assisted by Dr. Adolph K. Thiel (no relation to Walter Thiel, the A.4 engine expert who was killed during the first RAF raid on Peenemünde), a Paperclipper from Germany, who was with Ramo-Wooldridge. Together they "tinkered up" an IRBM, using as many ICBM systems as possible.

Because the IRBM would have to be transported overseas, the cargo hold dimensions of the Air Force C-124 transport became the determining factor, just as the A.4 had been sized by the dimensions of the German railway system.

The result was a proposed ballistic missile 8 feet in diameter and 65 feet long with a range of 1,750 miles. It would use the Atlas Mark 2 reentry nose cone, a single 150,000-pound combustion chamber developed for the Atlas booster stage, and an all-inertial jam-proof guidance system developed by the AC Spark Plug Division of General Motors with the GE/Burroughs radio-inertial guidance system as a redundant backup J.I.C. (Just In Case).

If the ICBMs were named Atlas and Titan after mythological deities, then the IRBM was obviously Thor, the Norse god of war.

Did anyone really want it?

Schriever did. He signed off on it and took it to General Powers at ARDC, who took it to the Air Staff in the Pentagon and thence to the new Secretary of the Air Force, Donald A. Quarles.

On September 24, 1955, President Eisenhower suffered a severe heart attack in Colorado. That was as nothing compared with what went on when the Army and the Navy learned about the Air Force Thor at about the same time.

# Jupiter and Polaris

In late 1955 trouble was brewing in Washington. Interservice rivalries are not unusual, but this was the first time a real controversy had arisen because of ballistic missiles.

The Army had Dr. von Braun and the German Paperclippers at Huntsville's Redstone Arsenal under the command of Maj. Gen. John B. Medaris. The Redstone tactical ballistic missile, the American V-2, was flying at Cape Canaveral and was in production under contract with the Chrysler Corporation.

The Navy had maintained a quiet interest in ballistic missiles from the start. Naval officers were interested in the German work at Peenemünde in 1942 where 21-centimeter solid-propellant rockets had been launched from the deck of a submerged submarine, the U511, which had been under the command of Dr. Ernst Steinhoff's brother. The Peenemünde "Project Test Stand XII" was a plan to tow V-2 rockets in sealed, submerged containers close to enemy coasts, in a favorable position to launch from the sea.

As mentioned earlier, a V-2 was launched from the deck of the aircraft carrier U.S.S. *Midway* on September 6, 1947. Although Operation Sandy was "successful," naval officers were cautious about proceeding with any project involving the launch of liquid-propellant ballistic missiles from seagoing vessels. Why? Because of the results of a rarely discussed experiment known as Operation Pushover. North of the Navy Launch Area at White Sands Proving Ground lay a twisted pile of scrap metal that had once been a simulated navy aircraft carrier deck. Before the Navy allowed Operation Sandy to take place, Operation Pushover had been conducted. A fully fueled V-2 rocket had been placed on this simulated carrier deck and the motor ignited to the pre-stage or low-thrust level. Then two legs of the firing stand had been blown away, allowing the fueled V-2 to fall over on the simulated deck. The objective was to see what would happen to an aircraft carrier if a V-2 failed at takeoff.

I understand that it was a spectacular "event." The wreckage of Operation Pushover may have been cleaned up and sold off as scrap since I last saw it over three decades ago, but the event must indeed have been spectacular because the damage to the simulated carrier deck was severe. It obviously caused naval officers to rethink any grandiose plans they might have been formulating for shipboard launchings of large liquid-propellant ballistic missiles.

Be that as it may, the Navy had developed the Martin Viking rocket, an American replacement for the dwindling supply of captured V-2s. Much of the research work carried on by the 12 Viking rockets launched by the Glenn L. Martin Company for the Navy between 1949 and 1955 was concerned with measurements of the ionosphere 50 and more miles above the surface of the earth, where radio waves are deflected back to the ground, making long distance radio communications possible. The Navy has always had a consuming interest in how electromagnetic signals (radio) propagate through the earth's upper atmosphere because, prior to having communications satellites, the Navy required reliable high-frequency radio communication with its ships at sea. Viking rocket Number 4 had been launched from the aft deck of the U.S.S. *Norton Sound* off Christmas Island in the Pacific on May 11, 1950.

In essence, the Navy had maintained a quiet interest in ship-launched ballistic missiles but apparently was waiting for rocket technology to develop a less hazardous vehicle. Thus, the Navy had a Special Projects Office in being for just such a contingency.

Furthermore, yet another committee had been formed by President Eisenhower in 1955. Chaired by Dr. James R. Killian of MIT, who was later to become Eisenhower's first presidential science advisor, the Killian Committee was charged with evaluating the true posture of the Soviet military establishment. The report it gave to Eisenhower in late 1955 was sobering. The Soviets were developing the 1,000-mile Sandal, an improved version of the 600-mile Shyster tactical ballistic missile. Thus, the USSR could bring all of Europe and the United Kingdom under the direct threat of nuclear black-mail from Shysters based within the Soviet Union. NATO and the free-world structure of alliances would be jeopardized. Thus, an American IRBM based in England was no longer merely an attrac-tive proposition but was becoming a necessity for national and NATO security.

When Schriever's proposal to develop the Thor IRBM within the national priority status of WDD's ICBM program hit the Joint Chiefs of Staff, both the Army and the Navy raised a fuss. The result was that the Joint Chiefs (with the Army member dissenting) rec-ommended to Secretary of Defense Charles E. Wilson that the IRBM program be divided, with the land-based version being the Air Force's responsibility while the seagoing version would be the Navy's.

With his Joint Chiefs of Staff in disagreement and turmoil, Secre-tary Wilson took his usual course of action by issuing decisive orders. Having come to the position of Secretary of Defense from the presidency of General Motors Corporation, "Engine Charlie" Wil-son was known, feared, cursed, but always respected as a tough boss who made tough decisions. In this case, Wilson issued a directive to the secretaries of the three armed services on November 8, 1955. In retrospect, Wilson's decision appears to have been designed to buy a little time, cool off the debate, introduce some sort of rational-ity into the situation, and get people working instead of squabbling.

Wilson told the Air Force to proceed with IRBM Number One, the Thor, while the Army was to develop the liquid-propellant IRBM Number Two, called the Jupiter. The Army and Navy were jointly to develop a ship-launched version of the Jupiter.

Gen. Bennie Schriever was determined to get the Thor opera-tional first. By the end of November 1955 he had assigned Thor to Col. Charles H. Terhune, Jr., a mechanical engineering graduate of Purdue and Cal Tech. He told Terhune to prepare a preproposal briefing for potential prime contractors—airframe, propulsion, guidance, reentry vehicle, ground support equipment, assembly, and testing—and do it "within a few days."

Terhune followed orders and came through. The contract to develop the Thor IRBM, WS-315A, was awarded to Douglas Aircraft Company on December 27, 1955. Douglas had built the Nike SAM system and had turned down the Titan ICBM contract to go for the IRBM. They got it. Dr. Maxwell G. Hunter was assigned as chief engineer with instructions to build and fly ASAP. Hunter had about a year to complete all the groundwork. The schedule left no margin for mistakes.

Hunter set about the work with a small cadre of engineers and an impossible schedule. He planned to build the first test missile on production tooling while simultaneously developing all the ground support equipment. Thor was given a numerical designation as a bomber, B-75, later changed to SM-75. Douglas gave it the model number DM-18. (The USSR is not alone when it comes to strange and nonsequenced designations for ballistic missiles.) But Hunter had the luxury, if one can call it that, of having the preliminary design completed already for a missile 8 feet in diameter and about 64 feet long, using the Rocketdyne MB-1 rocket engine with 150,000 pounds of thrust. The AC Spark Plug all-inertial guidance system was specified, with the Bell Labs radio-inertial system as an alternate. The GE Mark 2 heat sink reentry body was to be carried. All Hunter and Douglas had to do was build it. But it was still a very high risk project, one that probably could not be attempted thirty years later because of excessive caution and a growing penchant of engineers, military men, and politicians to make no mistake whatsoever and choose the path of least risk.

But Medaris and von Braun had not been idle in Huntsville. Always the visionary as well as the practical engineer, von Braun had initiated studies for a Redstone missile follow-on that would be an IRBM capable of carrying a thermonuclear warhead to a range of 1,500 miles. This vehicle, using the available Rocketdyne 150,000-pound engine, would have been 95 inches in diameter and 65 feet long. A range of 1,500 miles was still considered to be "tactical" and within the roles and missions of the Army. However, a 1,500-mile range was beginning to encroach on Air Force bombing turf.

When the Navy came into the Jupiter partnership in December 1955, some changes had to be made in the Army's proposed IRBM. The Navy was concerned about the length of the vehicle because of the difficulties involved in handling and launching such a monster at sea. The Navy wanted a shorter, more manageable missile. Naval officers were a bit skittish about the whole thing. In fact, the Navy didn't really like the idea of a liquid-propellant ballistic missile at all. The Operation Pushover results haunted naval officers. The Army didn't care if something happened and the missile blew up on the launch pad; the launch crew could be protected, and another clearing or level patch of ground could be found to erect and launch another missile. As one Navy officer pointed out, "The Army has never had to worry about having a battlefield sink." The Navy went along with the liquid-propellant Jupiter because it was a foot in the door. Other technology was coming along, especially in the area of solid-propellant rockets, and the Navy didn't want to be left out of the ballistic missile activity.

The result of the Army-Navy joint effort on IRBM-2 came out in February 1956 as a Jupiter configuration 105 inches in diameter and 58 feet long with a range of 1,500 miles. It used liquid oxygen and RP-1 hydrocarbon fuel.

The Army-Navy Jupiter team had an advantage over the Air Force Thor team. The Army had the Redstone missile, which could be used as a flying test bed for various Jupiter systems and, with minor modifications, for testing the Jupiter reentry nose shapes and materials. In order to take advantage of the high national priority assigned to the IRBM projects, the Redstone test missiles were called Jupiter-A (largely unmodified Redstones for testing guidance systems) and Jupiter-C (stretched Redstones carrying clustered solid-propellant upper stages capable of launching nose cone models to very high velocities and eventually putting satellites into orbit when permission was finally granted to do this).

But the Navy's Special Projects Office under Rear Admiral William "Red" Raborn wanted a real and a safe Fleet Ballistic Missile

(FBM) that wasn't a hybridized bastard, one that was designed with the Navy's unique requirements in mind. Raborn wanted to put the FBM in a submarine, where it would remain undetected until it could be launched from under water. The idea of putting liquid oxygen and RP-1 inside a submarine made naval officers nervous. Furthermore, a submarine capable of carrying the liquid-propellant Jupiter missile would have to be huge. Therefore, for the meantime, SP concentrated on putting the Jupiter on surface ships.

Launching a 1,500-mile ballistic missile from the moving and heaving deck of a surface warship was fraught with problems. The ship's motion would make it difficult to stabilize the missile during liftoff and to determine the azimuth. Determining the ship's exact position at the moment of missile launch was critical if the missile was to hit its intended target. Special electrical systems would be required. And means for producing liquid oxygen would have to be built into the ship.

Therefore, although the Navy had been told to cooperate with the Army in developing the liquid-propellant Jupiter, Raborn and the SP office began to investigate the possibility of using solid propellants instead.

The Navy had done a lot of research and development on large solid rocket motors using what is termed composite propellant—ammonium or potassium perchlorate as an oxidizer suspended in a polyurethane plastic binder that also served as a fuel, plus finely ground particles of aluminum along with other chemicals to act as burning rate stabilizers. The Army had built some large 31-inch diameter solid-propellant rocket motors in the Hermes B program and for the solid-propellant Sergeant missile developed by JPL. The Navy had monitored this work and done some large solid motor work on its own under Project Bumblebee, which dated back to 1945. Thus, the SP had its contractors draw up proposals for a "solid fuel Jupiter" consisting of a cluster of seven solid motors with a central core motor that would serve as a second stage. The proposed IOC was 1963. It was a long shot on the Navy's part because it didn't seem possible to Raborn's solid-propellant expert, Capt. Levering "Rosy" Smith who'd come to SP directly from commanding the

Navy's contingent at White Sands, that a suitable solid FBM could be developed to loft the thermonuclear warheads that were available at that time.

But Dr. Edward Teller was gently critical of Raborn's conservative thinking about warhead weights. By 1963, Teller predicted, a warhead much lighter than that proposed for Jupiter would be available. Raborn sent his SP officers to check this out but could get no agreement from the warhead experts. But he did get numbers that encouraged him to try for a small solid-propellant submarine-launched missile called Polaris.

A submarine-launched ballistic missile with a range of 1,500 miles isn't in the same class as a 5,000-mile ICBM, unless one remembers that a submarine is a mobile launching base that can be anywhere under the surface of the 70 percent of the earth's surface covered by oceans. A submarine can lie undetected off the Eurasian land mass in such a position that most of the USSR is within the range of a 1,500-mile FBM. In essence, the submarine becomes a manned first stage of an ICBM. Furthermore, unlike an ICBM missile silo whose exact location is known to the enemy, the submarine can't be located before it launches its missiles. Solid-propellant missiles can be launched within a few minutes, unlike liquid-propellant missiles, which may require up to 20 minutes to load and launch. And with a 1,500-mile range, the flight time is less than 15 minutes, giving the enemy far less time to react. The FBM is therefore a special category of the ICBM class.

But what should the Navy do? Withdraw from the joint Jupiter program and go for Polaris alone? Continue in the Jupiter program in case the small solid-propellant Polaris and the lightweight warheads didn't work out? Both paths had their upside and downside elements. Debate went on within SP for months.

Finally, Admiral Raborn decided to drop the Jupiter and go with Polaris. The Navy asked the Army if it wanted to drop Jupiter and help develop Polaris; the Army said no because that would have put its Huntsville team out of a job. So the Chief of Naval Operations bought off on Polaris. So did the Secretary of the Navy. Defense

Secretary Wilson agreed because it was obvious that the Jupiter was going to be a difficult shipboard weapon system, that the Navy would go along with Jupiter only with great reluctance, and that the SP had indeed come up with a workable FBM approach. On December 8, 1956, Wilson divorced the Navy from the Army's Jupiter IRBM program and told Raborn to go ahead with Polaris.

# Baptism by Fire

No series of tests of any new gadget proceeds without failures. Engineers expect failure and plan as best they can for them because each failure is literally treated as a learning experience. The first task is to pinpoint the cause of the failure so that changes can be made to prevent it from happening the same way again. Once the gadget is working properly, engineers will make one improvement or change at a time in order to make the gadget perform better. Rarely does a device meet all its specifications with the first prototype; it must be fine-tuned by the engineers to get it to do what it's supposed to do.

The general public seems to realize this, but politicians and representatives of the news media either do not or prefer to use the inevitable failures inherent in a test program to further their own narrow goals. In the case of the news media, accidents, failures, and disasters are their stock in trade.

No one knows how many experimental television sets fail or how many automobile tests turn out badly. These devices are relatively small and can be tested in isolation or secrecy. It was even possible to flight-test the early ballistic missiles in isolation at Peenemünde, Blizna, or even the wide-open spaces of White Sands. (One does not count Kapustin Yar or the other Soviet flight-test ranges; in the Soviet Union's closed society nothing is revealed that does not benefit the state, and if you happen to see a failure, you'd better keep quiet about it.) But when ballistic missiles become larger than the

V-2, thousands of people become involved, and the coastal launch site is plainly visible from nearby towns and even interstate highways, a flight test attracts attention. Since the chances for failure are great in a rocket test program, the news media can benefit from the usual spectacle, which adds excitement to their news reports and livens up the boring lives of most readers and viewers.

Thus, in spite of military secrecy and the need to preserve a certain degree of security for defense purposes, the American ICBM program has always operated with a television camera staring over its shoulder. Part of this was due to the hoopla over the American earth satellite program, Vanguard, which was gearing up for its first launches in 1957 at the same time the IRBM and ICBM flight-test programs got started. The military ballistic missile flight-test programs never were as open as the civilian-manned space flight program of NASA became, but anyone who wanted to find out what was going on certainly could do so, and usually within minutes.

This news media attention probably bothers the test engineers more than it distresses the military security people. The engineers, expecting failures, just don't want to have members of the press joggling their elbows when they've got a difficult job to do on an impossible deadline. Most military security personnel are simply paranoid about releasing *any* information because the punishments for compromising classified material are quite severe; in such circumstances, it's easier and safer to say no and keep nosy news types away. Some writers and reporters, however, know these things, make a serious attempt to respect the problems of the engineers and security people, try to learn the language and appreciate the problems, and as a result become the primary news sources for technical and engineering progress. But there are very few writers and reporters like Martin Caidin, Walter Cronkite, and Walter Sullivan.

Thus, the high-priority crash programs of WDD, SP, and Redstone Arsenal came to the attention of the news media in 1957, when the first big rockets appeared, looming over the sands of Cape Canaveral. The general public found out about it later in the year, when the Soviets used the R-7 to loft Sputnik I into orbit.

In early 1957, during the heady, peaceful days that marked the lull in the Cold War because of the seemingly passive posture of the Eisenhower administration, Thor, Jupiter, and Atlas were getting close to their scheduled first flight tests. A great deal of launch activity had already taken place at the Air Force Long Range Missile Test Center (later called the Eastern Test Range) stretching from Cape Canaveral southeasterly along the Bahamas and out over the Atlantic Ocean to Ascension Island more than 5,000 miles away. So no one paid much attention to what was really going on at the Cape because rockets were considered strange, wonderful, and futuristic gadgets to liven up television shows such as *Tom Corbett, Space Cadet* or Wernher von Braun's huge and fantastic spaceships on *The Wonderful World of Disney.* The "little stuff" at the Cape wasn't as glamorous or exciting as what was on TV.

The Cape was busy even in early 1957. Few people outside the aerospace industry knew that the Army Ballistic Missile Agency (ABMA)—as the Redstone Arsenal group under General Medaris and Dr. von Braun was designated in 1956—had flown 37 Redstone-based missiles from Cape Canaveral in support of the Jupiter IRBM project. One of these, a Redstone-boosted multistaged Jupiter-C, had made the longest rocket flight in the free world on September 20, 1956, when it launched a Jupiter test nose cone to an altitude of 700 miles and a range of more than 3,000 miles downrange from the Cape. Or that the Air Force Research & Development Command and North American Aviation had launched the first Navaho rocket-boosted ramjet cruise missile from the Cape in September 1953. Nor were people generally aware of the establishment of an Air Force Western Test Range at Point Arguello near Lompoc, California, where ICBMs could be lofted toward Kwajelein in the mid-Pacific. Or the ongoing Navy missile test center at Point Mugu, California, a few miles to the southeast down the coast.

So attention was slowly drawn to the Cape during early 1957 because these were BIG rockets and, being the first experimental prototypes, they often blew up. When they did, the failure was loud, fiery, and spectacular. It was almost tailor-made for television. Thus, during the period from early 1957 through 1959, the Cape got a lot of media attention during the period when most of the failures were taking place.

This led directly to the general perception of rockets that grew in the minds of the opinion makers and persists to this day. It was succinctly set forth by Tom Wolfe in his book *The Right Stuff:* "*Our rockets always blow up and our boys always botch it.*"

This, of course, was unfair as hell. It's a nontechnologist's or even antitechnologist's view of an ordinary, everyday engineering procedure. As such, it became a very popular belief, not among the American people who are smart enough about technology to know better, but among those technical illiterates who try to mold American opinion and who have trouble dealing with anything more complicated in the way of machinery than a knife and fork. Almost any device can be substituted for the word "rocket" in that quote if attention is given only to the first few tests of the new gadget. Until World War II aviation was treated in the same manner, and any plane crash rated an immediate front-page headline. Today that level of attention is given only to accidents involving airliners the size of a Boeing 737 or bigger.

Although an attempt was made to keep those early test flights secret, it was patently impossible to hide the fact that all the hotels and motels in Cocoa Beach and Melbourne would suddenly be booked solid and all the rental cars would be taken as hundreds of additional military officers and civilian engineers flooded into the area to take part in a flight test and to watch. Nor was there any way to hide the increased amount of overtime being put in by engineers and technicians who lived in the area and worked at the Cape. Anyone who knew any of those people could make a very good guess which ballistic missile was about to be flown because the overtime was put in by Douglas, Chrysler, General Dynamics, or Martin employees, depending on the missile. The scuttlebutt in the grocery stores, laundromats, and local bars would quickly confirm observations about whose employees were putting in the overtime. People who knew the layout of the Cape could also determine which missile was about to go on the basis of which launch area was most brilliantly floodlit at night. The local stringers for the news media kept a careful eye on all this and had much better information than the Air Force, which was responsible for Cape security, was happy about.

Jupiter did a little better during flight testing than it did in the rough-and-tumble war between the armed services. Defense Secretary Wilson's memorandum of November 26, 1956, had effectively stripped the Army of its long-range ballistic missile program, limiting Army tactical ballistic missiles to a range of 200 miles. Thus, the responsibility for the management of the Jupiter program went to Gen. Bernard Schriever's new Ballistic Missile Division, as WDD was redesignated, although the development and technical direction remained with ABMA in Huntsville.

The first Jupiter IRBM was launched from the Cape on March 1, 1957, and flew to a range of 60 miles, making it a "partial success." Powered by the Rocketdyne S-3D engine, a modification of the Atlas booster engine and similar except in detail to the Thor's MB-1 engine, the Jupiter's first full success came on its third flight on May 31, 1957, when the big ablative nose cone traveled 1,600 miles downrange, making Jupiter the first successful American IRBM. ABMA delivered the first operational Jupiter to the Air Force in August 1958, and more than 60 Jupiters were eventually based in Italy and Turkey until the missile system was retired in 1963.

The Jupiter represents the last military ballistic missile developed by the originators of the modern ballistic missile, Dr. Wernher von Braun and his team from Peenemünde. On July 1, 1960, the ABMA team was transferred to NASA to form the cadre of the George C. Marshall Space Flight Center, designers of the Saturn space-launch vehicles. Some 28 years after Wernher von Braun had gone to work for the German army to develop military ballistic missiles because it was the only way that he could develop rockets at all, he was finally free to concentrate on what he'd wanted to do all the time: work on space-going rockets.

The first Thor IRBM was on the launch pad in January 1957, a little over 12 months from the day the contract was signed. Max Hunter and his Douglas team had worked hard, and they had Missile Number 101 ready to test. On January 25, 1957, almost exactly 13 months from the go-ahead, the countdown got to zero and the single-chamber 135,000-pound Rocketdyne MB-1 ignited. The mighty Thor began to rise slowly from the launch pad. Then the liquid oxygen start tank, a small container of LOX used during the engine start sequence and later eliminated from the design, ruptured in the engine bay. Thor 101 settled slowly and majestically back down, crumpling into the flame bucket, and became engulfed in a fireball of burning LOX and RP-1.

It took four more Thor flight tests before Hunter had what he considered a fully successful flight on September 20, 1957, with Missile Number 105. On October 24, 1957, Flight Number 8 with Missile 109 went the full 1,500-mile range. Thor achieved IOC with the flight of Missile 140, the twenty-sixth flight, on November 26, 1958. The all-inertial guidance system put Thor 140 right on target, and the improved Rocketdyne MB-3 Basic rocket engine had produced 150,000 pounds of thrust. In getting to operational capability, 15 of the 26 flights were classed as malfunctions or partial successes.

Now it was the Atlas's turn.

The development of the Atlas proceeded through specific steps with specific "series" of missiles. The Atlas Series A used a dummy nose cone and was powered only by the two Rocketdyne 135,000-pound booster engines supplied by a single turbopump because the 60,000-pound Rocketdyne middle or sustainer engine wasn't ready for the first flight tests. The Atlas Series B added the sustainer, bringing the thrust up to 360,000 pounds, while the Atlas Series C had the Mark 2 heat sink nose cone, improved guidance, and increased range. The Atlas Series D had reduced weight and increased range; it was flown with both the Mark 3 reentry body and the Avco ablative nose cone. The first operational missile was the Atlas Series E with the Rocketdyne MA-3 rocket engine system with separate turbopumps for all three chambers and the thrust increased to 389,-000 pounds. Atlas Series F incorporated several small changes from the Atlas Series E to permit it to be stored partially loaded with RP-1 in a hardened silo and raised vertically to ground level for final loading and launch.

But this is getting slightly ahead of the story.

Atlas first had to go through its ordeal by fire.

Like the Soviet R-7 and the American Thor, Atlas had its early problems.

Atlas 4-A was on the Cape Canaveral launch pad in late May 1957. The first test, conducted on June 3, 1957, was a static test, a flight readiness firing during which the missile was held down, the engine started, and all systems checked without committing the missile to flight. All went well. Atlas 4-A was launched on June 11, 1957. Its two booster engines and two 1,000-pound vernier or steering engines were ignited properly with pyrotechnic igniters, the launcher hold-downs were released, and the missile rose off the launch pad. However, one of the two booster engines malfunctioned and produced only partial thrust. The autopilot fought to overcome the unbalanced thrust but failed. Atlas 4-A pitched hard over and became unstable. It threatened to land where it might do damage. So the Air Force Flight Safety Officer punched the pickle switch and shut off the propellant flow, then activated the flight safety explosives and blew the bird in the air so that only pieces would come down.

It was a fiery end to the first Atlas.

# Out of the Fire

Although the Soviet Union might not have had a real ICBM operational capability with Korolev's R-7 in late 1957, the communist country suddenly became a superpower overnight because, on October 4, 1957, Korolev used an R-7 ICBM to place the first artificial satellite, Sputnik I, into orbit around the earth.

This shocked the American people because the USSR was perceived as being a backward country peopled by uneducated peasants who couldn't even get a tractor to run properly. Any American pilot who had fought the MiG-15 jet fighter over Korea or any American infantryman who had tried to stop the Soviet T-34 tanks on the ground could have corrected this misconception at once if anyone had listened to them and believed them. Or if anyone had listened to some of us in the guided missile business at the time who were writing about Soviet capabilities in rocketry.

In 1954 the United States had announced its intention to launch one or more unmanned earth satellites during the International Geophysical Year, 1957–1958. The Soviets responded in a "me-too" fashion that they would also do that. Only a few people realized the Soviets could; everyone else thought it was just another empty communist boast from a culture that has always been paranoid and has always wanted to be perceived as leading the "wave of the future."

Some of us knew the Soviets were working on an ICBM. We also knew that any ballistic missile that could deliver a warhead to a range of 5,000 miles could also place an unmanned satellite in orbit. In

April 1957 I wrote *Earth Satellites and the Race for Space Superiority*, which was published in paperback by Ace Books in September 1957. In this book, which had been cleared for security by the U.S. Army, I pointed out that the Soviets would probably launch a satellite weighing at least 84 pounds and that they would use their ICBM to launch it. I was off by 100 pounds on the light side but absolutely correct in reporting what everyone else in the American aerospace industry knew about the use of the Soviet ICBM as a launch vehicle.

On the night Sputnik I was launched, October 4, 1957, I was called by the Denver stringer for United Press, who had read my book. I was asked about the consequences. I told him what I had written in my cleared book: that it confirmed the fact that the Soviets had an ICBM, meaning that the United States from then on would be vulnerable to ballistic-missile attack just as Britain had been with the V-2 rockets. The following day I was curtly fired by the Glenn L. Martin Company, where I was working on advanced designs of the Titan ICBM, not because I had violated security but because I had spoken to the press without getting permission to do so from the Martin Company. That was the end of my professional employment career as a rocket engineer in the aerospace industry. The fact that Dr. Wernher von Braun echoed my statement several days later meant little to me; it would have been far more difficult to fire *him!*

Basically, this incident was an example of the utter panic that gripped official Washington as a result of the American reaction to Sputnik.

The United States wasn't far behind in the ICBM race, but it was behind. It didn't help that the second Atlas, Missile 6-A, had been launched on September 25, 1957, and suffered yet another malfunction in propulsion and flight control.

And few people stopped to think that it would take the USSR some time to deploy its R-7 on railcars positioned on sidings along the Trans-Siberian Railroad, as they intended to do. In fact, the R-7 was a terrible ICBM, albeit an excellent heavy-lift space launch vehicle which was still in production as late as 1988. It would have been very difficult for the Soviets to support an R-7 ICBM force deployed as they had planned. But the R-7 had one thing going for it: The Soviets had it as a working ICBM, however crude, that had flown successfully with a warhead to the full range of more than 5,000 miles while the United States had nothing yet that would fly at all to that range, much less to satellite velocities.

If the impacts on the American Vanguard earth satellite program, on the American educational system, and on American preparedness were grave, the consequences for the American ICBM program were truly severe. The pressures on General Schriever, the Air Force, and Convair to get a successful flight of the Atlas became enormous. It's to the credit of Schriever and his BMD team that they didn't cave in to the political pressures but maintained their planned program. Schriever knew exactly what was going on in the USSR ballistic missile program; so did the Washington politicians, but they reacted while BMD acted. In retrospect, the abuse heaped upon President Eisenhower and his administration was ill founded. And the "missile gap" that became an election icon in 1960 was nowhere near as bad as it was portrayed on the American political battlefield.

The violent maneuvers of Atlas 4-A and 6-A proved conclusively that the pressurized airframe would withstand forces far in excess of design specifications. The A-Series not only validated the airframe design and proved the booster engines in flight, it added information to the storehouse of design knowledge that was slowly incorporated into the Atlas, making it still one of the most successful space-launch vehicles ever developed and second only to the Thor in this regard. Remember that Thor had a series of spectacular and expensive failures to start with too.

Atlas 12-A was launched successfully on December 17, 1957, which happened to be the 54th anniversary of the Wright brothers' first manned, controlled powered flight at Kitty Hawk (but no one noticed). Both booster engines performed properly, and the bird flew to its programmed range of 600 miles.

Four successes and two more failures were chalked up in the A-Series flight tests that ended on June 3, 1958, with the flight of Atlas 16-A. Atlas 13-A and Atlas 11-A broke up in flight late in booster operation because of aerodynamic heating that shorted out electrical circuits leading to the vernier steering engines. The A-Series also solved problems of the coupling of the autopilot with the bending frequencies of the stainless-steel balloon; a simple electronic filter was added to the autopilot. The booster engine turbopump gearbox failed due to frothing of the lubricant in the oil reservoir at high altitudes, and the reservoir was subsequently pressurized to eliminate that problem. This is just the sort of finicky fiddling with a prototype gadget that consumes so much engineering time and effort and is so abysmally boring to others.

By June 1958 the Rocketdyne 60,000-pound sustainer engine was ready, making the basic MA-1 propulsion system complete. The three-engine Atlas could now be tested. It performed far better than expected. Although the flight of Atlas 3-B on July 19, 1958, was a failure because of engine problems, Atlas 4-B was launched on August 2, 1958, and performed flawlessly, traveling 2,349 nautical miles down the range. Little problems with the sustainer engine kept coming up because of difficulties the engineers encountered in making it meet specifications; the most troublesome problems were with the turbopumps, which eventually led to a complete redesign. Some of these engine problems were the same as those experienced by the Thor, which used a similar single-chamber engine. The turbopump and engine problems of both Atlas and Thor were essentially solved by September 1958, and during the following 15 months more than 85 flight tests saw no recurrence of engine problems.

Regardless of the accelerated concurrency philosophy of BMD's program management, competent engineering would have eliminated the little problems eventually. Under BMD, the engineering "fine-tuning" was accelerated. R&D went on without interrupting or delaying the flight test schedule. This might have resulted in more failures than if a slower, more conservative approach had been taken. Jupiter certainly had its share of problems, but von Braun's team wasn't working under the same concurrency philosophy but more of an accelerated Peenemünde approach; thus, when successes and failures are totaled, it appears that the Jupiter had fewer, but that was because it was running to a different beat.

Thor became operational with the launch of November 5, 1958, from the Cape and was the first ballistic missile to be launched from the new Vandenberg Air Force Base at Point Arguello on the west coast on December 16, 1958. The first overseas Thor squadron became operational in Great Britain on April 22, 1960.

As Thor progressed and its problems were solved, it was quickly pressed into service as a launch vehicle to test reentry body shapes and materials as well as to launch Air Force satellites. BMD had been given responsibility for all Air Force military space activities because it was also responsible for the big ballistic missiles that also could be used as space boosters. The first of these was the Thor Able Model DM-1812-1, which carried an upper stage consisting of a modified Vanguard second stage with an Aerojet-General AJ10-40 propulsion system. The first bird malfunctioned, but the second and third propelled test nose cones more than 5,000 miles downrange on July 9 and July 23, 1958. On August 17, 1958, a Thor Able I made an unsuccessful attempt to launch a payload into orbit around the moon. Since that time, nearly 200 Thor-derived space launch vehicles have been used to orbit satellites and launch deep space probes so that today, the McDonnell Douglas Delta launch vehicle, directly descended from the Thor, is one of the free world's most inexpensive and reliable expendable launch vehicles.

Atlas was pressed into service early as a space launcher. On December 18, 1958, a year and a day after the first successful Atlas 12-A flight, Atlas 10-B put itself into orbit with a radio transmitter provided by the U.S. Army Signal Corps that broadcast President Eisenhower's Christmas greeting back to the earth from space, a worldwide first.

This flight was so secret that only a handful of people knew that it was not an ordinary 5,000-mile test shot. Travis Maloy, the Atlas test conductor at the Cape, was in on the secret, but not Curt Johnston, the Launch Complex 11 test engineer who was running the show. Maloy and several others had to work at night to make clandestine changes in the autopilot and several other systems. Some equipment had to be removed from Missile 10-B to lighten it, and arrangements had to be made so that the removed equipment would *appear* to be aboard and working properly. They even had to put a new nose on 10-B without anyone knowing it, and this required such minor modifications as installing new tubing from the top of the LOX tank to a LOX pressure sensor, a job that required the best Convair tube bender at the Cape to be brought into the picture to fabricate by feel and experience a new length of bent tubing for which no drawing existed.

When the countdown progressed to the point where certain green lights had to flash on consoles in the blockhouse, another man hidden in the basement with a switch panel sent false signals up to rewired consoles above. Since the radio-inertial guidance system had been modified, the personnel at the ground station reported no output from the missile. "We'll go without it," was the command, and the Cape's range safety officer concurred because he was in on the secret—and had to be. The last glitch was a report at T minus one minute that the electrical drain on the missile battery was low (because of all the electronic gear that had been covertly removed), and the reply was, "We'll go with it high."

At 6:02 P.M. Atlas 10-B lifted its 244,000 pounds off the pad and began its long flight, marking the first of many space missions yet to come that would use the Atlas as a booster. Somewhere out over the Atlantic it nosed into a trajectory parallel with the earth's surface and pushed on to 17,300 miles per hour, orbital velocity. The pen on the plotting board hooked to the tracking radars that was computing where 10-B would land went right off the edge of the chart. "Where did it go? Where is it going to come down?" were the questions that bombarded Maloy. It took about 15 minutes to establish that 10-B wouldn't come down at all for a long time. It was then that Maloy told Johnston, "It's going around the world." But Johnston had guessed this a few days before and had said nothing. Still playing the game, however, he cracked, "In orbit?"

Atlas 10-B was visible as well as audible. It was at last an answer to the Soviet R-7 core that had gone into orbit with Sputniks 1 through 3. It circled the earth for 33 days and reentered the atmosphere over Midway Island in the Pacific on January 21, 1959. The 5,000-mile ICBM had traveled 12,500,000 miles.

# Out of the Ground

A basic IRBM or ICBM launch capability doesn't necessarily mean that the capability can or will be used. A ballistic missile on a surface launch pad is terribly vulnerable to the blast effects of an enemy ICBM's warhead detonating nearby. The amount of damage that can be inflicted by a thermonuclear warhead is related to many factors—weapon yield in equivalent kilotons of TNT, the burst point above or under the ground, the distance from the burst point, terrain features, and current weather conditions, among others.

Two possible defenses of a ballistic missile force exist against preemptive missile attack: (1) keep the missile in a very strong underground silo until the first wave of the enemy attack is over, and (2) launch before the enemy's warhead reaches the silo.

The latter means a reaction time of less than 30 minutes, which is about the length of time it takes for an ICBM warhead to travel 5,000 to 8,000 miles. IRBMs launched 1,500 to 2,000 miles away from target provide considerably less warning time and require even less reaction time. All the early first-generation ICBMs—R-7, Atlas, and Titan—utilized "cryogenic," or supercold, propellants such as liquid oxygen that would continually boil away; therefore, they had to be loaded with LOX only minutes before launching. This in turn meant that a highly effective ballistic missile radar detection screen had to be established to detect and track an incoming ballistic missile attack.

Since the United States had already deployed a chain of high-powered radar stations across the arctic barrens of North America stretching from Alaska to Greenland, the Distant Early Warning (DEW) Line, these radar stations had to be modified and upgraded in order to detect ICBMs, which are much smaller than Tupolev Tu-16 Badgers, Tu-20 Bears, and Myasishchev Mya-4 Bisons, the only long-range bombing aircraft with which the Soviets could have launched an airborne bombing attack against North American targets in the 1954–1960 time period. This upgraded ballistic missile warning chain was called the Ballistic Missile Early Warning System (BMEWS) and could provide the United States with as much as 20 minutes' advance warning of a Soviet preemptive ICBM strike. Later developments utilized orbiting satellites, put up with space launch versions of the Thor, Atlas, and Titan, that could detect the infrared radiation from a missile launch itself.

The first option—protect the ICBM—was achieved in two ways by both the United States and the USSR. The first was to emplace the ICBM in a "hardened" launch silo buried deeply in sandy soil so that it could withstand the enormous shock and pressure of a megaton-range thermonuclear warhead exploding nearby. The second was to emplace the ballistic missile in a submarine that could lie undetected beneath the surface of the sea, therefore protecting itself by stealth with the philosophy of: "If you can't find it, you can't hit it." Like tracer bullets, however, this works both ways; the United States and the USSR developed submarine-launched ballistic missiles.

But the problem of providing a launch silo hardened against thermonuclear attack depended on two factors: (1) the ability of structural engineers to build a launch silo strong enough, and (2) the ability of ICBM engineers to build a missile that could be launched out of such a silo. The first was relatively easy to do: just pour a lot of reinforced concrete. The second wasn't so easy.

The Atlas missiles were steel balloons, and as the first-generation ICBMs, they were not designed to be launched from a hole in the ground. Although the Atlas Series B was a fully operational ICBM capable of its design range of 5,500 nautical miles, it had to be launched from prepared aboveground facilities, and the only two places that had these were the Cape and the Western Test Range of Vandenberg Air Force Base at Point Arguello, California. On September 9, 1959, the Air Force declared Atlas to be a fully operational ICBM although only two missiles were erected in R&D-style gantries at Vandenberg. The first truly operational Atlas was the Series E, which was launched on October 11, 1960, from the Cape.

Atlas E was designed to be emplaced in a horizontal "soft coffin" and stored horizontally. In order to be launched, it had to be lifted to a vertical position and fueled. This increased its reaction time and left it vulnerable to a preemptive strike.

Atlas F was almost identical to the Atlas E except that it was stored vertically in a hardened concrete silo, raised vertically to the surface, loaded, and launched.

The Atlas test program was completed on December 5, 1962, with the launch of Atlas 21-F from the Cape. The Atlas E featured a completely new propulsion system, the Rocketdyne MA-3, with individual turbopumps feeding each combustion chamber except the two 1,000-pound pressure-fed vernier engines. The thrust of the Atlas E Series was 389,000 pounds, an increase from the 360,000 pounds of the Atlas B Series. The full inertial guidance system, now using solid-state transistor components instead of the vacuum tubes of the early Atlas B Series, had reduced the CEP from 30,300 feet in 1958 to 910 feet.

By 1962, 126 Atlas missiles were deployed at Warren Air Force Base (AFB), Cheyenne, Wyoming; Offutt AFB, Omaha, Nebraska; Fairchild AFB, Spokane, Washington; Forbes AFB, Topeka, Kansas; Schilling AFB, Salina, Kansas; Lincoln AFB, Lincoln, Nebraska; Altus AFB, Altus, Oklahoma; Dyess AFB, Abilene, Texas; Walker AFB, Roswell, New Mexico; and Plattsburgh AFB, Plattsburgh, New York. An Atlas ICBM launch capability was preserved at Vandenberg AFB near Lompoc, California.

Although Atlas went on to become one of the U.S.'s space launch vehicles, a task for which it was never designed, it's interesting to note that this successful test program didn't proceed without some of the classical mistakes of rocket testing. One that seems to run through all ballistic missile testing is the part of Murphy's Law that states, "If a part can be installed backward, sooner or later someone will install it that way." Atlas 16-E maintained the tradition. When it was launched on March 24, 1961, from the Cape, no one knew that a technician had reversed the wiring for the vernier engine ignition system and the vernier tank pressurization system. Atlas 16-E took off without its two verniers burning but with pressurization gas pouring through the nozzles instead. At Booster Engine Cutoff (BECO), the verniers came on with a bang but with insufficient thrust to jettison the booster engines.

Then there was the classic Flight of the Seven Miracles, which occurred after the flight test program was long completed. An Atlas launched a Surveyor moon-landing spacecraft for NASA. Everything went wrong that could go wrong without causing a complete abort. The verniers went hard over, putting the Atlas into a roll; miraculously, something happened just before BECO at which time they went hard over in the opposite direction, canceling the roll. Numerous other technical miracles occurred, including overheating of the batteries by more than 200 percent; the mission was saved because the battery manufacturer had decided to make that particular battery lot with a little more temperature tolerance than was required and the test engineers had selected the one battery from that lot that exhibited much better temperature tolerance than the rest.

However, getting an ICBM to launch out of a silo had to be deferred to the parallel Titan ICBM program.

Titan I was propelled by liquid oxygen and RP-1 in both stages. Again, Titan I was to be emplaced vertically in a hardened concrete silo, lifted vertically to the surface by a high-speed elevator, loaded with propellants, and launched. Because of its self-supporting monocoque airliner-type airframe, it was a far more robust ballistic missile than the Atlas.

The first Titan I flew from the Cape on February 6, 1959, with only the LOX/RP-1 lower stage operable. The two-chamber engine, the Aerojet-General LR87-1, produced 300,000 pounds of thrust. After several failures, the full two-stage Titan I with the upper stage powered by an Aerojet LR91-1 rated at 80,000 pounds of thrust flew under radio-command guidance to 2,200 miles from the Cape. Probably to confuse the Soviets as much as they were confusing us with missile designations, the Titan I ceased to be the B-68/SM-68 and became the LGM-25A when it became operational at Lowry AFB, Colorado, on April 18, 1962. Titan I carried a 4-megaton thermonuclear warhead, much more powerful than the one on the Atlas. The missile was housed in a concrete silo with the then exceptional overpressure rating of 300 pounds per square inch. Titan I had a 20-minute reaction time. Titan I was deployed in 6 SAC squadrons with nine missiles each. Lowry AFB had two squadrons with silos out on the Colorado prairies; single squadrons were based at Beale AFB, California; Mountain Home AFB, Idaho; Ellsworth AFB, South Dakota; and Larson AFB, Washington. Titan I stayed in service until 1966.

However, Titan I was used to test the feasibility of a "hot silo launch." On May 3, 1961, a Titan I was launched from Vandenberg AFB, California, out of a silo with exhaust gas deflection tunnels to carry away the rocket blast of the first stage when ignited "in the hole." The success of this technique paved the way for Titan II.

Early in 1958 Robert Demaret, chief designer of the Titan program, and others at the Martin Company proposed to BMD the development of Titan II, using an Aerojet-General rocket engine burning Aerozine 50 (a form of unsymmetrical dimethyl hydrazine) and nitrogen tetroxide ($N_2O_4$), a combination that is noncryogenic, can be stored in the missile tanks indefinitely, and ignites spontaneously upon contact with the other liquid. Titan II was 7 feet longer than Titan I, had a second stage that was the same diameter (10 feet) as the first stage, and weighed 330,000 pounds. The Aerojet-General LR87-5 two-chamber first-stage engine produced 432,000 pounds of thrust and the Aerojet-General LR91-5 second-stage engine produced 100,000 pounds of thrust. Carrying an 18-megaton thermonuclear warhead (the largest ever flown on an American ICBM) inside a larger GE Mark 6 ablative reentry body, Titan II had a 60-second reaction time and could be launched "hot" out of a reinforced concrete silo.

As the LGM-25C, the Titan II first flew in November 1961 and was deployed in 1963. Fifty-four Titan II ICBMs stood guard over the United States for 25 years in silos at Davis-Monthan AFB, Tucson, Arizona; Little Rock AFB, Arkansas; and McConnell AFB, Kansas, before they were removed starting in 1987. The Titan IIs were older than some of the missile crews manning the underground bunkers. The silos were filled in with dirt.

The Air Force decided not to waste the 54 Titan IIs, however, and contracted with the Martin Company to refurbish them for use as expendable space launch vehicles.

In the meantime, the Air Force was keeping a close watch on what the Navy's SP office was doing with Polaris and solid-propellant ballistic missiles. Liquid oxygen is very transient, and the nitrogen tetroxide used in the Titan II is highly toxic. Basically, the Atlas and the Titan were huge flying sewer pipes, to use the derogatory term applied to them by the solid-propellant missile advocates. A solid-propellant ICBM offered the advantages of simplicity, safety, economy, and rapid reaction time. It could be fired "hot" right out of its hole in the ground. It could truly be a push-button missile. But the Air Force was primarily concerned with the directive given to it in 1954 to attain an ICBM capability in the shortest possible time. The quickest way was via the path of liquid-propellant rockets. Nevertheless, General Schriever and WDD began to see in late spring 1956 that Atlas, Thor, and Titan were well started. WDD/BMD wanted to ensure that the American ICBM program kept up with both advancing technology and a potential enemy, the USSR, which seemed to be developing a stable of ballistic missiles at an amazing pace.

H. R. Lawrence and Barney Adelman of Ramo-Wooldridge Corporation, WDD/BMD's civilian technical consultants, had accumulated data on solid-propellant research, run computer studies, and generally kept abreast of developments. When the Navy SP opted for a solid-propellant submarine-launched ballistic missile in 1955, Schriever set up a special committee to study the problems. On this committee were Lawrence and Adelman but also Dr. Clark B. Millikan of Cal Tech and Dr. George Kistiakowski of Harvard.

In October 1956 this committee recommended the development of a multistage, solid-propellant ICBM.

The early symptoms of "manageriosclerosis" had just begun to set in at BMD, although it wasn't recognized at the time. More than 5,000 people were now working directly for BMD. A bureaucracy was forming. Schriever pulled Col. Edward N. Hall, head of the Thor flight test team, off that project and put him to work on a further study of the solid-propellant ICBM.

Hall was a man of action. He was now forced to work alone without even a secretary. He tried to resign. Schriever refused to accept his resignation. So he went to Col. C. H. "Hap" Norton, assistant commander for technical operations at BMD and told him:

> *I'm no man for studies. I'm not going to study this thing. I can sit down and study until hell freezes over, and I'll wind up with nothing. If you ask me why I want to do something, I'll give you the same reason as a refrigerator manufacturer who knows his business: He's made a lot of refrigerators. I know why because I've flown a lot of rockets. As far as I'm concerned, this is a weapon system, not a study. We can build this as a weapon system right now!*

Norton didn't tell him not to proceed, so Hall went to work. He created his own department in BMD, choosing the letter Q because no one had taken that yet. At first he didn't have any people at all. But he designed a solid-propellant ICBM system. Those who were at BMD during those years still tell the story with awe—the solitary colonel who frequently worked through the night, completely caught up in the fascination of what he was doing. He projected his thinking into the future: "We'll need a deterrent and we'll want it to be a threat twenty-four hours a day, seven days a week. It should have a life expectancy of at least fifteen years." With these concepts in mind, Hall tackled the ICBM system from a cost-effective standpoint, figuring that it would require far fewer people to run it, maintain it, and support it, far less land for basing its silos, and far less money to upgrade it as technology progressed and better components such as guidance systems became available. He developed a "stable" of solid-propellant ballistic missiles. The ICBM he called Sentinel, the shorter-range IRBM Minuteman, and the tactical MRBM Scout.

When the Air Force Scientific Advisory Board in the Pentagon started talking about a ballistic missile for deployment on European roads and highways, the Navy's SP office under Adm. William Raborn proposed a land-based Polaris system. Hearing this, BMD went to work because a land-based long-range ballistic missile *had* to be an Air Force bird. The Air Force wasn't about to permit a chink in its roles-and-missions armor that might allow the Navy or even the Army back into the land-based long-range ballistic missile mission that the Air Force had spent so much time and effort getting and then building. Col. Ed Hall suddenly found a lot of allies.

By this time General Schriever was completely sold on the concept because the Minuteman would be a second-generation ICBM capable of remaining in place for a long time. Like many other visionary military leaders before him who saw what had to be done, Schriever literally put his career on the line. He took Hall to Washington in late 1957 to make a round of presentations. They went through the whole Pentagon organization, layer after layer, even successfully fielding the questions and objections of the Air Force Scientific Advisory Board, whose warhead expert, Kistiakowski, felt that it was too much of a gamble to count on smaller warheads in the 1960s. The Sentinel and the Scout didn't survive an all-day bloodletting conference on February 10, 1958; the Minuteman did and had its range stretched to intercontinental mileage.

Schriever requested $150 million to develop WS-133A, the Minuteman, for the fiscal year starting in July 1958. The Air Force would give him only $50 million. A lot of skepticism stood in the way of the Minuteman. It was "pushing the state of the art" in solid-propellant propulsion, miniaturized guidance systems, and small warheads.

So Schriever literally called in all his favors up to and including the Secretary of Defense. He asked for an additional $100 million if he could prove the Minuteman concept within six months. On

January 7, 1959, Defense Secretary Neil McElroy gave the Air Force permission to spend $184 million on the Minuteman during that fiscal year.

In spite of the work that Admiral Raborn, Captain Smith, and the Navy's SP office were doing with the Polaris, Schriever and his team had to prove that the larger and more powerful Minuteman would work. Their careers were on the line.

# Out of the Tube and Silo

The immediate Air Force BMD reaction to the Navy proposal to adopt the Polaris submarine ballistic missile, the Fleet Ballistic Missile or FBM system, as a land-based system was simply because of the outstanding progress made by Raborn's SP office.

Using a technology management charting and control method known as PERT that had been developed specifically for the Polaris, the Navy's concurrency program was proceeding with great speed. In September 1956 the Atomic Energy Commission (AEC) estimated that a suitable warhead for the Polaris would be available by 1965 with an even chance of attainment by 1963; a year later the AEC said it would be ready by 1960. Over the strong objections of Adm. Hyman Rickover, Raborn's SP commandeered the SSN-589 nuclear attack submarine U.S.S. *Scorpion* on the ways at the Electric Boat Company, Groton, Connecticut. Its hull was sliced in two, a 130-foot section was added midships to house 16 Polaris launch tubes, and the redesignated SSBN-598 U.S.S. *George Washington* was launched on June 9, 1959.

But the skepticism in high places was due to the abysmal failure of the first Polaris test missiles. This didn't upset General Schriever and his team; they'd been through that sort of thing in their own ICBM/IRBM program. They knew the cause of the failures would be found and corrected.

Building the first large operational solid-propellant ballistic missile

wasn't easy. Fortunately, the Navy and Lockheed engineers had previous work to rely upon. Back in the 1940s, the GE Hermes program had pioneered large solid-propellant rocket motors with the Hermes RTV-A-10, which was 31 inches in diameter. The Army had carried on with the XM-15 Sergeant battlefield missile intended as a replacement for the unwieldy liquid-propellant SSM-A-17 Corporal. By 1959, Thiokol Chemical Corporation in Ogden, Utah, was developing a solid-propellant rocket motor for Sergeant that was 31 inches in diameter. With a few modifications, this basic XM-15 rocket motor was used as the first stage of an Air Force reentry test vehicle known as the X-17. It was also used as the basis for the first Polaris test vehicles, the FTVs.

Lockheed, the Polaris prime contractor, had modified the XM-15 as needed to test various Polaris features such as the "jetavator" steering rings that would deflect the exhaust of the first and second stages, thus providing steering.

The first Polaris test vehicles had been launched from the Navy's Point Mugu test facility near Oxnard, California. Here on January 11, 1958, the first successful FBM test flight was made with a Polaris not fully loaded with propellant. A Polaris dummy had been successfully launched by compressed air from a simulated ship silo at the San Francisco Naval Shipyard in November 1957. And on March 28, 1958, the first launching of a large Polaris test vehicle from an underwater tube had been made off San Clemente Island, California.

But for the Polaris test vehicles and the Polaris FBM itself, the flight tests would be made from the Cape.

The Polaris area was seventy acres just south of the Cape's point. To the south were some Jupiter launch pads, while a line of Atlas gantries and pads stretched off to the north. The principal inhabitants of the Polaris area were snakes and mosquitoes. In this small area, Raborn's people and Lockheed built not only the three Polaris launch pads but the Polaris shipboard motion simulator. The Polaris industrial area included a dozen buildings such as a hangar, an engineering lab, a machine shop, and a heating plant. Here, the large solid motors were assembled into missiles only 800 yards from the launch areas. If the Navy had a really big explosion, the Navy facility would go with it.

The first full-scale Polaris, the AX-1, a bottle-shaped vehicle 28 feet long and 54 inches in diameter, was ready at the Cape on September 24, 1958. It didn't carry a combat guidance system or a live warhead, but it was a Polaris. In full view of a lot of Navy brass, it lifted off after several holds and roared into the Florida sky. But at 40,000 feet it blew up. Missile parts showered the Navy area. The Range Safety Officer hadn't destroyed it. A $25 piece of electronic equipment in the Polaris autopilot had failed.

Back in the Pentagon a week later, an SP staff officer told the assembled Polaris officers and civilians:

> *The best way to explain what we found is to tell a little story. Right out of college, I went to work as a government bank examiner. I had to go around with a team and count money. I was taken into a bank vault by a bank officer. He kicked a pile of money bags and they jingled. He said I could count them if I wanted, but they just usually just kicked them; if they jingled, they were okay. Well, I decided I didn't like that idea. When I opened a bag, I found the shiniest new washers I'd ever seen. So in the Polaris program we've been kicking these bags that the contractors have handed us without looking inside. Now we're starting to look, and we're finding lots of shiny new washers.*

Raborn thought about this and said, "We had a lot of criticism here, and that's good. We discovered our weaknesses. But let that stop here in this room. Let's get the hell out of here and get to work."

Two weeks later Polaris AX-2 was on the pad. It went off like a Fourth of July Roman candle. The first stage sat on the pad, billowing smoke. The second stage had ripped loose and was thrashing around the sky. The Range Safety Officer blew it, and again pieces showered the area, starting a few grass fires this time. Firemen not only had to pour water on the fire but had to use their axes to kill the dozens of snakes that fled into the Polaris area from the fiery palmetto patch.

"It's like a newly married ensign," Raborn remarked. "It just doesn't want to go to sea."

The problem was caused by a $10 explosive bolt that had gone off prematurely.

Tighter quality controls were immediately put into place.

And Raborn acted at once to eliminate the distracting "brass factor" by prohibiting high-ranking naval officers as sightseers at the Cape during the tests. He didn't want his officers and engineers to be distracted by VIPs.

The trouble continued with AX-3, and Raborn himself obeyed his own command by staying away. On December 30, 1958, AX-3 performed beautifully through most of the first stage burn, then went head over heels. The Range Safety Officer destroyed it. Thanks to radio telemetry, the SP and Lockheed discovered that the heat from the burning propellant was melting the tail of the missile, causing the Polaris to suffer from a "hot bottom."

Admiral "Red" Raborn was stubborn. He decided to gamble and stay on the launch schedule. After all, failures were something you learned from. So he smiled at the Pentagon admirals, told them not to worry, then went home at night and worried for everyone.

AX-4 suffered the same fate. Two months of laboratory tests followed, but the results weren't in hand soon enough to prevent the failure of AX-5 on February 27, 1959. By this time another failure of a Polaris test vehicle was no longer newsworthy; it was commonplace. It was noted only in the outer ring of the Pentagon, where the Air Force generals grinned and the admirals found it very difficult to smile at all. When Raborn was advised to knock off the testing for a while, he too smiled but refused to budge. Even the Chief of Naval Operations, Adm. Arleigh Burke, refused to cave in to the pressures from other flag officers and continued to back Raborn.

AX-6 was something new. It had a *lot* of fixes in it. All the lab tests said this one would work. But no lab test can equal an actual flight. On April 20, 1959, AX-6 lifted off the pad at ignition, roared into the sky, staged perfectly, and dropped its nose cone exactly where it was supposed to 300 miles downrange.

In Washington 1,500 miles away, the red-haired admiral smiled.

The rest was just finicky engineering work and technical upgrades as technology progressed.

On July 20, 1960, a Polaris A-1 missile was launched from the submerged SSBN-598 U.S.S. *George Washington* and flew 1,200 miles down the Atlantic Test Range to an impact well within the design CEP.

The SSBN-598 U.S.S. *George Washington* was declared operational on November 15, 1960. Within a few years, 41 Polaris boats were at sea, each carrying 16 Polaris missiles. Although the first A-1 Polaris missiles had only a 1,200-mile range and a large CEP, making them suitable only against large urban areas, subsequent developments of the A-series Polaris, the larger follow-on Poseidon, and the 4,300-mile Trident made the FBM into perhaps the ultimate intercontinental ballistic missile.

The rest of the Polaris story, like the rest of the ICBM story, is one of continual improvement, progress, refinement, and fine-tuning.

However, the land-based solid-propellant ICBM—the WS-133 and its SM-80 Minuteman—was proceeding with unusual speed and success as the Air Force watched and learned from the Navy's Polaris flight tests. The official Request for Proposals on WS-133 brought forth no less than 14 responses. The Boeing Aerospace Company was selected as the prime contractor in October 1958. A lot of possibilities were then looked at and rejected. The use of lighter-weight plastic motor casings was deferred until later in the program; steel casings were selected initially because of their known characteristics. The initial plans to base the Minuteman on railway trains went as far as surveying suitable sidings, but it was rejected, only to be picked up by the Soviets at a later time. Another concept that went in the wastebasket was the use of the three stages in different combinations to provide a family of missiles with different ranges and warhead capabilities.

To reduce the risk of developing the large solid-propellant stages, three contractors were selected. It wasn't precisely the same as the redundancy of the Atlas/Titan ICBM program, and had any of the three failed to work, the Minuteman would have been in deep trouble.

The first stage was to be built by Thiokol Chemical Company in Ogden, Utah. As the M55 motor, it would produce 200,000 pounds of thrust and use polybutadyene AA binder (a form of Thiokol synthetic rubber) with powdered aluminum additive and ammonium perchlorate (AP) as an oxidizer. The casing was fabricated from D6AC steel and used four small nozzles that swiveled, a breakthrough that was different from the Polaris jetavators.

Aerojet-General, the makers of the first solid-propellant rocket-assisted takeoff (RATO) units during World War II, built the 60,000-pound second stage, which used polyurethane and AP as well as swiveling nozzles. Like the Thiokol first stage, it had a D6AC steel motor casing. By 1962 Aerojet had developed a new second stage using a forged and machined titanium casing.

The third stage was built by Hercules. It was a 35,000-pound motor using a special high-performance composite AP propellant and the radically new glass-fiber filament-wound casing.

The Avco Mark 5 reentry body carrying a 1.3 megaton thermonuclear warhead was fitted to the Minuteman.

On September 15, 1959, exactly on schedule, a short-grain tethered Minuteman was launched out of a simple silo without exhaust gas ducts, proving that the missile could be fired out of a simple hole in the ground. It was the first time observers saw the unique smoke ring that precedes the Minuteman coming out of its hole in the ground. On February 1, 1961, the first full-up Minuteman scored a 100 percent success by delivering its warhead 4,600 miles downrange from the Cape.

But not all was success. A few months later a Minuteman gained the dubious honor of just clearing the silo lip before it blew up in the biggest explosion ever seen at the Cape until the space shuttle Challenger disaster.

By December 1962, Minutemen were in their holes in the ground at Malmstrom AFB, Montana. Eventually Minuteman I LGM-30B (with the lightweight titanium second stage) equipped the next four wings at Ellsworth AFB, South Dakota; Minot AFB, North Dakota; Whiteman AFB, Missouri; and Warren AFB, Cheyenne, Wyoming, where it was centered around the old Atlas complexes. Minuteman I filled 800 silos by June 1965.

Minuteman II, LGM-30F, was a longer and heavier missile using an improved Aerojet second stage, a new solid-state electronic autopilot and all-inertial guidance system, an Avco Mark 11 reentry body with a 2-megaton warhead, and Tracor penetration aids to confuse any Soviet ballistic missile defense systems. Minuteman II flew in September 1964 from the Cape and was in the ground at Grand Forks AFB, North Dakota, in 1966. Eventually, Minuteman II replaced Minuteman I entirely and was upgraded with the Mark 12 reentry body, improved silo hardening, and penetration aids.

Minuteman III, LGM-30G, came along late in the 1960s and used glass fiber filament-wound motor casings instead of metal and mounting Multiple Independently-targetable Reentry Vehicles (MIRV) with three 350-kiloton warheads and a CEP of less than 600 feet.

By 1977, 550 Minuteman III missiles were in silos, along with 54 Titan II missiles and 450 Minuteman II missiles. The Atlas ICBM and the Titan I ICBM forces had been retired.

At that point, the American ICBM effort reached its peak.

 38

# Travail and Trouble at Tyuratam

Having challenged the United States and stimulated the American ICBM program both with Nikita Sergeyevich Khrushchev's missile-rattling diplomacy and Sergei Pavlovich Korolev's revelation of the existence of the R-7 Semyorka through the launches of several Sputniks, the USSR forged ahead with plans not only to become a world power with its long-range ballistic missiles but to attain overwhelming military superiority over the United States.

There is no question that the successful launch of the Sputniks with the R-7 and the subsequent buildup of the Soviet ICBM force catapulted the Soviet Union almost overnight to a perceived position as a superpower. The USSR continued to build its ICBM force over the next twenty years. And the United States reacted to it until the Minuteman III force was in the field. At that point, the United States felt it had enough warheads on ICBMs, on Submarine-Launched Ballistic Missiles (SLBMs), and in its B-52 bombers—the "triad"—to achieve deterrence by being able to take out nearly all strategic targets in the USSR. The Soviets just kept building rockets.

In 1959 Soviet Premier Nikita Khrushchev activated an entirely new fifth armed service within the Soviet Ministry of Defense: a separate Strategic Rocket Forces *(Raketnyye Voyska Strategicheskovo Naznacheniya)*. The RVSN had responsibility for all land-based ballistic missiles with a range of 1,045 kilometers or more. The world's first and only separate strategic missile force, it was under the direct control of the Politburo through the Minister of Defense, who was a member. However, it appears that all Soviet nuclear weapons, including missile warheads, remain under the control of the KGB. The first commander of the RVSN was Chief Marshal of Artillery Mitrofan I. Nedelin.

Having seen the impact of Sputnik I on the world, Khrushchev realized something stated clearly in a report from the American RAND Corporation, "Preliminary Design of an Experimental World-Circling Spaceship," issued on May 12, 1946: "To visualize the impact on the world, one can imagine the consternation and admiration that would be felt here if the U.S. were to discover that some other nation had already put up a successful satellite."

Yet another report, "The Time Factor In The Satellite Program," written by Dr. James Lipp and issued by RAND Corporation on October 18, 1946, went on to say: "The psychological effect of a satellite will in less dramatic fashion parallel that of the atomic bomb. It will make possible an unspoken threat to every other nation that we can send a guided missile to any spot on earth."

Khrushchev probably hadn't read these reports, but he understood the psychological impact of the ICBM as exhibited by the Sputniks Korolev had launched with the R-7.

Basically, it came down to the fact that the Soviet Union, a third-class power, could be perceived as and maintain a position of a world-class superpower on the basis of an ICBM force that could threaten any other nation on earth. In addition to being backed up by armed forces boasting 6 million men under arms, the RVSN meant that the USSR could throw its weight around. It did so for thirty years. It is still doing so and will remain hazardous to life on this planet as long as it has a first-strike ICBM capability.

However, this capability didn't come easily. Korolev might have given Khrushchev the R-7 ICBM, but it turned out to be an un-wieldy and unreliable weapons system.

It's difficult if not impossible to track all the failures in the Soviet ballistic missile program. The Soviets are just beginning to talk about them more than thirty years later. However, the United States did establish a long-range radar station in Turkey to keep track of the flights of Soviet missiles; those radars, however, weren't able to discern the failures on the pad or shortly after launch. It took surveillance satellites to get that information, orbiting platforms with sensors continually scanning for the infrared and electromagnetic signatures of rocket exhausts and explosions. (Even low-order chemical explosions such as those experienced in rocket failures generate an electromagnetic pulse, albeit far weaker than the EMP from a nuclear explosion.) We know of at least six failures of the R-7 before its first successful long-range flight in August 1957. We know of other failures following this. I am sure that the intelligence organizations of the United States know far more about this sort of thing, but they haven't released their information. However, much can be inferred from the pace of the Soviet program. For example, after launching two successful Sputniks in 1957 and conducting at least one successful full-range test of the R-7, only one successful launch to orbit (Sputnik 3) was made in 1958, followed by no orbital flights and three lunar shots in 1959. Korolev was obviously having the usual sort of teething troubles with the R-7.

A semibiographical—i.e., sanitized by the Soviets—film of Korolev's life, *The Taming of Fire,* was released by Mosfilm in 1972. In it, the actor playing Korolev counterattacks his competitors, namely the engineer Chelomei, and some of the Politburo politicians by saying, "You think only Atlas missiles can explode? We are building the most powerful machines in the world!" The reference to Atlas failures could be construed as setting the time of this statement, if Korolev ever made it at all, as sometime in late 1957 or early 1958. We do know of a series of R-7 launch failures in 1958, some of them involved with integrating a new upper stage onto the R-7 for space launch purposes.

The biggest one that we do know a great deal about and that the Soviets have now admitted took place, occurred on the night of October 23–24, 1960. It was in the launch window for a minimum-energy flight to Mars. Khrushchev was in New York City and was scheduled to make a speech before the UN. He'd arrived on the Soviet liner *Baltika,* and one of the sailors revealed that several spaceship models were aboard, but they were never shown to anyone because nothing happened in space. Then the tracking ships, which the Soviet Union used in lieu of the land-based tracking stations set up around the world by the United States, began returning to port. Khrushchev flew home after banging his shoe on the desk in the UN General Assembly. On October 25, 1960, Moscow announced the death in a "plane crash" of Marshall Mitrofan Nedelin, chief of the RVSN.

Two launch attempts had been made, one on October 10, 1960, and the second on October 14, 1960. Both had failed at high altitude. The third failure was a bigger one. It was reported in several places by several Soviets—the controversial "Penkovskyi Papers" published in the west in 1965 after the spy Penkovskyi was executed in Moscow; the second from the diaries of the KGB official and defector Peter Deryabin; a third report in 1976 from Dr. Zhores Medvedev who also reported the nuclear waste disaster in the Urals in 1958; and the last from Khrushchev's own posthumously published memoirs. It has since been confirmed by the Soviets under the apparently relaxed situation of glasnost.

On the evening of October 23, 1960, an R-7 was on the pad at Tyuratam. The countdown reached zero. The R-7 misfired. Korolev and the ground crew wisely decided to stay in the blockhouse. However, the cream of Soviet space scientists and missile marshalls was there, and they'd seen two failures thus far. Marshall Nedelin apparently got into a loud argument with Korolev, the chief designer. Nedelin was Korolev's boss. At about midnight, Nedelin finally overruled Korolev and gave the order to go out and inspect the R-7 on the pad.

At that time the R-7 used hypergolic leads—slugs of self-igniting liquids in the propellant lines leading to each combustion chamber—to ensure ignition of all 32 thrust chambers. A loaded R-7 that has just misfired with no known cause is the sort of hazardous and deadly machine one does not approach, orders or not.

Korolev's deputy, Mikail Yangel, a rocket engineer who had penetrated Peenemünde as a spy, went out to the pad with Nedelin and his staff. But Yangel got extremely nervous with all the rocket propellant and missile explosives armed and ready; he retired to a small fireproof hut near the launch pad to have a smoke and calm his nerves. Just as he lit up, the R-7 blew up.

Probably a faulty valve had finally come unstuck and opened. Whatever happened, 30 tons of rocket propellant produced a huge, low-order explosion. It must have lit up the sky for a hundred kilometers around the Baikonyr Cosmodrome, as the Soviets were calling the site even though it was a long way from the little village of Baikonyr.

Several hundred people were killed on and around the pad, including Nedelin and his military staff. Also killed were many of Korolev's engineers and probably most of the launch crew who were soldiers in the RVSN. (RVSN troops were involved in launching most of the Soviet space vehicles in the 1960s and 1970s, which is one reason why Soviet space shots were rare during periods when ballistic missile tests were in progress.)

A comparable disaster at Cape Canaveral would have been the explosion of the NASA Saturn-Ib, the "little Saturn."

A later analysis of the failure came from a report by Sergey Pilyugin, a Soviet rocket engine designer. There had been a flaw in the fuel feed system. An indication of the failure rate of the R-7 can be gained from the information that it took two years to get the failure rate down to 25 percent.

Dr. Charles S. Sheldon II was the doyen of Soviet space watchers in the U.S. Library of Congress until his untimely death on September 11, 1981. Sheldon estimated that if Soviet launch vehicle failure rates were comparable to those in the United States—a reasonable assumption, since the basic technology was the same on both sides of the ocean and had come from the same fountainhead at Peenemünde—the failure counts for Soviet launches between 1957 and 1967 should have been forty-nine. The official record shows two.

This did not keep the Soviets from continuing to develop a growing stable of ICBMs of increasing size, reliability, and accuracy.

The table in the appendix shows the characteristics of all known Soviet ballistic missiles.

Many of these are known only because the Soviets have paraded them through Red Square during May Day or November 3 each year. Some reports from defectors such as Viktor Suvarov claim that many of these ballistic missiles were merely "dimensional replicas"—i.e., dummies—based on the standard Soviet practice that "the enemy should see only what the Motherland wishes to show them." For example, there is no indication that the SS-10 (NATO code name Scrag) ever became operational even though it was paraded through Red Square in May 1965; it has not been seen since 1971. The Soviets hinted that it was capable of placing a thermonuclear weapon in orbit but were very defensive in their insistence that it did not violate any UN treaty restrictions on space weapons, which, they said, did not prohibit their production, only their use. The Soviets claim that every ICBM is a space weapon because all such missiles fly through space and that their use is permitted under all treaties.

On the other hand, the SS-7 Saddler has never been seen except in a propaganda movie of a silo-launched missile. It may be the basic missile behind the Soviet Fractional Orbital Bombardment System (FOBS), which is capable of launching a thermonuclear warhead into low earth orbit and then deorbiting the warhead at the proper point in the orbit to cause impact on a target. A FOBS warhead never makes a complete orbit, hence the "fractional orbital" part of its name. Thus, the Soviets have the capability to launch a FOBS missile that could attack the continental United States from the south rather than through the BMEWS missile detection system emplaced in arctic North America.

The Soviet FOBS may have been retired from service. Landsat photographs of the Tyuratam space launch center in Khazhastan show an area on its western side that Soviet space expert Charles P. Vick says is a military launch area primarily assigned to the missile designer Chelomai. Early photos show an array of launch silos in this area, whereas more recent photos, including those taken by American astronauts from the space shuttle Orbiters, indicate that these silos have been filled in and largely unused, judging from the condition of roads and railways serving that part of the cosmodrome.

Although most people believe that the United States was the first to deploy a submarine-launched ballistic missile (SLBM) system, again the Soviets were the first to do it. Their development program began in 1953. Tests were conducted first with an SS-1B Scud land-based liquid-propellant missile launch from tubes on land and then in a rebuilt Zulu-class submarine. At least seven Z-class submarines were rebuilt in the Zhadanov yard in 1955–1956 with an 11-meter section spliced into the hull for two launch tubes. These were followed in 1958–1961 by twenty-two Golf-class submarines built for the first Soviet SLBM specifically designed for the mission, the SS-N-4 Sark which used hypergolic liquid propellants, carried a one-megaton warhead, and was about 15 meters long and 1.8 meters in diameter, just big enough for three of them to fit in launch tubes between the keel and the top of the conning tower sail of the Golf-class submarines. The Sark was blown out of the surfaced submarine by six solid charges, and the ignition of the liquid-propellant engines took place in the air above the submarine. The range was about 600 kilometers, permitting the Soviets to bring most coastal American cities within range of SLBM attack if it hadn't been for the noisy Soviet submarines and the high level of American antisubmarine warfare technology. The plans and data for the SS-N-4 Sark were passed to the People's Republic of China before the rift in 1960.

The Soviets appear to have kept the dangerous hypergolic liquid-propellant SLBMs for nearly twenty years because the first known solid-propellant SLBM produced by the Soviets was the SS-N-17, which was first seen being launched from a Yankee-class submarine in 1977. The improved SS-N-20, with twelve MIRV warheads and a range of 8,300 kilometers, is probably the SLBM deployed aboard the huge Soviet Typhoon-class submarines. These 25,000-ton giants with titanium hulls are 170 meters long and have twenty launch tubes forward of the conning tower. This means that the Soviet Union's SLBM force can hide in territorial waters off the Soviet Union and attack any location in North America. In 1988 at least five Typhoons were at sea near or under the Arctic ice pack north of Murmansk.

In spite of glasnost and perestroika, the Soviet Union in 1988 continues the development and production of new ICBM models. They are now up to SS-25. They have the means to deliver by ICBMs and SLBMs more than 10,000 thermonuclear warheads. As one American arms negotiator recently remarked in frustration, "We arm, they arm. We disarm, they arm."

# Other Players

Although the United States and the Soviet Union were the two nations primarily engaged in the race to obtain the ICBM, it quickly became apparent to other countries that it would be beneficial to be missile powers for various reasons.

Some of them made it. Some of them didn't. However, as the years go by, we shall see more nations joining the ICBM club as the technology, worked out with so much sweat and money by the United States and the USSR, slowly moves from high technology to low technology. Some countries simply won't build ICBMs because they can buy them more cheaply from those countries willing to sell them. Both the United States and the USSR have sold their ballistic missile systems to their friends. Other nations won't become ballistic missile powers simply because they can't afford to buy missiles or because they see no need to do so.

One of the first countries to attempt to build its own ballistic missile system was Great Britain. As one of the victorious Allies of World War II, Britain had the opportunity to get its share of the German war technology booty, including the V-2 rocket. The best the British were able to do, however, was to get the Germans to fire some V-2s for Operation BACKFIRE. After fighting two world wars and saving the free world twice in as many generations, the British were both exhausted and nearly bankrupt. Their industry had been bombed and some of it destroyed. They had overextended themselves everywhere. The British Empire was in its final throes of disintegration, a process that had started at about the turn of the century. The unusual thing about the British was that they were quite different from the other empire builders of history; even as they were building the British Empire, they sensed and expressed the belief that it was probably quite transient. This was perhaps best expressed by Rudyard Kipling in his Victorian ode, *Recessional.*

However, in 1955 the British government ordered the development of the Blue Streak Long-Range Ballistic Missile (LRBM), which would be based on the emerging Atlas technology and other missile hardware licensed from the United States. This was before the nationalization of the British aerospace industry, so the de Haviland Propeller Company got the prime contract for Blue Streak while de Haviland Aircraft was made responsible for the airframe and Sperry Gyroscope Co. Ltd. for the all-inertial guidance system. Propulsion was to be furnished by Rolls Royce, which licensed the Atlas booster engine technology from North American Rocketdyne.

The result was a missile 61 feet, 6 inches long, and 10 feet in diameter made from stainless steel and weighing loaded about 199,000 pounds. It was propelled by two Rolls Royce RZ.2 gimbaled thrust chambers each producing 137,000 pounds of thrust, and two Armstrong Siddeley PR.23 vernier engines each producing 500 pounds of thrust. Propellants were LOX and RP-1. A heat sink nose cone similar to the GE Mark 2 would be used to carry a British-designed thermonuclear warhead to a range of 2,500 miles, bringing all of the Soviet Union west of the Ural Mountains within striking distance of Blue Streaks launched from the British Isles. Blue Streak would be silo-stored and lifted vertically for surface launch on an azimuth-aligned elevator launch table built by Morfax.

The chief development centers for Blue Streak were Hatfield for the airframe and systems integration, Spadeadam Waste for rocket engine testing, and Woomera, Australia, for flight testing.

Many well known British rocket engineers were involved in Blue Streak because they felt that at last Britain would be developing into a missile and space power. Blue Streak attracted such well known rocket men as A. V. "Val" Cleaver, who ran the Spadeadam rocket test stands and proved out the Rolls Royce RZ.2 engines.

The RAF Bomber Command would have operated Blue Streak squadrons both inside and outside the British Isles.

Several Blue Streaks were built and flight tested at Woomera, but not before the British government canceled the program in favor of buying the U.S. Skybolt missile system. Skybolt was an air-launched ICBM dropped from a bomber. In the late 1940s the British had developed a "V-bomber" force consisting of the Vickers Valiant, the Handley Page Victor, and the Avro Vulcan. Skybolt was to be mounted on the huge delta-winged Vulcan bomber.

The U.S. government pulled out of Skybolt. When the Kennedy administration took over in 1961, Robert McNamara, then Secretary of Defense, canceled Skybolt, leaving Great Britain with only an aging force of Thor ICBMs.

As a result of the hastily called 1962 Nassau Conference in the Bahamas, President John F. Kennedy agreed to sell Polaris A-3 SLBMs for installation on British-built SSBNs of the Royal Navy. An important feature of this agreement was that the British would provide the guidance system, penetration aids, warheads, and reentry bodies, thus permitting them to maintain control over targeting. The RN Polaris missiles each carry three 200-kiloton thermonuclear warheads in MIRVs, and the British Chevaline Program is intended to keep these missiles effective into the twenty-first century. But the RN has only four submarines of the Resolution class; the fifth boat was canceled. This means that the Royal Navy can guarantee to have only one boat on patrol at any given time. However, although replacement boats were scheduled to start construction in 1987, only four replacements are planned.

The contractors for Blue Streak kept at it, however, proposing the Blue Streak as the first stage for an all-European space launch vehicle, the Europa, which finally died in 1973 when the French Ariane launch vehicle became available. At that point British rocketry died and hasn't been resurrected since. Personally, I feel this was a great waste since I had worked on many aerospace projects with British designers and found them to be brilliant, innovative, and daring. Many of the old British rocket engineers died shortly after Blue Streak/Europa was canceled forever, and undoubtedly the demise of

British rocketry had something to do with that. A person who has given a lifetime to a professional technical field only to see it torn apart by an uncaring government bureaucrat sometimes doesn't have very much left to live for, and most of the British rocket engineers werc idealists.

The French, however, decided to go their own way under Charles de Gaulle, pulled out of NATO, opted to develop their own nuclear weapon capability, built a strong aerospace industry that produced the Dassault Mirage-IVA delta-winged supersonic bomber as the main linchpin of their nuclear *force de frappe,* and began a broad rocket research program in 1959 that was designed to provide an all-French land-based and submarine-launched ballistic missile force. The French wanted their own hardware so they wouldn't be dependent on other countries. Having seen what had happened to Great Britain, one can hardly blame them for this approach.

The *Sol-Sol Balistique Stratégique* (SSBS), or surface-to-surface ballistic missile, program was started with the Société pour l'Étude et la Réalisation d'Engins Balistiques (SEREB), a consortium, as the prime contractor, Nord Aviation for the airframe, Nord and Société Nationale d'Étude et de Constructions de Moteurs de Aviation (SNECMA) for propulsion, Direction des Poudres for the solid propellant, Sud Aviation for the reentry vehicle, and Sud Aviation and Société pour l'Étude de la Propulsion par Réaction (SEPR) for the gimballed nozzles. Later, when the French nationalized their aerospace industry, this was all combined into the Société Nationale Industrielle Aérospatiale, known simply as Aérospatiale, and became their Division Systèmes Balistiques et Spatiaux.

In 1966 the first missile, the S-112 test vehicle with a dummy second stage, was launched from a test silo. Testing of S-01 two-stage prototypes followed. The first SSBS prototype, the S-02, was launched in May 1969. IOC was reached in the summer of 1971 when the full force of two groups of nine silos was ready. The 1me Groupement des Missiles Stratégiques is located on the Plateau d'Albion in Haute Provence, France, with the administrative center at St Christol airbase five kilometers away and the two launch control centers underground at Rustrel and Reilhannette. The launch silos are protected by 8 meters of reinforced concrete, and the S-2 missiles are hot-launched out of the silos.

The SSBS S-2 is 14.8 meters long, 1.5 meters in diameter, and has a launch weight of 32,000 kilograms. Its range of 2,750 kilometers puts all of Europe west of the Ural Mountains within reach of its 1.2-megaton thermonuclear warhead, developed independently by the French.

Rather than follow the British lead and buy American Polaris SLBMs from the United States and possibly run into problems with supply of missiles and components, France developed its own *Mer-Sol Balistique Stratégique* (MSBS), sea-to-land strategic ballistic missile. The French contractors were essentially the same. The dimensions of the first solid-propellant M-1 MSBS missiles were similar to those of the SSBS, being 10.4 meters long by 1.5 meters in diameter. However, since the M-1 was smaller, its liftoff weight was only 18,000 kilograms and its two-stage solid-propellant booster could send its 500-kiloton French thermonuclear warhead to a range of 2,500 kilometers. Like the American Polaris system, sixteen MSBS missiles are deployed in each Sous-marin Nucléaire Lance-Engin (SNLE) nuclear submarine. The first such French submarine to receive its MSBS missiles was *Le Redoutable,* which was declared operational in December 1971.

Later versions of the MSBS increased the range, warhead weight, and warhead yield.

In the 1970s France definitely became an independent ballistic missile nation with eighteen SSBS land-based IRBMs and eighty MSBS submarine ballistic missiles in service.

China was the fourth major power to develop its own ballistic missiles. Little was known about the ballistic missile program of the People's Republic of China, but we did know that a very knowledge-able Chinese-American rocket pioneer left the United States and returned to China in 1955. Dr. Hsue-shen Tsien was one of Dr. Theodore von Kármán's students at Cal Tech and one of the found-ers of the Jet Propulsion Laboratory. Because of Tsien's expertise in aerodynamics and jet propulsion, von Kármán nominated him for membership on the Air Force Scientific Advisory Group. But in spite of Tsien's skills, high reputation, and contributions to the rocket program of the United States, he was accused of being an alien communist and a danger to his adopted country. Tsien was arrested by the Immigration and Naturalization Service in 1950, kept in custody for two weeks, and held in the United States against his will for five years under constant threat of deportation. Finally in 1955, he was deported to China in a bitter mood over what he felt was unjust treatment. The Chinese government, of course, was delighted to get him. He became the director of the Institute of Mechanics in Beijing and a member of the Academia Sinica. There were rumors that Tsien had led the development effort that resulted in the People's Republic of China detonating its own missile-borne nuclear device at Lop Nor on October 27, 1966. And, because of his expertise in rocketry, he has probably been one of the leaders in the PRC ballistic missile program.

Back in the 1950s, before the great rift occurred between the communist Soviet Union and the communist People's Republic of China, the Soviet Union had given the PRC some SS-3/R-3 Shyster ballistic missiles and the plans for the SS-N-4 Sark submarine-launched ballistic missile. The Chinese under Tsien started from there, redesigning the R-3 to lengthen it and increase its range to approximately 750 miles. By 1966 between fifty and ninety of these missiles, called the CSS-1 by United States intelligence organizations and Dong Feng 2 (East Wind), or DF-2, by the Chinese, were deployed against the Soviet Union in northern China. They each carried the 20-kiloton Chinese atomic warhead. The DF-2 was used to launch the first Chinese satellite on April 24, 1970.

The first true Chinese ballistic missile was the CSS-2 or DF-3, which quickly followed the DF-2 (the Chinese designation DF-1 was apparently never assigned) and was ready in 1971. While the DF-2 had used the classical LOX/RP-1 liquid propellants, the DF-3 started the Chinese trend of using UDMH and $N_2O_4$ storable liquids as propellants. The DF-3 is 67 feet long and 8 feet in diameter, a Chinese Thor, except that its rocket engine uses four combustion chambers. It carries a 3,300-pound 1-megaton thermonuclear warhead to a range of 1,550 miles. The PRC had deployed twenty of them against the Soviet Union in 1971, threatening most of the Soviet Asiatic cities.

Full membership of China in the ICBM club came in 1975 with the flight of the DF-4 (CSS-3) two-stage ballistic missile capable of carrying the same 3,300-pound 1-megaton thermonuclear warhead to a range of 4,350 miles. The DF-4 was basically a CSS-2 with an upper stage. Now China could target any location in the Soviet Union and reach some parts of the United States as well.

But the true Chinese ICBM came along about 1980 with the DF-5 (CSS-4), which could throw a 7,000- to 11,000-pound 5-megaton thermonuclear warhead to a range of 5,000 miles. The first stage engines, a four-chambered unit burning storable liquids, produces a thrust of 616,000 pounds, while the second stage produces 154,000 pounds of thrust. The DF-5 is 107 feet long and 10.9 feet in diameter with a liftoff weight of 420,000 pounds. It's basically a Chinese Titan II in most respects, and the PRC's commercial space launch company is offering it as a launch vehicle capable of placing a 6,000-pound satellite into a 125-mile low earth orbit. The PRC has launched and recovered six satellites, being one of three countries that have done this (the other two being the United States and the USSR).

The People's Republic of China also deployed a submarine-launched ballistic missile system on four submarines with two more planned. Each "Xia" (U.S. code name) submarine carries twelve CSS-N-3 SLBMs, probably Chinese designs based on the Soviet SS-N-4 Sark. These SLBM boats are apparently stationed in the western Pacific with their missiles targeted on the eastern USSR, but later deployments into the South China Sea and the Indian Ocean can be expected.

China is not only a ballistic missile power, but the PRC has reportedly entered into an agreement with Brazil to produce and launch space vehicle versions of its ballistic missiles there, and Brazil/China reportedly agreed to supply the DF-3 to Iraq in 1989. The agreement fell through in 1990, but this is the sort of ballistic missile proliferation that we can expect to see in the years to come.

It won't be helped by the fact that Israel and the Republic of

South Africa have concluded a joint development agreement for the Israeli solid-propellant IRBM, about which little is known at the time of this writing.

Thirty years after the United States and the USSR sweated through the technology development, ICBM technology is out there loose in the world in 1990.

# *What Next?*

For all intents and purposes, this story of the ICBM and the ballistic missile must stop here. Once the USSR and the United States got the ICBM, it was a matter of continual minor improvements in subsystems; the basic world-girdling weapon was in existence. The fact that France and China were able to duplicate this technology in a short period of time means that ballistic missile technology matured about 1965–1970. But where do things go from here? Can we expect more great ballistic missile breakthroughs? That depends on one's perception of "war."

The conduct of warfare—the waging of armed conflict, the use of physical force to coerce an opponent to do it your way—is not a simple matter. Save for a few people who studied and wrote about war—Sun Tzu, Caesar, Napoleon, Jomeni, Clausewitz, the Mahans, von Moltke, du Picq, von Schlieffen, Foch, and Fuller—the study of war and its causes was usually considered to be depraved and somehow antisocial until World War II gave us the atomic bomb and the ballistic missile, the combination of which is now termed the "ultimate weapon." The realization dawned on serious students of warfare such as Gen. Sir John Hackett that "the concept of total war between sovereign national states was now matched with a technique of total destruction." A further realization by Col. Trevor DuPuy and others shows that there must be a convergence between the capabilities of a weapon and the doctrine that governs its use. We may not have achieved that yet with the ICBM because no war has been fought with ICBM weapons. Hopefully, because the weapon of nearly total destructive capabilities is now in hand, total war will no longer be fought, but for other reasons than fear.

The slow development of the ballistic missile during its first quarter century, something we've traced herein, motivated other students of warfare such as Herman Kahn and his Hudson Institute to develop patterns of thinking about the conduct of war and to test them insofar as possible in structured "war games." Never in the history of the human race has so much intellectual effort been devoted to wars, how wars are fought, and how to prevent wars. Herman Kahn's concept of escalation remains as valid as the basic principles of Sun Tzu and the principles of war first codified by John F. C. Fuller. Wars happen, but they occur as a result of definite escalatory steps. A country or its leaders can stop at any step up the ladder; the important factor is not to jump steps and not to go any higher than is necessary to achieve the basic goals.

In the meantime, under the threatening umbrella of the nuclear explosive, delivered either by air or by ballistic missile, there has hardly been a day since the guns stopped firing in 1945 when a war of some kind has not been taking place somewhere on this planet. These wars have reverted to "limited armed conflicts"—they are now called "armed conflicts" because the Charter of the United Nations says that all its signatories have pledged not to engage in "war"—in which conventional guns and high explosives, perhaps with some chemical and biological agents, were the primary weapons. Nuclear explosives have not been used except in one unconfirmed case of a Sino-Soviet border conflict in 1969 when all indications pointed to the Soviet use of a nuclear weapon. Ballistic missiles have been used in some limited armed conflicts, but their warheads carried conventional high explosives.

Whether or not this situation will continue remains to be seen. But the experience of military professionals clearly indicates that any available weapon will certainly be used at some point.

But, in a like manner, the history of warfare shows that every offensive weapon eventually results in the creation of a defense against it.

A defense now exists against long-range artillery shells—and a ballistic missile is merely a modern extension of long-range artillery, whose history goes back to the use of the thrown rock, the first missile weapon as contrasted to the club which was the first shock weapon. The classical first defense against any missile weapon is a deep hole—a foxhole or bunker. The next defense is armor, which is an extension of the earthen protection of the hole. The ultimate defense against the missile weapon is another missile weapon that can intercept and destroy the assaulting missile.

In 1944 no defense existed against the V-2, which arrived at supersonic speeds. But the elements of a defense against the V-2 existed: radar and other sensors to locate and track the V-2 and another rocket-propelled missile to intercept and destroy it in flight. It wasn't impossible to do this in 1944; it was only very difficult and very expensive.

It was shown to be possible in the 1960s, when it was no longer difficult but only expensive.

In the 1980s ballistic missile defense became possible and affordable, if expensive. The Soviet Union deployed an antiballistic missile (ABM) force around Moscow in the late 1960s. It has continually upgraded this ABM system since that time and at the moment is the only nation that possesses an ABM system. The United States began to deploy an ABM system to protect the Minuteman missile silos in the Dakotas but then ceased work and scrapped it.

On March 23, 1983, President Ronald Reagan played a trump card in the technological war with the Soviet Union by establishing a new strategic doctrine that would eventually replace the Mutually Assured Destruction (MAD) doctrine that had existed to that time between the United States and the USSR. The United States would build a new antiballistic missile system to defend itself. The resulting Strategic Defense Initiative (SDI) was facetiously labeled "Star Wars" by the liberal news media and immediately set upon as unworkable by the left-wing political elements of American academia, who had never built anything but lab equipment, much less a weapon. In spite of this opposition, the Strategic Defense Initiative Office (SDIO) has quietly gone about solving the technological problems connected with two basic sorts of ballistic missile defense. The impact of SDI on the Soviet Union has been profound because in essence the United States changed the course of a technological war and placed extreme pressure on the Soviet Union and its "short blanket economy" (when the shoulders get the blanket, the feet get cold). The current climate of Soviet glasnost and perestroika is probably a direct result of pressures on the USSR to either eliminate or reduce the intensity of this threat to its expensive ICBM force without which it would be a third-class world power.

The first ABM technique is the "kinetic kill," or "hard kill," approach of launching an interceptor against an incoming ICBM warhead and literally killing it by impact or the physical shock wave of a nearby explosion. It is antiaircraft artillery technically upgraded for use against much faster and smaller ICBM reentry bodies. Given enough kinetic kill vehicles, it's certainly possible to knock out a percentage of the attacking force, just as antiaircraft artillery and interceptor fighters can shoot down a percentage of attacking bombers. While it is certainly true, according to the Trenchard doctrine, that "the bomber will always get through," the attacker does not know *which* bomber will get through to *which* target. Military planners do not like to go to war facing this sort of uncertainty. A verity of combat states that a good defense can always prevail over an offense; the converse is that any defensive position can be overwhelmed by an offensive force, provided the attacker is willing to pay the price.

A study of warfare indicates that nearly all past wars have started with the attacker barely having enough offensive power, and in many cases not enough to realistically do the job. All attackers have always counted on a short war and usually do not have the capabilities to carry on a conflict for more than six weeks. Thus, faced with limited attack capabilities—and no military man has ever had enough offensive power to do the job as he believed it should be done—the risk becomes almost unacceptably high if any sort of workable defense exists and you don't know how good it might be against your assault.

A defense can and does win. We have recent examples in the Battle of Britain, Stalingrad, and Hanoi/Haiphong.

This may sound a bit simplistic. Perhaps it is, because the whole matter of war planning and war gaming is *not* a simple undertaking. We have neither the time nor the space herein to go into the manifold techniques of war gaming.

Two well known factors always affect conflicts, and there is no way planners can adjust for them. The first of these is the so-called "haze of battle," which may be summed up in the phrase, "No plan survives the first contact." The second is the "friction of war," which means that things take longer to do than planned and is the military equivalent of Cheop's Law of Engineering: "Nothing *ever* gets built on schedule or within the budget."

However, a new weapon has entered the picture in the past two decades: the directed-energy weapon (DEW). This is exemplified by the high-powered laser and the particle beam weapon. Both types of DEW are under intense development by the United States and the USSR. They work. It is likely that the United States could deploy an ABM system utilizing ground-based DEWs; the USSR may also be able to do this.

No defense is perfect, however, and the SDI and ABM systems were never touted as being perfect. But they would provide the same sort of defense against ballistic missiles that currently exists with conventional weapons: a chance to blunt the attack and make it too expensive or too risky for the attacker to contemplate with impunity. A defense is adequate if each side looks at the other every morning and says, "No, not today."

This, of course, is an example of Herman Kahn's analysis of war in what he called the post-industrial society. (Actually, there is no such thing as a post-industrial society because no modern society can exist today without an industrial infrastructure, but I can no longer argue this point with Herman Kahn.) To put it in other terms, before a nation resorts to military action these days, it must answer three questions:

1. Can we win?
2. What will it cost?
3. Is it worth it?

The United States learned this in southeast Asia; the USSR learned it in Afghanistan, although they still have troops there as of this writing.

The purpose of a ballistic missile defense, now technically feasible, changes the equation of the second question for a potential enemy.

Protracted general wars, even without nukes, have a proven tendency to drive one or both adversaries into bankruptcy.

This is why we may never see the widespread use of the ICBM just as we have seen no widespread use of either chemical or biological weapons.

One can hope.

And one can act to counter the effectiveness of an ICBM by defensive measures because, in spite of all good intentions, disarmament has never worked in the past to prevent wars and probably will not work in the future as long as there is any chance for national leaders to believe that the answers to all three questions stated above are to their advantage.

However, the frightening possibility no longer lies with a massive United States/USSR thermonuclear exchange with ICBMs and SLBMs but with a "man on horseback" in a smaller nation who acquired an IRBM or ICBM capability by means of purchase or indigenous development.

Eventually the technology or the weaponry may be available to smaller nations. Ballistic missile and nuclear warhead technology is a Pandora's box; it has been opened and is loose in the world. No way exists to put it back in the box and hold the lid closed. No restrictions on technology transfer can keep the know-how within national borders. Once an engineer knows that another engineer has done something, said engineer can proceed with the assurance that he, too, can do it because the laws of the universe are the same everywhere. Also, engineers can be acquired and learned from. The history of the ICBM has proved this many times. Both the United States and the USSR profited by co-opting the German rocketeers, and the Chinese program owes a great deal to the fact that the United States deported one of its top Chinese-born experts in aeronautics and propulsion.

A MAD doctrine of defense can work—and did work—when only two major powers are involved and three or four smaller players exist. It cannot work when men on horseback get ballistic missiles or when these weapons fall into the hands of people who *hate* their neighbors with an intensity and passion not well understood elsewhere.

The development of the ICBM has followed rather prosaic and well-beaten historic paths. If history does not repeat itself but the patterns of history do, the ICBM as an offensive weapon will lead to the deployment of a defense against it.

This, of course, will happen because the ICBM was developed by military artillery officers with the help of idealistic engineers who saw the ballistic missile as the only way to get into space, which is what they really wanted to do in the first place while hoping that the ballistic missile matter would somehow take care of itself. It turned out that indeed the ballistic missile could open the door to space, but it was too expensive and used the wrong operational philosophy.

The rocket engineers, consciously or otherwise, worked to bring to reality the predictive writings of Jules Verne, who in his 1865 novel *De la Terre à la Lune (From the Earth to the Moon)* had the artillery officers and manufacturers of the Baltimore Gun Club build a cannon that would shoot a projectile to the moon. As we have seen, a gun to do this would have been too long, but a rocket can be used to self-propel a long-range artillery shell to the same lunar target. That is what has been used between 1945 and today to put things into space.

Shooting things into space on top of a big artillery shell is no longer the only way to do it. But that's another story.

# Postscript

# Saddam's Scuds

Since the writing of the text of this book in 1989, ballistic missiles have been used in armed conflict. Granted, these were Soviet Scuds, which are not ICBMs. However, the people who used them apparently had not learned the lessons that have been discussed in this book.

The German V-2 was not a weapon of military significance. If the Germans had been successful in mating the V-2 and its offspring with nuclear warheads, World War II might have ended quite differently. Or, if the Germans had deployed the V-2 earlier, they might have had an impact upon Operation Overlord, as Eisenhower discussed in *Crusade In Europe*. The German V-2, therefore, turned out to be a terror weapon that was primarily used in a missile version of the discredited and unworkable Trenchard doctrine. This British-developed theory calls for an air war in which indiscriminate area bombing of large cities is used to break the morale of the civilian population.

Massive aerial bombing of cities didn't work. The equivalent V-2 barrages against Paris, Antwerp, and London did little damage of a military nature. However, many noncombatant civilians were killed or injured.

If this sounds like the Scud attacks by Iraq against Israeli and Saudi Arabian urban areas in January 1991, it is no accident. History is indeed repeating itself because Saddam Hussein did not learn the lessons of the German V-2.

The German V-2 played an insignificant military role in World War II, and the Scud reprised the role in 1991.

The Soviet SS-1 Scud is a direct descendant of the German V-2. It was designed in the late 1940s and deployed by the Soviet Army in the 1950s. It was intended for use as a tactical theater weapon carrying a nuclear warhead. It is smaller than the V-2, has a smaller warhead capability, and uses different rocket propellants. But it has about the same range and accuracy. When the Soviet Union sold its obsolete Scuds to Third World nations such as Iraq, Syria, and Egypt, the nuclear warheads were not part of the deal. So the recipients had to be satisfied with mounting conventional high explosive warheads onto their Scuds.

The use of Soviet-made SS-1C Scud-C ballistic missiles by Saddam Hussein's Iraqi Army against Tel Aviv, Riyadh, and Dhahran in January 1991 was not the first time that this ballistic missile was launched in Middle East conflicts. Egyptian troops fired three Scuds into the Sinai during the Yom Kippur War in 1973, but all three missed their targets. In November 1975, the Syrian Army was reported to have flown a Scud to a range of 250 kilometers.

A ballistic missile without a nuclear warhead can be only a terror weapon used for psychological warfare. In terms of its cost, the complexity of its system, and the amount of material required to build and launch it, it is a very inefficient way to send less than 200 kilograms of ordinary high explosive 200 kilometers. However, it may be the *only* way to deliver high explosives to an enemy target if bombing aircraft cannot do the job because of air defenses. But unless it has the accuracy of a cruise missile or a smart bomb—and, as we've seen, the Scud does not possess this accuracy—it is a weapon of total military uselessness. The Scud attacks did not cow the civilian populations of Tel Aviv, Riyadh, or Dhahran any more than the German V-2 caused the collapse of civilian morale in London.

But suppose a Scud was carrying a chemical or biological warhead instead? Would it be more effective?

It is unlikely that it would.

As the Germans discovered with the V-2, getting the warhead to explode at the right instant is critical. Fusing a ballistic missile warhead is a difficult technical problem. Even Adolf Hitler recognized this, and he was no technical genius. No evidence exists *at the time of this writing* that the Iraqis have managed to solve the fusing problem involved with effectively delivering a chemical warhead by Scud.

If the warhead is not activated at the proper microsecond, its chemical payload does not become properly distributed for maximum effect. Maximum effect includes the element of time because all chemical agents lose their effectiveness quickly. The best way to deliver chemical agents is to release large quantities of the agent in a short period of time upwind of the target.

A ballistic missile is also a poor way to deliver a biological payload. Such biological warfare agents as disease organisms must have a very short lifetime; otherwise, they can become a serious problem for the user. Biological agents can backfire unless careful vectoring methods are used to distribute them. A ballistic missile is a very poor way to do this: A "Typhoid Mary" is far more effective.

If the Scud delivered a small nuclear warhead, of course, its effectiveness as a destructive weapon is enormously increased. Whether or not it becomes militarily decisive depends on where, when, and how a nuclear-tipped Scud is used.

So much for the military effectiveness of a short-range ballistic missile.

But Scud was politically effective. Its use as a terror weapon by Saddam Hussein threatened to expand and complicate the conflict. In terms of the political and diplomatic effort required to counter the Scud as a terror weapon, it might be viewed by some as a success, even though the diplomatic and political effort succeeded.

The importance of the Scud attacks during January 1991 lay not in the effectiveness or lack thereof of the ballistic missile as a weapon. These attacks revealed to all the world that an effective, reliable, and workable defense against ballistic missiles exists.

As discussed herein, prior to 1991 the only way to eliminate a ballistic missile threat was to destroy the launchers. Although it is an expensive and often deadly hunting game that involves very expensive fighter-bomber aircraft and does not always find all the launchers, this method of defense was used in the Kuwait War as it was in World War II.

However, a new element was introduced in Saudi Arabia and Israel. The Patriot battlefield air-defense system proved conclusively that a ballistic missile could be intercepted in flight and destroyed. Ballistic missile defense works. Less than fifty years after the first launch of the first military ballistic missile, the German A.4 (V-2), a defense against it was used and it worked.

The Patriot system was designed to shoot down airplanes. Congress nearly killed it in 1980 by refusing to appropriate funds to continue its development and deployment with the U.S. Army. It was a very expensive and complicated system to perfect. Once it was in the hands of the troops, a bright engineer or group of engineers discovered that the Patriot could be used to intercept incoming ballistic missiles. This required a revision of the software that commanded the computer that ran the phased-array radars and the missile guidance systems. This improvement to the Patriot system was completed for a total cost of $150,000,000!

The contentions expressed in the final chapter of this book now have a much higher probability of coming to pass since a defense against the ballistic missile exists and has been proved in actual field use in warfare.

The interception of a Scud by a Patriot is a far more difficult task than the interception of an incoming ICBM. The time of flight of a Scud is shorter than that of an ICBM. The time available for the Patriot to intercept and kill the Scud is shorter than that needed to kill an ICBM. Reaction times are critical when someone is shooting at you. The difference between a Patriot killing an incoming Scud and a ballistic missile defense system—SDI or "Star Wars"—killing an ICBM is one of degree, not kind.

People sitting in front of their television sets around the world watched while the Patriots killed the Scuds. The few Scuds that got through in the absence of a Patriot defense caused civilian casualties and domestic destruction to which television viewers could relate: Here were Scud-blasted people who looked like them and lived like them. These people had been hurt and killed by ballistic missiles because a defense was not available. Their homes, which looked like the viewers' homes, were being destroyed or damaged until the Patriots were brought in to stop the Scuds. The viewers only had to look around, without using much imagination, to realize that a Scudlike attack could happen to *them*.

But they also realized that ballistic missiles could be stopped. They saw it happen on television. And they realized that their lives and homes were vulnerable without a Patriotlike defense.

When the technology is available and the public demands its application, the job gets done.

SDI, Star Wars, Patriot Shield, or whatever one wants to call it will now be built to protect us. It can also protect anyone else in the world. The ballistic missile, the long-range artillery shell, will no longer be an instrument of terror.

By the end of the 1990 decade, the naked threat of ballistic missile attacks will be only a memory.

# APPENDIX

## Soviet Ballistic Missiles
## (Up to SS-20 & SS-N-18)

*Notes:* All data are in metric units. Storable liquid propellants are usually unsymmetrical dimethyl hydrazine (UDMH) as a fuel and either nitrogen tetroxide ($N_2O_4$) or inhibited fuming nitric acid (IFNA) as an oxidizer.

**NATO Designation**   None
**Soviet Designation**   R-1, 8-Zh-38
**Dimensions**   14.036 m × 1.651 m
**Weight**   12,900 kg
**Propellants**   Liquid oxygen and alcohol
**Range**   200 km
**Warhead**   1,000 kg high explosive
**Remarks**   Soviet-built German A.4 (V-2)

**NATO Designation**   Scunner
**Soviet Designation**   R-2, K-1, A-1, Pobeda
**Dimensions**   ? × 1.651 m
**Weight**   ?
**Propellants**   LOX and alcohol
**Range**   500 km
**Warhead**   1,000 kg high explosive
**Remarks**   Korolev's uprated A.4; also V2A research rocket

**NATO Designation**   SS-1B Scud
**Soviet Designation**   R-5
**Dimensions**   10.5 m × 0.85 m

**Weight**   4,500 kg
**Propellants**   Storable liquids
**Range**   150 km
**Warhead**   Nuclear or conventional
**Remarks**

**NATO Designation**   SS-1C Scud
**Soviet Designation**   R-5 (?)
**Dimensions**   11.25 m × 0.85 m
**Weight**   6,300 kg
**Propellants**   Storable liquids
**Range**   280 km
**Warhead**   Nuclear or conventional
**Remarks**   Sold to WarPac, Egypt, Iraq, Libya, Syria

**NATO Designation**   SS-2 Sibling
**Soviet Designation**   A-2
**Dimensions**   ?
**Weight**   ?
**Propellants**   ?
**Range**   ?
**Warhead**   ?
**Remarks**   Identified only in U.S. congressional documents

**NATO Designation**   SS-3 Shyster
**Soviet Designation**   ?
**Dimensions**   21 m × 1.65 m
**Weight**   26,000 kg
**Propellants**   LOX and alcohol/kerosene
**Range**   1,200 km
**Warhead**   Nuclear or conventional
**Remarks**   May also be the R-2 or Pobeda

NATO Designation    SS-4 Sandal
Soviet Designation    R-3, V1
Dimensions    22.4 m × 1.65 m
Weight    28,000 kg
Propellants    Storable liquids
Range    1,800 km
Warhead    1 MT nuclear
Remarks    Emplaced in Cuba in 1962; sold to China before 1960


NATO Designation    None
Soviet Designation    R-4
Dimensions    ?
Weight    ?
Propellants    LOX and alcohol
Range    ?
Warhead    1,000 kg conventional
Remarks    "Peenemünde Pfiel" (Arrow) proposal


NATO Designation    None
Soviet Designation    R-10 (G-1)
Dimensions    19.8 m × 1.6 m
Weight    18,600 kg
Propellants    LOX and alcohol
Range    920 km
Warhead    Conventional
Remarks    Plywood-sheathed ablative warhead


NATO Designation    None
Soviet Designation    R-12
Dimensions    ?
Weight    ?
Propellants    LOX and alcohol

**Range**   2,400 km
**Warhead**   1,000 kg conventional
**Remarks**   Multistaged version of R-10

**NATO Designation**   ?
**Soviet Designation**   R-14
**Dimensions**   23.6 m × 2.74 m
**Weight**   71,000 kg
**Propellants**   LOX and alcohol
**Range**   2,900 km
**Warhead**   3,000 kg
**Remarks**   Last Grottrüp group design

**NATO Designation**   SS-5 Skean
**Soviet Designation**   ?
**Dimensions**   25 m × 2.44 m
**Weight**   60,000 kg
**Propellants**   Storable liquids
**Range**   3,500 km
**Warhead**   1 MT nuclear
**Remarks**   IOC 1961; first displayed Moscow, November 1964

**NATO Designation**   SS-6 Sapwood
**Soviet Designation**   R-7, 8-K-63
**Dimensions**   30.5 m × 10.3 m
**Weight**   300,000 kg
**Propellants**   LOX and kerosene
**Range**   10,000 km
**Warhead**   3,000 kg, 15 megatons nuclear
**Remarks**   First USSR ICBM; Sputnik/Vostok/Voskhod/Soyuz
     booster

**NATO Designation**   SS-7 Saddler
**Soviet Designation**   ?

**Dimensions**   31.8 m × 2.8 m
**Weight**   102,000 kg
**Propellants**   Storable liquids
**Range**   11,000 km
**Warhead**   25 megaton nuclear
**Remarks**   Silo hot launch; may also be FOBS weapon; never displayed

**NATO Designation**   SS-8 Sasin
**Soviet Designation**   ?
**Dimensions**   24.4 m × 2.74 m
**Weight**   77,000 kg
**Propellants**   Storable liquids
**Range**   10,460 km
**Warhead**   5 megaton nuclear
**Remarks**

**NATO Designation**   SS-9 Scarp
**Soviet Designation**   ?
**Dimensions**   36 m × 3.1 m
**Weight**   190,000 kg
**Propellants**   Storable liquids
**Range**   12,000 km
**Warhead**   25 megatons nuclear (biggest ever)
**Remarks**   Largest Soviet ICBM to its time; first fitted with multiple warheads

**NATO Designation**   SS-10 Scrag
**Soviet Designation**   ?
**Dimensions**   38 m × 2.74 m
**Weight**   170,000 kg
**Propellants**   Storable liquids
**Range**   12,000 km

**Warhead**  ?
**Remarks**  Three-stage liquid; shown May 1965; did not go operational

**NATO Designation**  SS-11 Sego
**Soviet Designation**  ?
**Dimensions**  19 m × 2.44 m
**Weight**  48,000 kg
**Propellants**  ?
**Range**  10,500 km
**Warhead**  25 megaton nuclear
**Remarks**  Container only seen in 1973; missile never seen

**NATO Designation**  SS-12 Scaleboard
**Soviet Designation**  ?
**Dimensions**  11.5 m × 1.1 m
**Weight**  8,000 kg
**Propellants**  Storable liquids
**Range**  800 km
**Warhead**  Nuclear
**Remarks**  Highly mobile "shoot and scoot" tactical missile

**NATO Designation**  SS-13 Savage
**Soviet Designation**  ?
**Dimensions**  20 m × 1.7 m
**Weight**  35,000 kg
**Propellants**  Solid
**Range**  8,000 km
**Warhead**  1 megaton
**Remarks**  First USSR solid ICBM, IOC 1968

**NATO Designation**  SS-14 Scapegoat/Scamp
**Soviet Designation**  ?

**Dimensions**   10.8 m × 1.4 m
**Weight**   12,000 kg
**Propellants**   Solid (?)
**Range**   4,000 km
**Warhead**   ?
**Remarks**   Top two stages of SS-13? Land-based Soviet "Polaris"? Never seen outside of container. Scapegoat is missile, Scamp is system

**NATO Designation**   SS-15 Scrooge
**Soviet Designation**   ?
**Dimensions**   18.3 m × 1.3 m (estimated)
**Weight**   28,000 kg (estimated)
**Propellants**   Solid
**Range**   5,000 km (estimated)
**Warhead**   ?
**Remarks**   Shown Moscow 1965; world's largest mobile missile system; never seen outside its travel container

**NATO Designation**   SS-16
**Soviet Designation**   RS-14
**Dimensions**   20 m × 1.7 m
**Weight**   36,000 kg (estimated)
**Propellants**   Solid
**Range**   9,000 km
**Warhead**   Single 2 megaton nuclear or three MIRV
**Remarks**   "Soviet Minuteman" 3-stage solid; silo-launched

**NATO Designation**   SS-17 Spanker
**Soviet Designation**   RS-16
**Dimensions**   24.4 m × 2.5 m
**Weight**   65,000 kg
**Propellants**   Storable liquids

**Range**  10,000 km
**Warhead**  3 MIRV, 200 kiloton nuclear each
**Remarks**  Cold-launched from silo; first MIRVed Soviet ICBM


**NATO Designation**  SS-18 Satan
**Soviet Designation**  RS-20
**Dimensions**  37 m × 3.2 m
**Weight**  220,000 kg
**Propellants**  Storable liquids
**Range**  12,000 km
**Warhead**  8 MIRV 2 megaton nuclear each; CEP 180 meters
**Remarks**  Largest USSR ICBM; 310 deployed


**NATO Designation**  SS-19 Stiletto
**Soviet Designation**  RS-18
**Dimensions**  27 m × 2.5 m
**Weight**  78,000 kg
**Propellants**  Storable liquids
**Range**  10,000 km
**Warhead**  6 MIRV 1 megaton each
**Remarks**  1,000 old SS-11 silos got SS-19s


**NATO Designation**  SS-20 Saber
**Soviet Designation**  RSD-10 Pioneer
**Dimensions**  10.5 m × 1.4 m
**Weight**  13,000 kg
**Propellants**  Solid
**Range**  5,700 km
**Warhead**  3 MIRV 600 kilotons each
**Remarks**  Available as a commercial space launch vehicle


**NATO Designation**  SS-N-4 Sark
**Soviet Designation**  ?

**Dimensions**   15 m × 1.8 m
**Weight**   20,000 kg
**Propellants**   Storable liquids
**Range**   600 km
**Warhead**   1 megaton nuclear
**Remarks**   Deployed on Class Z, G, and H submarines

**NATO Designation**   SS-N-5 Serb
**Soviet Designation**   ?
**Dimensions**   12.9 m × 1.42 m
**Weight**   17,000 kg
**Propellants**   Storable liquids
**Range**   1,600 km
**Warhead**   1 megaton nuclear
**Remarks**   Deployed on Class G and H submarines

**NATO Designation**   SS-N-6 Sawfly
**Soviet Designation**   ?
**Dimensions**   13 m × 1.8 m
**Weight**   19,000 kg
**Propellants**   Storable liquids
**Range**   3,000 km
**Warhead**   1-2 megaton nuclear
**Remarks**   Deployed on Class Y submarines

**NATO Designation**   SS-N-8
**Soviet Designation**   ?
**Dimensions**   17 m × 2 m
**Weight**   40,000 kg
**Propellants**   Storable liquids
**Range**   9,200 km
**Warhead**   2 megatons nuclear
**Remarks**   Deployed on Class D submarines

NATO Designation   SS-N-18
Soviet Designation   ?
Dimensions   ?
Weight   ?
Propellants   Solid
Range   ?
Warhead   ?
Remarks   Deployed on Typhoon Class submarines

## *Unknowns*

The following missile designations have appeared in the literature. However, it has not been possible to tie them in with any known Soviet missile.

8-K-84 or UR-100, supposedly both an ICBM and an ABM
S-200 SAM and ABM
S-125 SRBM

# Bibliography

Alexander, George. "Atlas Accuracy Improves as Test Program Is Completed." *Aviation Week & Space Technology,* 25 February 1963.

Bergaust, Erik. *Reaching for the Stars.* New York: Doubleday, 1960.

Braun, Wernher von, and Ordway, Frederick I. III. *History of Rocketry & Space Travel.* New York: Crowell, 1966.

Brennan, William J. *Milestones in Cryogenic Liquid Propellant Rocket Engines.* American Institute of Aeronautics and Astronautics Paper No. 67–978, October 1967.

Clausewitz, Carl von. *On War.* New York: Penguin, 1967.

Daniloff, Nicholas. *The Kremlin and the Cosmos.* New York: Knopf, 1972.

Dannau, Wim. "Les Fusées de von Braun." *Historia,* No. 276, November 1969, pp. 60–70.

Dornberger, Walter. *V-2.* New York: Viking, 1954.

DuPuy, Col. Trevor N. *The Evolution of Weapons and Warfare.* London: Jane's, 1980.

Emme, Eugene M., ed. *The History of Rocket Technology.* Detroit: Wayne State University Press, 1964.

Ferrill, Arthur. *The Origins of War.* London: Thames & Hudson, 1985.

Friedman, Col. Richard S., et al. *Advanced Technology Warfare.* New York: Harmony Books, Crown, 1985.

———.*The Pocket Encyclopedia of Spaceflight in Color.* New York: Macmillan, 1967.

———.*The Illustrated Encyclopedia of Space Technology.* New York: Salamander Books, Crown, 1981.

Gunston, Bill. *The Illustrated Encyclopedia of the World's Rockets & Missiles.* London: Salamander, 1979.

Gurney, Lt. Col. Gene. *Rocket and Missile Technology.* New York: Franklin Watts, 1964.

Hackett, Gen. Sir John. *The Profession of Arms.* New York: Macmillan, 1983.

Hartman, Edwin P. *Adventures in Research: The History of Ames Research Center, 1940–1965.* Washington, D.C.: National Aeronautics and Space Administration Publication NASA SP-4302, 1970.

Hartman, Tom, and Mitchell, John. *A World Atlas of Military History, 1945–1984.* New York: Da Capo, 1985.

Henshall, Philip. *Hitler's Rocket Sites.* London: Robert Hale, 1985.

Hoffman, S. K. *Development of Engines for the U.S. ICBM's and IRBM's.* American Rocket Society Paper 2090-61, October 1961.

Johnson, David. *V-1/V-2: Hitler's Vengeance on London.* New York: Stein & Day, 1981.

Kármán, Theodore von, with Lee Edson. *The Wind and Beyond.* Boston: Little, Brown, 1967.

Kennedy, Gregory P. *Vengeance Weapon 2: The V-2 Guided Missile.* Washington, D.C.: Smithsonian Institution Press, 1983.

Klee, Ernst, and Merk, Otto. *The Birth of the Missile: The Secrets of Peenemünde.* New York: Dutton, 1965.

Ley, Willy. *Rockets, Missiles, and Men in Space.* New York: Viking, 1968.

Oberg, James E. *Red Star in Orbit.* New York: Random House, 1981.

Ordway, Frederick I. III, and Sharpe, Mitchell R. *The Rocket Team.* New York: Crowell, 1982.

Pretty, Roland, ed. *Jane's Pocket Book of Missiles.* New York: Macmillan, 1975.

Rhodes, Richard. *The Making of the Atomic Bomb.* New York: Simon & Schuster, 1986.

Scott, Harriet Fast, and Scott, William F. *The Armed Forces of the USSR.* Boulder, Colo.: Westview Press, 1979.

Sun Tzu. *The Art of War.* Translated by Samuel B. Griffith. New York: Oxford University Press, 1982.

Suvarov, Viktor. *Inside the Soviet Army.* New York: Berkley, 1984.

Thomas, Shirley. *Men of Space, Vol. 1.* New York: Chilton, 1960.

Verne, Jules. *De la Terre à la Lune.* Originally published 1865. New York: Fawcett, 1958.

Walmer, Max. *An Illustrated Guide to Strategic Weapons.* New York: Salamander Books, Prentice-Hall, 1988.

Weinberger, Caspar W. *Report of the Secretary of Defense to the Con-*

*gress, Fiscal Year 1983.* Washington, D.C.: Department of Defense, February 8, 1982.

————. *Hermes Guided Missile Research and Development Project, 1944–1954.* U.S. Army Ordnance Corps and General Electric Company, September 25, 1959.

————. *Diversity, Adversity, Success: 18 Years of U.S. Missiles, Lark to Atlas-Mercury.* San Diego: General Dynamics/Astronautics, March 1962.

————. *The Thor History, Douglas Report SM-41860.* Santa Monica, Calif.: Missile & Space Systems Division, Douglas Aircraft Corporation, February 1964.

————. "For Freedom's Sake: From Frustration to Fruition." *Challenge,* General Electric Company, vol. 3, no. 2, Summer 1964.

————. *History, Astronautics Division, General Dynamics Corporation,* press release, San Diego, Calif., 1966.

————. *Review of the Soviet Space Program.* Report of the Committee on Science and Astronautics, House of Representatives, Ninetieth Congress, Washington, D.C.: U.S. Government Printing Office, 1967.

————. *Soviet Space Programs, 1976–80.* Committee on Commerce, Science, and Transportation, Washington, D.C.: United States Senate, December 1982.

————. *Space Technology of China.* Beijing: Ministry of Astronautics of the People's Republic of China, 1985.

————. *Long March Launch System.* Beijing: Ministry of Astronautics of the People's Republic of China, 1985.

————. "Soviet Aerospace Almanac." *Air Force,* vol. 70, no. 3, March 1987.

————. *Soviet Military Power: An Assessment of the Threat.* Washington, D.C.: Department of Defense, 1988.

————. "Soviet Aerospace Almanac." *Air Force,* vol. 72, no. 3, March 1989.

————. *Development of the USAF Thor and Atlas Re-entry Vehicles.* Valley Forge, Penn.: Missile and Space Vehicle Department, General Electric Corporation, undated.

# Index